Governors State University
Library Hours:
Monday thru Thursday 8:00 to 10:30
Friday 8:00 to 5:00
Saturday 8:30 to 5:00
Sunday 1:00 to 5:00 (Fall
and Winter Trimester Only)

Interdisciplinary Language Arts and Science Instruction in Elementary Classrooms: Applying Research to Practice

Interdisciplinary Language Arts and Science Instruction in Elementary Classrooms: Applying Research to Practice

Edited by

Valarie L. Akerson
Indiana University

LAWRENCE ERLBAUM ASSOCIATES, PUBLISHERS
2007   Mahwah, New Jersey   London

Lawrence Erlbaum Associates
Taylor & Francis Group
270 Madison Avenue
New York, NY 10016

Lawrence Erlbaum Associates
Taylor & Francis Group
2 Park Square
Milton Park, Abingdon
Oxon OX14 4RN

© 2008 by Taylor & Francis Group, LLC
Lawrence Erlbaum Associates is an imprint of Taylor & Francis Group, an Informa business

Printed in the United States of America on acid-free paper
10 9 8 7 6 5 4 3 2 1

International Standard Book Number-13: 978-0-8058-6003-0 (Softcover) 978-0-8058-6002-3 (Hardcover)

Library of Congress Cataloging-in-Publication Data

Interdisciplinary language arts and science instruction in elementary classrooms :
    applying research to practice / edited by Valarie L. Akerson.
        p. cm. -- (Teaching and learning in science series)
    ISBN 978-0-8058-6002-3 (alk. paper) -- ISBN 978-0-8058-6003-0 (alk. paper)
    -- ISBN 978-1-4106-1758-3 (alk. paper)
    1. Language arts--Correlation with content subjects. 2. Science and the
humanities. 3. Interdisciplinary approach in education. I. Akerson, Valarie L.

    LB1575.8.I555 2007
    372.6--dc22   2006036439

Visit the Taylor & Francis Web site at
http://www.taylorandfrancis.com

Contents

PREFACE

Ideas for *Interdisciplinary Language Arts and Science Instruction in Elementary Classrooms: Applying Research to Practice* originated early in my career as both an elementary teacher and as a university elementary science educator. As an elementary teacher, I was somewhat amazed that many of my colleagues did not enjoy teaching science as much as I did, yet loved teaching reading and writing. From working with them, I began to notice that there could be many connections between language arts and science instruction. I began to connect children's literature to my science instruction, and began to use science journals and children's writing to both assess their understanding of content and to track the development of their ideas during science units. As we worked and planned together, my teacher colleagues began to see how they could use science activities as purposes for reading and writing instruction in their own classrooms.

As a university faculty member, I have retained the pleasure of working with elementary teachers, and have continued to notice the incredible work they do every day. Many of these teachers strive to use interdisciplinary language arts and science instruction to enable them to both improve their students' understandings of science and language arts concepts, and to ensure that they have time to include science teaching into a crowded elementary curriculum. However, I have often wondered about the influences of such interdisciplinary instruction on children's learning, as well as the best approaches to help teachers use effective instruction.

The purpose of this book, then, is to provide elementary teacher educators, aspiring teacher educators, and prospective and practicing teachers, with evidence-based approaches to interdisciplinary language arts instruction, as well as with the means to recognize the influence of such instruction on their students' knowledge. I hope that elementary teachers and students everywhere will benefit from this overview of current research in interdisciplinary and language arts instruction.

There have been numerous recommendations for using interdisciplinary language arts and science instruction. We have previously made recommendations for such instruction that include (a) choose meaningful themes, (b) balance thematic with disciplinary instruction, (c) make interdisciplinary connections logical, natural, and appropriate, and (d) include experiences that will help students meet goals and objectives of both disciplines (Dickinson & Young, 1998). However, we still need research support that these, and others' recommendations, enable the best language arts and science interdisciplinary instruction. We also need research to support that such strategies positively influence elementary students' understandings of language arts and science objectives. Therefore, the chapters in this book provide research evidence, and subsequent synthesis, of effective strategies for using interdisciplinary language arts and science instruction.

OVERVIEW

The book is divided into four sections. Part I, "Introduction to Interdisciplinary Science and Language Arts Instruction," includes the introduction to the book, a chapter on historical perspectives on interdisciplinary instruction, and a sociocultural perspective on scientific learning and learning science. In Chapter 2, Janet Richards shares an overview of prior recommendations for interdisciplinary instruction, as well as historical definitions for such instruction. In Chapter 3, Troy Sadler provides a foundation of the sociocognitive perspective of language and science and the roles language plays in doing and learning science and in reporting and persuading others about science, technology, society, and environmental issues.

Part II, "The Influence of Interdisciplinary Science and Language Arts Instruction on Children's Learning," provides research reports that describe the influence of interdisciplinary language arts and science instruction on elementary students' learning. Research on the use of science notebooks and the influence on students' understanding is shared in Chapter 4 by Judith Morrison. Chapter 5, by David Crowther and John Cannon, describes research on the use of Think-How-Conclusion (THC) and notebooking strategies for effective use of writing in the elementary and middle school classroom. In Chapter 6, Deborah Powell and Roberta Aram describe research on primary students' use of writing as a published version to learn science, carrying beyond science writing in notebooks. David Crowther, Michael Robinson, Amy Edmundson, and Alan Colburn share research-based strategies for English language learners in

Chapter 7. The section concludes with Chapter 8—a report by Carol Giles on the interdisciplinary inquiry classroom in the primary grades.

In Part III, "Research on Preparing Elementary Teachers to Use Interdisciplinary Science and Language Arts Instruction," research is presented that describes preparing teachers to use effective strategies for interdisciplinary language arts and science instruction. Chapter 9 by William Bintz and Sara Moore presents their research on using award-winning literature to teach math and science to grade 4–8 students. In Chapter 10, Janet Richards and Kim Shea share research on a teacher preparation program that emphasizes interdisciplinary instruction. In Chapter 11, Judith Morrison discusses the use of science notebooks to promote teachers' understandings of formative assessment. In Chapter 12, Ingrid Graves and Teddie Phillipson-Mowrer share research-based strategies for using critical literacy to prepare preservice teachers to use interdisciplinary instruction. In Chapter 13, Susan Britsch and Daniel Shepardson share research conducted from their professional development program with elementary teachers that was designed to promote elementary teachers' use of multimodal science instruction. Lucia Lu then follows in Chapter 14 with research from a teacher education program that combined science and mathematics within the instruction of language arts. Part III concludes with Chapter 15 by Valarie Akerson, on the use of action research to promote appropriate interdisciplinary language arts and science instruction by preservice teachers.

Each chapter in Parts II and III ends with "Applications to Classroom Practice" and "For Further Thoughts" sections to help the reader apply the research to the classroom.

In Part IV, "Conclusions and Recommendations," Valarie Akerson and Terrell Young synthesize the research from the previous sections. Implications are drawn for the influence of interdisciplinary language arts and science instruction on elementary student understanding, as well as appropriate preparation models to help teachers improve their interdisciplinary language arts and science instruction. Recommendations are also made for future research in this area.

REFERENCE

Dickinson, V. L., & Young, T. A. (1998). Elementary science and language arts: Should we blur the boundaries? *School Science and Mathematics, 98,* 334–339.

ACKNOWLEDGMENTS

The development of any volume depends on numerous individuals, and this one is no exception. Without interactions with so many amazing elementary teachers over the beginning of my career, it is certain that this work would never have been undertaken. It has been my extreme pleasure to work with so many dedicated elementary teachers that strive to teach science as well as language arts in an interdisciplinary fashion to their students.

I have also had the greatest of pleasure working with science education and literacy education university faculty members, many of whom have contributed to this volume, and all of whom have influenced my view of interdisciplinary language arts and science instruction. I must give my thanks to my "interdisciplinary" colleagues for your influence on my ideas, and sharing your research with me.

It is also necessary for me to thank Norman Lederman. I thought he was done teaching me once I graduated, but to my extreme pleasure, he has continued to be an important and helpful influence on my career. It was a phone call from him that prompted the development of this volume. After I received tenure and promotion at Indiana University, he called and said to me "it is about time in your career that you start working on a book. Get a prospectus ready." And so I did...thank you, Norm!

Of course, nothing is complete without my amazing and supportive husband, Wayne, and my extremely cool and intelligent son, Alec. They are infinitely more patient and calm than I, and still put up with me in the best of ways. Thank you, Wayne and Alec for reminding me what is truly important in life!

Part I

INTRODUCTION TO INTERDISCIPLINARY SCIENCE AND LANGUAGE ARTS INSTRUCTION

This section introduces the topic of the book, helping the reader conceptualize the problems inherent in approaching interdisciplinary instruction, as well as identifying reasons why interdisciplinary language arts and science instruction is appropriate for elementary classrooms. In Chapter 1, Akerson and Young explore the difficulties elementary teachers have in finding time to teach science, their backgrounds for teaching science, the definitions of interdisciplinary instruction, and scientific literacy. Richards, in Chapter 2, discusses historical perspectives of interdisciplinary instruction, provides a theoretical basis for such instruction, and provides an overview and interpretation of various sorts of interdisciplinary instruction. In Chapter 3, Sadler describes a sociocultural perspective on interdisciplinary science and language arts instruction, contextualized within scientific literacy. Within this view of scientific literacy, a major component is literacy itself in terms of communication in the written and oral forms.

Why Research on Interdisciplinary Language Arts and Science Instruction?

Valarie L. Akerson
Indiana University

Terrell A. Young
Washington State University

It can be reasonably argued that the main goal in any elementary classroom is to produce literate readers and writers. Indeed, language arts subjects can take most of the elementary school day. Typically, time has been a constraint to the teaching of much science in elementary classrooms (Fitch & Fisher, 1979), even when elementary teachers desire to emphasize science in their classrooms (Akerson, 2001). However, use of other content areas such as science to promote literacy and to support learning is recommended and encouraged by the International Reading Association (IRA) and the National Council of Teachers of English (NCTE). The *National English Language Arts Standards* recommend that language arts serve the goals of purposeful communication through reading, writing, speaking, and listening (IRA & NCTE, 1996). Science can provide a purpose for reading, writing, speaking, and listening. Indeed, Tower (2005) found that fourth-grade students were able to note the purpose of writing for science in their classroom—in helping to communicate their findings through written means.

There have been recommendations for elementary teachers to use literacy strategies to improve their science teaching (e.g., Akerson & Young,

2004; Crowther & Cannon, 2004; Thier & Davis, 2002). One compelling reason to consider interdisciplinary language arts and science instruction is the evidence showing cognitive parallels between the two subjects (Baker & Saul, 1994; Gaskins & Guthrie, 1994; Glynn & Muth, 1994; Keys, 1994; Rivard, 1994; Romance & Vitale, 1992). Casteel and Isom (1994) state that the interrelated connection between language arts and science ensures improved science learning by beginning with what students and teachers know about the reading and writing process. There are claims that engaging in reading and in conducting science requires similar process skills of observation, identification, using background knowledge, making inferences, and drawing conclusions (Padilla, Muth, & Lund Padilla, 1991). There are many interdisciplinary language arts and science teaching strategies described in journals such as *Science and Children* that are accessible to elementary teachers. However, students can be engaged in language arts activities that do not support science content learning, and vice versa.

Given the goals for elementary teaching to produce students who can effectively read and write, it is not surprising that elementary teachers' backgrounds are generally much stronger in language arts than in science. One solution to this problem is to help teachers use their strengths in language arts to improve their teaching of science. What is continuing to be determined through research are appropriate ways to use interdisciplinary language arts and science instruction to promote learning by elementary students in both subjects, and ways to help teachers most effectively use interdisciplinary language arts and science instruction. In a recent report, Yore, Bisanz, and Hand (2003) provided a review of the literature on research on the language arts and science instruction. They described the need to think about the use of language in scientific literacy research because we all communicate ideas through language. They describe research on the development of oral and written language with science education, such as teacher questioning, and writing to learn strategies. They make recommendations for future research that document effective interdisciplinary science and language arts instruction, and the influence on students' understandings that will improve their scientific literacy. Hapgood, Magnusson, and Palincsar (2004) found that primary-grade children are capable of experiencing scientific inquiry, and of improving their understandings of content through that inquiry through scaffolded teacher mediation with properly designed texts that students used to develop understandings and reasonings. Palincsar, Magnusson, Collins, and Cutter (2001) similarly found that inclusion students could similarly make growths in their science and literacy understandings through appropriately guided inquiry instruction. Romance and Vitale

(2001) described a multiyear study conducted at grades 2–5 that explored the effectiveness of an IDEAS curriculum that replaced a traditional reading/language arts curriculum with a science emphasis interdisciplinary language arts curriculum. Students who participated in this program improved in both their reading achievement and in science content understandings as measured on standardized tests. They also held more positive attitudes and self-confidence toward reading and science. Likewise, Morrow, Pressley, Smith, and Smith (1997) found that students who were provided with science-related reading opportunities gained more in both reading and science achievement than did a control group.

Saul (2004) edited a book that provided a rationale for interdisciplinary science and literacy instruction, and several sections describing recommended strategies for choosing trade books, scientific writing strategies, evaluating text materials, and reaching teachers. With all of these excellent recommendations for such interdisciplinary instruction, and rationales for such instruction, a volume that describes research on developing teachers' strategies for interdisciplinary science and language arts instruction, as well as the influences on students' understandings of language arts and science content, is timely, and is what this book sets out to do.

OUR DEFINITION OF INTERDISCIPLINARY INSTRUCTION

The terms used to describe cross-disciplinary approaches of instruction have varied meanings. We are choosing to use the term "interdisciplinary" so we can emphasize maintaining the distinct differences between language arts and science, while combining instruction in one discipline to support learning in the other (Lederman & Niess, 1997). With interdisciplinary instruction, each discipline maintains its integrity, while connections between the disciplines are made explicit. Determining where one discipline ends and the other begins remains possible. With interdisciplinary instruction in science and language arts, it is possible to note which language arts tools are being used for science instruction and how science activities are being used to promote language learning. Yore (2004) stated, "Oral and written communication and the processes of speaking, listening, writing, and reading are highly valued within the scientific community; scientists who communicate well are successful in gaining support from members of their own communities, funding agencies, and the wider society" (p. 76). Therefore, there is support for interdisciplinary instruction from scientists themselves. For example, an elementary classroom studying outer space may use language arts skills of reading and writing to search for and organize information and that would be the language arts portion of the day. Science would be used to provide motivation for the book research. However, during another part of the day, students would be involved in investigations and manipulating materials to help them learn science content related to outer space. Language arts skills of reading, writing, and oral communication could support the investigations. These skills provide tools for recording observations and evidence, and holding discussions about the meanings of investigations.

Thematic instruction is the variety that is most often used in elementary schools. Elementary teachers can visit many teacher supply stores and purchase professionally developed "thematic units" recommended for different grade levels. With thematic instruction, an overall motif or theme pervades the classroom. *Benchmarks for Science Literacy* (AAAS, 1993) and *National Science Education Standards* (NRC, 1996) recommend broad themes such as "systems," "models," "constancy and change," and "scale." These themes describe ways of thinking about science, and permeate throughout different science content areas. More typically, thematic units for an elementary classroom are developed around topics, such as "outer space," about which science, language arts, math, art, music, and physical education activities could take place. These thematic units provide a muddled notion of what a theme is and is not, because when teachers use the thematic units from professionally prepared curricula, they are actually teaching topics rather than science themes. Should the teacher decide to use such "thematic units" that are typically available, the instruction could use interdisciplinary approaches of instruction. Each discipline could be separated under the umbrella of "outer space." However, a more common approach in an elementary classroom may be that of attempted integration within the thematic unit. Instead of being able to define boundaries between the disciplines, such "thematic" instruction focuses on relating all activities to the theme without regard to the objectives and goals of individual disciplines. Too frequently, activities are chosen simply because they match the theme. Although teachers may congratulate themselves and say they use thematic instruction to teach both science content and language arts, in fact, they often do not teach much science at all. Often they are actually using a "theme," or topic such as outer space to develop reading or writing lessons that they believe help to teach science, but the science discipline is not approached using recommended strategies (NRC, 1996) or to meet science goals or *Benchmarks* (AAAS, 1993). Thus, although they believe they are using an integrated approach, they are inappropriately defining integration because although language arts goals are being met, the same activities do not allow students to meet science learning goals. The science goals are lost in the language arts instruction under the guise of integration. Students who participate in such a unit may view science as a body of knowledge about which they must read or write and will not experience inquiry activities to help them learn science processes.

Although elementary children do not initially divide their school day or lives into different disciplines, it becomes important for them to recognize the differences in, and to develop in-depth understandings of, different disciplines. Without in-depth understandings of individual disciplines, it is difficult to develop an integrated or interdisciplinary awareness of the connections between disciplines (Lederman, 1994). Without a teacher who approaches instruction in each of the disciplines in a manner true to the standards and goals of those disciplines, students will be unlikely to develop a strong understanding of those individual disciplines. Therefore, we recommend interdisciplinary language arts and science instruction through which connections are made between the disciplines and are used to support the learning of the other discipline, while maintaining the integrity of each separate discipline. Such instruction highlights the distinctions as well as the connections between the disciplines. The chapters in this book explore how teachers can effectively deliver interdisciplinary language arts and science instruction and the influence of such instruction on elementary students' knowledge.

Literacy and Science Literacy

Elementary teachers strive to help their students become literate readers and writers. According to national reforms (AAAS, 1990), elementary teachers should also strive to help their students become scientifically literate. Proponents of interdisciplinary instruction have stated that by combining language arts and science instruction, teachers can concurrently develop language literacy and scientific literacy. Is it possible to help elementary students develop both scientific and language literacy through interdisciplinary instruction? First we need to explore what it means to develop scientific literacy as well as language literacy, and then research practices that purport to concurrently develop literacy in both disciplines.

If teachers are to help students become scientifically literate, they must have an understanding of scientific literacy. Defining the term "science literacy" is not simple. Bybee (1997) stated that the term *science literacy* has different meanings for different people. Science literacy, according to Bybee, is

> best defined as a continuum of understanding about the natural and defined world, from nominal to functional, conceptual and procedural,

and multidimensional. This unique perspective broadens the concept to accommodate all students and gives direction to those responsible for curriculum, assessment, research, professional development, and teaching science to a broad range of students. (p. 86)

The *National Science Education Standards* (NRC, 1996) recommend that a scientifically literate person know science as inquiry, science subject matter, the relationship between science and technology, science in personal and social perspectives, the history and nature of science, as well as unifying concepts and processes. The *Standards* also recommend that students present and share their results with other students. Presenting and sharing results with other students directly connect to general literacy goals of developing effective written and oral communication skills by students using their skills in language arts to present and share science investigation results with other students.

Lemke's (2004) definition also includes an interdisciplinary focus of language literacy skills with scientific understanding:

> Science literacy includes the ability to interpret visual displays of information. We need to help [students] understand the conventions that connect verbal text with mathematical expressions and graphs and diagrams of all kinds….Students need not only to do hands-on science and talk and write science in words; they also need to draw, tabulate, graph, geometrize, and algebrize science in all possible combinations. (Lemke, 2004, 41)

Yore's (2004) definition also ties together the language arts and science disciplines by connecting "big ideas" of science to the communication skills inherent in language arts:

> Science literacy…. Involves critical thinking, cognitive and metacognitive abilities, and habits of mind to construct understanding in the specific disciplines, the big ideas or unifying concepts of the disciplines, and the communications to share these understandings and to persuade others to take informed action. (p. 83)

Language literacy also has many definitions, ranging from being able to write one's name to having the ability to read at a certain level to more sophisticated definitions. A generally accepted definition is the following by Venezky (1995):

> [The] ability to read and write in a designated language, as well as a mindset or way of thinking about the use of reading and writing in

everyday life. It differs from simple reading and writing in its assumption of an understanding of the appropriate use of these abilities within a print-based society. Literacy, therefore, requires active, autonomous engagement with print and stresses the role of the individual in generating as well as receiving and assigning independent interpretations to messages. (p. 142)

Within the language arts, there are various related literacies. Two literacies directly related to science instruction are content literacy and information literacy. McKenna and Robison (1997) defined content literacy as "the ability to use reading and writing for the acquisition of new content in a given discipline." Three cognitive components underlie this ability; (a) literacy skill, (b) prior content knowledge, and (c) content specific knowledge. For example, in science, students need to be able to read, interpret, and create charts, graphs, diagrams, and tables. The second related literacy, information literacy, is especially important in thematic instruction, because information literacy is the ability to access, evaluate, and use information from a variety of sources (National Working Party for Information Literacy, 1997). The following basic information literacy goals enable students to use information effectively; (a) construct strategies for locating information, (b) locate and access information, (c) organize and apply information, and (d) evaluate the information-gathering process and the final product. These skills provide students with a meaningful link between the curriculum and the real world and need to be integrated into all curriculum areas.

But can literacy in both disciplines be developed concurrently? There are similarities between language arts and science literacy that may make meeting this goal possible. One similarity is that students must be able to purposefully use language arts and science. Another is that each discipline recommends that students actively interact. In language arts, students must actively interact with and make meaning of print; in science, students must actively interact with and make meaning of investigations.

The differences between the disciplines are greater. To be literate in language arts, students need to be able to accurately generate and interpret printed and oral language. To be literate in science, students need to have a basic understanding of the natural and defined world, subject matter, science processes and inquiries, and the nature of science itself. Although language arts skills can be used to develop science literacy, they are not enough to help students understand what they need to meet science objectives. Although science activities can serve as common experiences and motivation for using and developing language arts literacy, they do not, in and of themselves, help students become literate in written and oral communication. Because the disciplines of science and language arts have different goals and objectives, the assumption that students, especially elementary students, can naturally become literate in language and in science solely through thematic instruction using integrated instruction is erroneous. Language arts and science are different disciplines, and although instruction in one can complement the other, the expectation that instruction in one can substitute for separate instruction in both is mistaken. Science and language arts goals and objectives complement one another. Science can be used to provide common experiences about which students can communicate both orally and through written work. Language arts can provide tools for recording and communicating results of inquiry. Elementary teachers feel stronger in their language arts teaching. Using strengths in language arts can, thus, be a key to improving elementary science teaching. When elementary teachers understand that science can play a crucial role in developing their students' general literacy, it may demand greater focus in the classroom. However, using language arts methods cannot be a substitute for science inquiry, nor can it be used to help students meet all science goals and objectives. Goals and objectives of both science and language arts must be considered and assessed if both disciplines are to be given their fair treatment in elementary schools, and if elementary teachers hope to help students meet both *National English Language Arts Standards* (IRA & NCTE,1996) and *National Science Education Standards* (NRC, 1996).

Yore (2004) crafted the following criteria to guide teachers' selection and design of language tasks for science inquiry instruction:

1. Insure that any attempt to enhance students' speaking, listening, reading, and writing is based on compatible models of language arts and science learning as interactive and constructive.
2. Make language tasks and instruction pay off now and later by using authentic communicative strategies that enhance fundamental and derived literacy, are applicable in later life, and recognize the limitations of some "cute" activities.
3. Make debating, reading, and writing instruction an integral part of any science program and science course by starting in upper primary grades and continuing into middle school, secondary school, and university science courses with developmentally appropriate cognitive and metacognitive goals.
4. Provide explicit strategy instruction for the language arts similar to any embedded instruction of requisite science processes, laboratory procedures, or safety rules.

5. Select language tasks that encompass the range of genre, information sources, and communication technologies encountered by real scientists and science-literate adults. (p. 86)

Although these recommendations seem sound, we still need research to define both the best ways to implement interdisciplinary language arts and science instruction, and the influence of such instruction on students' understanding of science and language arts objectives.

REFERENCES

Akerson, V. L. (2001). Teaching science when the principal says "Teach language arts." *Science and Children, 38*(7), 42–48.

Akerson, V. L., & Young, T. A. (2004). Nonfiction know-how: Surefire strategies for effectively using nonfiction trade books in your science classroom. *Science and Children, 41*(6), 48–51.

American Association for the Advancement of Science. (1990). *Science for all Americans.* New York: Oxford University Press.

American Association for the Advancement of Science. (1993). *Benchmarks for science literacy.* New York: Oxford University Press.

Baker, L., & Saul, W. (1994). Considering science and language arts connections: A study of teacher cognition. *Journal of Research in Science Teaching, 31,* 1023–1037.

Bybee, R. W. (1997). *Achieving scientific literacy: From purposes to practices.* Portsmouth, NH: Heinemann.

Casteel, C. P., & Isom, B. A. (1994). Reciprocal processes in science and literacy learning. *The Reading Teacher, 47*(7), 538–545.

Crowther, D. T., & Cannon, J. (2004). Strategy makeover: K-W-L to T-H-C. *Science and Children, 42*(1), 42–44.

Fitch, T., & Fisher, R. (1979). Survey of science education in a sample of Illinois schools: Grades K–6 (1975–1976). *Science Education, 63,* 407–416.

Gaskins, I. W., & Guthrie, J. T. (1994). Integrating instruction of science, reading and writing: Goals, teacher development, and assessment. *Journal of Research in Science Teaching, 31,* 1039–1056.

Glynn, S. M., & Muth, K. D. (1994). Reading and writing to learn science: Achieving scientific literacy. *Journal of Research in Science Teaching, 31,* 1057–1073.

Hapgood, S., Magnusson, S. J., & Palincsar, A. S. (2004). Teacher, text, and experience: A case of young children's scientific inquiry. *The Journal of the Learning Sciences, 13,* 455–505.

International Reading Association & National Council of Teachers of English. (1996). *Standards for the English language arts.* Newark, DE: Author.

Keys, C. W. (1994). The development of scientific reasoning skills in conjunction with collaborative writing assignments: An interpretive study of six ninth-grade students. *Journal of Research in Science Teaching, 31,* 1003–1022.

Lederman, N. G. (1994). Midnight madness. *The Association of the Education of Teachers in Science Newsletter, 28*(1), 1–3.

Lederman, N. G., & Niess, M. L. (1997). Integrated, interdisciplinary, or thematic instruction? Is this a question or is it questionable semantics? *School Science and Mathematics, 97*, 57–58.

Lemke, J. L. (2004). The literacies of science. In E. W. Saul (Ed.), *Crossing borders in literacy and science instruction* (pp. 33–47). Newark, DE: International Reading Association.

McKenna, M. C., & Robison, R. D. (1997). *Teaching through text: A content literacy approach to content area reading.* New York: Longman.

Morrow, L. M., Pressley, M., Smith, J., & Smith, M. (1997). The effect of a literature based program integrated into literacy and science instruction with children from diverse backgrounds. *Reading Research Quarterly, 32*, 54–77.

National Research Council. (1996). *National science education standards.* Washington, DC: National Academy Press.

National Working Party for Information Literacy. (1997). *Information literacy in New Zealand schools and libraries.* Christchurch, New Zealand: Author.

Padilla, M. J., Muth, K. D., Lund Padilla, R. K. (1991). Science and reading: Many process skills in common? In C. M. Santa & D. E. Alvermann (Ed.), *Science learning–Processes and applications* (pp. 14–19) Newark, Delaware: International Reading Association.

Palincsar, A. S., Magnusson, S. J., Collins, K. M., & Cutter, J. (2001). Making science accessible to all: Results of a design experiment in inclusive classrooms. *Learning Disability Quarterly, 24*, 15–32.

Rivard, L. P. (1994). A review of writing to learn in science: Implications for practice and research. *Journal of Research in Science Teaching, 31*, 969–983.

Romance, N., & Vitale, M. R. (1992). Using videodisk instruction in an elementary science methods course: Remediating science knowledge deficiencies and facilitating science teaching attitudes. *Journal of Research in Science Teaching, 29*, 915–928.

Romance, N. R., & Vitale, M. R. (2001). Implementing an in-depth expanded science model in elementary schools: Multi-year findings, research issues, and policy implications. *International Journal of Science Education, 23*, 373–404.

Saul, W. (2004). *Crossing borders in literacy and science instruction: Perspectives on theory and practice.* Arlington, VA: NSTA Press.

Thier, M., & Davis, B. (2002). *The new science literacy: Using language skills to help students learn science.* Portsmouth, NH: Heinemann.

Tower, C. (2005). What's the purpose? Students talk about writing in science. *Language Arts, 82*, 472–483.

Venezky, R. L. (1995). Literacy. In T. L. Harris & R. E. Hodges (Eds.), *The literacy dictionary: The vocabulary of reading and writing* (p. 142). Newark, DE: International Reading Association.

Yore, L. D. (2004). Why do future scientists need to study the language arts? In E. W. Saul (Ed.), *Crossing borders in literacy and science instruction* (pp. 71–94). Newark, DE: International Reading Association.

Yore, L. D., Bisanz, G. L., & Hand, B. M. (2003). Examining the component of science literacy: 25 years of language arts and science research. *International Journal of Science Education, 25,* 689–725.

2

Interdisciplinary Teaching: History, Theory, and Interpretations

Janet C. Richards
University of South Florida

> For interdisciplinarians "knowledge is not certain and held by authorities...knowledge is relative to a context and acquired through inquiry" — Haynes, 2002 (p. XIV)

Despite the current renewed interest in interdisciplinary curricula across the United States and Canada, there are limited explicit descriptions in the literature regarding what is taught in these programs and how it is taught. More seriously, there are few research-based bodies of evidence that attest to the greater learning that occurs through interdisciplinary structures as opposed to traditionally organized curricula (Grossman, Wineburg, & Beers, 2000).

The chapters in this volume help address gaps in our knowledge of interdisciplinary initiatives. As a composite corpus, they illuminate an array of interdisciplinary teaching interpretations, and shed light on various learning contexts in which interdisciplinary practices take place. The chapters also depict some common themes and shared configurations that cut across teaching milieus. In addition, the chapters highlight benefits and strengths of specific interdisciplinary models, and help to alert readers to problems that can occur when educators enter into the realm of subject integration. Thus, as a comprehensive collection of teaching philosophies and experiences, the volume serves to broaden awareness of the benefits and limitations of interdisciplinary teaching, and reveals some of the dynamics that occur when interdisciplinary theory is put into practice.

This chapter provides a framework for the research and teaching initiatives presented in the volume by offering a chronological overview and a theoretical synopsis of interdisciplinary pedagogy. The chapter also discusses how interdisciplinary approaches are tied to current learning theories, and practitioner wisdom.

The chapter delineates varied interpretations of interdisciplinary teaching and discusses definitions related to each scheme. In addition, the chapter offers insights into an exemplary interdisciplinary themed inquiry where disciplines were not simply juxtaposed. Instead, concepts and modes of thinking in one discipline enriched students' understandings in another discipline and also served to help students research vital questions. The chapter also supplies an imaginative metaphor that helps expand understanding of the holistic nature of interdisciplinary modes of discovery. In addition, the chapter presents a visual representation analogy that helps to illuminate dimensions of interdisciplinary pedagogy. The chapter concludes with a summary that connects interdisciplinary teaching to beliefs about how human beings learn best, notions of what constitutes knowledge, and views about how knowledge is constructed.

INTERDISCIPLINARY TEACHING HAS A LONG HISTORY

Interdisciplinary teaching is not new. Historical support for interdisciplinary teaching resides in the work of Dewey (1897a, 1897b), Bruner (1963), and Piaget (1972), who recommended a holistic view of learning (Lake, 2005). Although "the word interdisciplinary did not enter the English language until the opening decades of the twentieth century" (Klein, 2005, p. 1), a radical approach to teaching was originally proposed as early as 1918, when scholars noted that education should ensue from students' interests rather than from disciplined subjects (Walker, 1996). Later, two forward thinking educators, Harold Rugg (1939), and George Counts (1932), suggested that at least part of the school curriculum should be organized around broad issues of American life and international issues.

The progressive education movement of the 1930s also supported an integrated curriculum, which proponents sometimes labeled as a *core curriculum* (Vars, 1987). However, what was known then, as a core curriculum was not comprised of conventional subjects required for high school graduation, but, rather, consisted of discussions about socially relevant topics, such as juvenile delinquency and family values.

By the middle of the century, interdisciplinary teaching was no longer considered a radical concept. In fact, in 1935, the yearbook "for the National Educational Association focused on 'Integration: Its Meaning and Application'" (Grossman, Wineburg, & Beers, 2000, p. 7).

The work of Florence Stratemeyer (1957) and her colleagues at Teachers College Columbia University, New York, also advanced understanding about interdisciplinary initiatives. Stratemeyer's research documented teachers' struggles to implement interdisciplinary curricula that included too little time, limited resources, noncommitted teachers, district requirements, and the challenges of interpreting or replicating interdisciplinary methods with few models to observe and emulate.

At present, although there is not a consensual accord, interest in interdisciplinary curricula has re-emerged throughout the United States and Canada where in both countries, this approach is equated with school reform. For example, U. S. discussions about interdisciplinary programs are often found in *Phi Delta Kappan*, *Educational Leadership*, and *Education Week* and in British Columbia, Canada's blueprint for school renewal, *British Columbia Year 2000* (Grossman, Wineburg, & Beers, 2000).

CONTEMPORARY THEORIES OF LEARNING SUPPORT INTERDISCIPLINARY INITIATIVES

Interdisciplinary methods are linked to an increased understanding of human development (Goodlad, 2000). Several contemporary theories of learning support an interdisciplinary approach. Broadened notions of literacy extend views of learning to include all of the myriad ways humans give and receive meaning. Learners have opportunities to employ all sign systems (i.e., multiple literacies), such as music, the visual arts, dance, technology, drama, and oral and written discourses to communicate and make sense of their world (Richards & McKenna, 2003).

Multiple intelligence (MI) theory explains how learners can call on eight (or more) intelligences that serve as a foundation for subject integration. Operating from these intelligences, labeled linguistic, musical, logical-mathematical, spatial, bodily kinesthetic, interpersonal, intrapersonal, and naturalist, allows learners to search for meaning and to problemsolve across a wide range of subject areas (Gardner, 1983; Boix Mansilla, Miller, & Gardner, 2000).

Neuroscientific studies also offer support for interdisciplinary teaching. Scientists interested in brain-based research suggest that optimal levels of learning only occur when students are fully immersed in an educational experience and can consider multiple views and connections across subjects (Caine & Caine, 1991). In fact, some research suggests that the human brain actively seeks patterns and therefore, "the brain may resist learning fragmented facts that are presented in isolation" (Lake, 2005, p. 6).

In addition, constructivist theory posits that learning is always interdisciplinary and that students learn more when they work with peers and teachers to problem solve, interpret, analyze, and reflect on broad concepts. Constructivists believe that learning is best accomplished through authentic experiences (Lake, 2005).

Teachers' Views of Interdisciplinary Curricula

Although little scientific research has documented teachers' points of view toward interdisciplinary methods, an additional rationale for interdisciplinary pedagogy is situated in practitioners' commonsense wisdom (Lake, 2005). Today's teachers often find it difficult to manage an integrated curriculum in United States' skills-driven classrooms. However, many teachers perceive an interdisciplinary approach as a solution to an overpacked fragmented curriculum (Lake, 2005). They also espouse subject integration as an adroit response to federal and local school district mandates that place an inappropriate emphasis on test-taking skills and direct teachers to concentrate on reading instruction to the detriment of content subjects. For example, teachers recognize they can connect reading lessons to the discipline of science because in both subjects, students question, hypothesize, compare, contrast, evaluate, and infer. To illustrate this ease of integration, Zemelman, Daniels, and Hyde (1998) describe a best practices fourth-grade interdisciplinary literacy/science inquiry in which students used reading and writing in a variety of ways to learn about the desert. Students wrote letters to children in Arizona, read *Desert Dog* (Kjelgaard, 1956), and listened to excerpts from *I'm in Charge of Celebrations* (Baylor, 1986), which poetically celebrates the pleasures of observing nature. They also kept records of data, compared hypotheses, and created graphs, charts, and drawings that documented what they had learned.

ADDRESSING CONFUSIONS IN THE LITERATURE

What Exactly is Interdisciplinary Teaching?

Interdisciplinary teaching often is described as a philosophy, a methodology, and as a process of connecting subjects; however, it entails much more than making connections. Schindler (2002) asserts, "there is no single best interdisciplinary pedagogy" (p. 233). Haynes (2002) concurs and emphasizes, "Interdisciplinary pedagogy...is not synonymous with a single process, set of skills, method, or technique. Instead, it is concerned primarily with fostering in students a sense of self-authorship and a situated, practical and perspectival notion of knowledge that they can use to respond to complex questions, issues, or problems" (p. XVI). Klein (1990) notes that this purposeful unification of subject areas allows students and teachers to address multifaceted issues that cannot be addressed through single-subject fragmented modes of teaching.

In a practical sense, interdisciplinary pedagogy may be considered a synthesis of two or more disciplines that has the potential to establish a new level of discourse and to produce constructions of knowledge that might not be attained through single-subject teaching (DeZure, 2005). In its purest form, interdisciplinary teaching refers to inquiries in which students and teachers work together to solve common problems, construct knowledge, and come to conclusions (see Vygotsky, 1978).

Extending Our Understanding of Interdisciplinary Teaching

Boix Mansilla, Miller, and Gardner (2000) help extend our understanding of exemplary interdisciplinary teaching by providing three essential features of an interdisciplinary framework. These features are; "(1) an emphasis on knowledge use; (2) a careful treatment of each discipline involved; and (3) appropriate interaction between disciplines" (p. 25–25). They further clarify interdisciplinary teaching with this statement:

> We propose that disciplines like history or science are not collections of certified facts; rather they are lenses through which we look at the world and interpret it. (p. 18)

To illustrate their premise, they depict an authentic themed unit of inquiry focused on Nazi Germany and the Holocaust in which middle school students employed two different lenses to explore problems, events, and "truth." Operating from an historical stance, students studied historical narratives and artifacts to answer research questions that included, "How did things come to be the way they were in Nazi Germany?" and "How did people experience the societal changes in Germany at that particular time?" (p. 19).

In addition, students employed scientific theory and laws to shed light on questions such as, "Is race a tenable biological concept?" and "What are the biological foundations of distinctions in the human race?" (p. 19). Thus, in this middle school setting, multidisciplinary modes of inquiry worked in tandem and synergistically informed each other. Students examined questions that could not be explored through individual discipline efforts. In addition, students were motivated to investigate complex issues, using history and science. That is, they employed the disciplines of history and science in the service of learning about a phenomenon rather than reducing these subjects to discrete facts, memorized definitions, and simplistic explanations. Furthermore, "concepts and modes of thinking in one discipline enrich[ed] students' understanding in another discipline" (Boix Mansilla, Miller, & Gardner, 2000, p. 29). For an enlightening theoretical and practical discussion relevant to this themed unit of inquiry and also to the broader topic of interdisciplinarity, see Boix Mansilla, Miller, and Gardner, 2000).

Abell (2002) also heightens our perceptions of interdisciplinarity by supplying an imaginative and amusing metaphor that contrasts a discipline-specific representation of teaching with an interdisciplinary model of instruction. The imagery employed in the metaphor facilitates our understanding of how a holistic approach helps students acquire multiple perspectives about a phenomenon.

> My favorite metaphor for interdisciplinary teaching is the pie. Discipline-specific education will teach you everything you need to know about the slice. You'll learn how to sharpen knives, know how apply tools (like spatulas) to extract data, and how to use discreet vocabulary to discuss these matters. But interdisciplinary instructors are not interested in slices; they are interested in the pie as a totality. How was the crust made? What spices will be needed? Deep analysis of the "filling" will be called for, as well as a study of cross-cultural traditions of pie-making and of the pie as a symbol in American culture. …More important, in this program of pie, we would eat pie whenever possible. Every faculty meeting, every student colloquium, on any occasion we could think of, we would devour pie of every description, form, and kind, Of course, in order to consume pie, we would have to make it: and we would spend a great deal of time teaching our students how to concoct one for themselves. In this way, our attention would be focused not only on concepts, but also on the creation and the shared experience of that creation (i.e., our discussions and activities would engage both artist and audience). But the deepest reason for all this pie eating would be that you are what you eat; and by eating all this pie, we would become one with our object of study. We would embody it. (p. 141–142)

Nancy Grace (2002) is another scholar who supplies an enlightening analogy to evoke our thinking about the interdisciplinary teaching paradigm. Grace describes a glass visual representation created by Marcel Duchamp in 1918, known as "Small Glass." The piece, part of the permanent collection of the Museum of Modern Art in New York City, invites viewers to circle the work and gaze into the various round, oblong, and rectangular glass shapes contained inside. "Not only can viewers peer from various vantage points at the world around them...they can also peer at themselves. Because the object is in continual motion, the images of oneself and others perpetually shift and transform" (Haynes, 2002, p. XVI).

The Many Forms and Interpretations of Interdisciplinary Teaching

Notwithstanding Boix Mansilla, Miller, and Gardner's (2000) informative discourse regarding two disciplines that were purposely and skillfully brought together to address a multifaceted problem, Abell's (2002) creative integrated pie metaphor, and Grace's (2002) reflective and refractive "Small Glass" analogy, many initiatives in U.S. classrooms that are labeled as interdisciplinary take varied forms. Not surprisingly, these diverse configurations do not correspond to purist definitions of what constitutes an interdisciplinary approach (Wentworth & Davis, 2002). "There is a lack of common definitions about what constitutes interdisciplinarity" (Grossman, Wineburg, & Beers, 2000, p. 10). One reason is that "over the course of the 20th century, the range of interdisciplinary practices widened and diversified and the underlying concepts became more pluralistic" (Klein, 2005, p. 1). For example, depending on grade level (primary through higher education), initiatives described as interdisciplinary range from simplistic to sophisticated and include the following:

- Engaging in team teaching at any grade level.
- Connecting science or social studies with reading and language arts in primary and elementary classrooms.
- Forming field-based education courses and school/university partnerships.
- Organizing general college courses of study around a theme, problem, or topic, such as American studies, general education studies, comparative civilization analysis, global studies, cultural studies, environmental studies, study abroad programs, women's studies, and multiculturalism perspectives.
- Infusing avant garde concepts (e.g., gender issues, gay and lesbian topics, and feminist points of view) into previously designed higher education curricula.
- Forming cohort groups at any level.

- Adding a service learning component to university courses (e.g., tutoring struggling readers, or volunteering in community agencies, such as Head Start or Big Brothers and Sisters Neighborhood Centers).

Sorting Out Definitions

In addition to the proliferation of activities that have surfaced as authentic interdisciplinary representations, during the past half-century, variations in terms have been employed to denote an interdisciplinary continuum (Gavelek, Raphael, Biondo, & Wang, 2002). For example, consider the following terminology:

- Multidisciplinary teaching
- Transdisciplinary teaching
- Themed units of inquiry
- Nested integration
- Synergistic teaching
- Webbed curricula
- Cross-curricular approaches
- Integrated curricula

Some authors use several of these terms synonymously to denote an interdisciplinary approach (e.g., see Bonds, Cox, & Gantt-Bonds, 1993; Hamel, 2000; Richards & Shea, 2006a, 2006b; Roth, 2000). In contrast, other writers take great care to employ a single term. Often, within single volumes, common definitions of interdisciplinary methods are absent and similar terms are used in different ways (Grossman, Wineburg, & Beers, 2000). A listing of some of the terminology and their brief definitions are presented in the following section. Readers will note the difficulty of distinguishing the terminology in relationship to their definitions and the difficulty of separating the terms according to differences in approaches. For additional information on terms and descriptions related to interdisciplinary teaching, refer to Fogarty, 1991, and Fogarty and Stoehr, 1995.

Terms and Definitions

A *multidisciplinary approach* is defined as a juxtaposition of disciplines that can guide students toward "further interdisciplinary understanding" (Boix Mansilla, Miller, & Gardner, 2000, p. 33). Subject matter is not altered— disciplines are only contrasted. A multidisciplinary approach involves "the sequential presentation of topic drawn from separate disciplines" (Wentworth & Davis, 2002, p. 16). According to Renyi (2000), a multidisciplinary approach is the use of one discipline at a time "to analyze different features and aspects of a work for different [or similar] purposes" (p. 43). An example of a multidisciplinary approach is studying a painting using art history methods and chemical analysis to verify that a specific artist created the painting during a specific time period (Renyi, 2000).

A *transdisciplinary program* operates as a gestalt, or a holistic scheme that considers all aspects of an entire structure, such as Communism, World War II, Global Warming, or World Hunger.

The terms *cross-curricula* and *integrated curriculum* often are used as synonyms for the term interdisciplinary (e.g., in the title, "What is Interdisciplinary/Cross Curricular Teaching?") (http://www.edu-place.com/rdg/red/literacy/interd0.html).

Nested integration "takes advantage of natural combinations. This could be accomplished in a lesson in the circulatory system by having the lesson focus on both the circulatory system and the concept of systems" (Merickel, 2005, p. 184).

Synergistic teaching moves beyond connecting subjects. All subjects are taught in a fashion that makes them appear indivisible (Bonds, Cox, & Gantt-Bonds, 1993). Students and teachers relate knowledge and skills acquired in one area of study to new areas of learning. For example, teachers and students studying volcanoes might connect their knowledge of geography, history, mathematics, world cultures, and the visual arts to volcanic studies. Curricula areas are blurred. Content transcends curricula boundaries. All knowledge is considered connected.

A *Webbed* curriculum employs a themed unit of inquiry to integrate subject matter. Broad themes, such as outer space and medieval life provide opportunities for teachers of diverse disciplines to address common topics and concepts.

A *themed unit of inquiry* approaches a topic from several disciplinary perspectives (Richards & McKenna, 2003). Primary and elementary curricula often offer themed units of inquiry, such as studying various states in the United States through the disciplines of history, geography, music, and the visual arts.

SUMMARY

Movements to fashion interdisciplinary curricula in the United States have intermittently surged and declined throughout the 20th century at all levels of education (Goodlad, 2000; Grossman, Wineburg, & Beers, 2000). Advocates of interdisciplinary pedagogy contend that teaching isolated facts and separating subjects artificially compartmentalizes learning, and fails to prepare students for a rapidly changing society (Shoemaker, 1989). Therefore, they recommend an interdisciplinary approach to "help students acquire the mental agility and critical thinking skills needed for success in the modern world" (Korey, 2005, abstract).

Despite these accolades and tributes, a single definition of interdisciplinary teaching remains elusive, most likely because the fluid nature of interdisciplinarity dictates that a single definition is inappropriate (Applebee, Burroughs, & Cruz, 2000). Furthermore, studies that examine students' achievements attained in interdisciplinary programs are lacking and supply inconclusive evidence (Field & Snow, 2002; Walker, 1996). "Claims by practitioners of the benefits of interdisciplinarity approaches are numerous and diverse, but the preponderance of the evidence regarding outcomes is often anecdotal" (Newell, 1998, p. 537). It is safe to say that at this time, the pedagogical value of interdisciplinary curricula remains unresolved (Korey, 2005).

Yet, as Goodlad (2000) notes, "interdisciplinary teaching is a worthy concept that has come around once more to challenge the supremacy of separate subjects as the way to organize curricula" (foreword, p. xi). In theory, interdisciplinarity promises to counterbalance fragmentation of curricula and to mitigate the considerable emphasis on memorization of facts and information that define too many of our nations' schools.

What is clear in the literature is that the concept of interdisciplinary teaching is bound to philosophical beliefs about how human beings learn best. Interdisciplinarity is also tied to notions of what constitutes knowledge, and is connected to views about how knowledge is constructed. Interdisciplinarians believe that truth is not absolute. Rather, truth is socially constituted and situated in specific contexts. Therefore, in any authentic interdisciplinary course of study, students are encouraged to see issues or topics from multiple perspectives. Thus, just as in Marcel Duchamp's (1918) "Small Glass" visual representation, "interdisciplinarity becomes a prism through which students can interpret the natural, social, and cultural worlds in which they live and operate in them in informed ways. In this sense interdisciplinary is not an end in itself but a means of addressing problems or examining phenomena that are relevant to the societies in which we live" (Boix Mansilla, Miller, & Gardner, 2002, p. 31).

APPLICATIONS TO CLASSROOM PRACTICE

In 1957, Florence Stratemeyer and her colleagues at Teachers College Columbia University, New York, documented teachers' dilemmas to implement interdisciplinary curricula. Teachers'concerns included too little time, limited resources, noncommitted teachers, district require- ments, and the challenges of interpreting, or replication interdisciplinary methods with few models to observe. How do these issues fit with your own concerns about teaching through an interdisciplinary approach? How might you attempt to solve these dilemmas?

FOR FURTHER THOUGHT

1. Why do you think there are so many definitions of interdisciplinary teaching?
2. What is your personal definition of interdisciplinary teaching?
3. How does your personal definition of interdisciplinarity connect to your beliefs about teaching, learning, and human development?
4. This chapter supplies two metaphors about interdisciplinary teaching methods; a pie and Marcell Duchamp's "Small Glass" visual represen- tation. Create your own metaphor or visual repesentation about inter- disciplinary approaches to teaching and learning. In what ways does the act of creating your metaphor or visual representation help you develop insights about interdisciplinary teaching?

REFERENCES

Abell, J. (2002). Being there: Performance as interdisciplinary teaching tool. In C. Haynes (Ed.), *Innovations in interdisciplinary teaching* (pp. 141–153). Westport, CT: Oryx Press.

Applebee, A., Burroughs, R., & Cruz, G. (2000). Curricular conversations in ele- mentary school classrooms: Case studies of interdisciplinary instruction. In S. Wineburg & P. Grossman (Eds.), *Interdisciplinary curriculum: Challenges to implementation* (p. 93–111). New York: Teachers College.

Baylor, B. (1986). *I'm in charge of celebrations*. New York: Athenium Books for Young Readers.

Boix Mansilla, B. V., Miller, W., & Gardner, H. (2000). On disciplinary lenses and interdisciplinary work. In S. Wineburg & P. Grossman (Eds.), *Interdisciplinary curriculum: Challenges to implementation* (pp. 17–38). New York: Teachers College.

Bonds, C., Cox, C., & Gantt-Bonds, L. (1993). Curriculum wholeness through syn- ergistic teaching. *The Clearing House, 66* (7), 252–254.

Bruner, J. (1963). *The process of education*. Cambridge, MA: Harvard University Press.

Caine, R., & Caine, G. (1991). *Making connections: Teaching and the human brain*. Alexandria, VA: Association for Supervision and Curriculum Development.

Counts, G. (1932). Dare the school build a new social order? *Teachers College Record, 26*, 815–826.

Dewey, J. (1897a). *Experience and education.* London: Collier Books.

Dewey, J. (1897b). *My pedagogic creed.* New York: Kellogg.

DeZure, D. (2005). Interdisciplinary teaching and learning. *Essays on Teaching Excellence.* [Publication of the Professional & Organizational Development Network in Higher Education]. Retrieved December 2005, from http://www.unm.edu/~castl/Castl_Docs/Packet1/Interdisciplinary

Field, M., & Snow, D. (2002). Transforming interdisciplinary teaching and learning through assessment. In C. Haynes (Ed.), *Innovations in interdisciplinary teaching* (p. 256–274). Westport, CT: Oryx Press.

Fogarty, R. (1991). *The mindful school: How to integrate the curricula.* Palatine, IL: Skylight Publishing.

Fogarty, R. & Stoehr, J. (1995). *Integrating curricula with multiple intelligences: Teams, themes, and threads.* Palentine, IL: Skylight Publishing.

Gardner, H. (1983). *Frames of mind: The theory of multiple intelligences.* New York: Basic Books.

Gavelek, J., Raphael, T., Biondo, S., & Wang, D. (2002). Integrated literacy instruction. In M. Kamil, P. Mosenthall, P. D. Pearson, & R. Barr (Eds.), *Handbook of reading research* (Vol. 3, p. 587–607). Mahwah, NJ: Lawrence Erlbaum Associates.

Goodlad, J. (2000). Foreword. In S. Wineburg & P. Grossman (Eds.), *Interdisciplinary curriculum: Challenges to implementation* (pp. xvi–xii). New York: Teachers College.

Grace, N. (2002). Margaret Sanger, Marie Curie, Maya Angelou, Marcel Duchamp, and Mary Belenky teach a women's studies course: A discussion of innovative interdisciplinary approaches to feminist pedagogy. In C. Haynes (Ed.), *Innovations in interdisciplinary teaching* (p. 154–178). Westport, CT: Oryx Press.

Grossman, P., Wineburg, S., & Beers, S. (2000). In S. Wineburg & P. Grossman (Eds.), *Interdisciplinary curriculum: Challenges to implementation* (pp. xvi–xii). New York: Teachers College.

Hamel, F. (2000). Disciplinary landscapes: Interdisciplinary collaboration: A case study. In S. Wineburg & P. Grossman (Eds.), *Interdisciplinary curriculum: Challenges to implementation* (p. 74–92). New York: Teachers College.

Haynes, C. (2002). (Ed.). *Innovations in interdisciplinary teaching.* Westport, CT: Oryx Press.

Kjelgaard, J. (1956). *Desert dog.* New York: Holiday House.

Klein, J. (1990.) *Interdisciplinarity: History, theory and practice.* Detroit: Wayne State University Press.

Klein, J. (2005, September). *Interdisciplinarity one century later.* Paper presented at the College of Education, Wayne State University, Detroit MI. Retrieved December 2005, from http://ed_web3.educ.msu.edu/news/events/05/klein.htm

Korey, J. (2005). *Successful interdisciplinary teaching: Making one plus one equal one.* Proceedings of the 2nd International Conference on the Teaching of

Mathematics, University of Crete, Greece. Retrieved December 5, 2005, from http://uuw.math.uoc_gr/~ictm2/Proceedings/ic.

Lake, K. (2005). *Integrated curriculum: School improvement research series.* Portland, OR: Northwest Regional Educational Laboratory.

Merickel, M. (2005). Integration of the disciplines: Ten methodologies for integration. Retrieved December 2005, from http://oregonstate.edu/instruction/ed555/zone 3/tenways.htm

Newell, W. (1998, March). *The place of interdisciplinary studies in higher education today.* Paper presented at the Association of American Colleges and Universities and the Association for Integrative Studies, Chicago, IL.

Piaget, J. (1972). The epistemology of interdisciplinary relationships. In L. Apostel, G. Berger, A. Briggs, & G. Michaude (Eds.), *Inter-disciplinarity: Problems of teaching and research in universities* (pp. 127–139). Paris: Organization for Economic Cooperation and Development.

Renyi, J. (2000). Hunting the quark: Interdisciplinary curricula in public schools. In S. Wineburg & P. Grossman (Eds.), *Interdisciplinary curriculum: Challenges to implementation* (pp. 39–56). New York: Teachers College.

Richards. J., & McKenna, M. (2003). *Integrating multiple literacies in K–8 classrooms: Cases, commentaries and practical applications.* Mahwah, NJ: Lawrence Erlbaum Associates.

Richards, J., & Shea, K. (2006a). Moving from separate subject to interdisciplinary teaching: The complexity of change in a preservice teacher K–1 early field experience. *The Qualitative Report, An International On-Line Journal.*

Richards, J., & Shea, K. (2006b). Interdisciplinary teaching in the primary grades: Preservice teachers' dilemmas and achievements connecting science, the arts, and reading. In V. Akerson (Ed.), *Research on interdisciplinary language arts and science instruction in the elementary classroom* (pp. 173–196). Mahwah, NJ: Lawrence Erlbaum Associates.

Roth, K. (2000). The photosynthesis of Columbus: Exploring interdisciplinary curriculum from the students' perspectives. In S. Wineburg & P. Grossman (Eds.), *Interdisciplinary curriculum: Challenges to implementation* (pp. 112–133). New York: Teachers College.

Rugg, H. (1939). *Democracy and the curriculum: The life and program of the American schools.* New York: The John Dewey Society.

Schindler, R. (2002). Interdisciplinarity and the adult/lifelong learning connection: Lessons from the classroom. In C. Haynes (Ed.), *Innovations in interdisciplinary teaching* (pp. 221–235). Westport, CT: Oryx Press

Shoemaker, B. (1989). Integrative education: A curriculum for the twenty-first century. Oregon School Study Council, ED 311 602.

Stratemeyer, F. (1957). *Developing a curriculum for modern living.* New York: Teachers College Press.

Vars, G. (1987). *Interdisciplinary teaching in the middle grades: Why and how.* Columbus, OH: National Middle School Association.

Vygotsky, L. (1978). *Mind and society: The development of higher mental processes.* Cambridge, MA: Harvard University Press.

Walker, D. (1996). Integrative education. *ERIC Digest No. 101,* January 1996, University of Oregon, Clearing House on Educational Management.

Wentworth, J., & Davis J. (2002). Enhancing interdisciplinarity through team teaching. In C. Haynes (Ed.), *Innovations in interdisciplinary teaching* (pp. 16–37). Westport, CT: Oryx Press.

Zemelman, S., Daniels, H., & Hyde, H. (1998). *Best practice: New standards for teaching and learning in America's schools* (2nd ed.). Portsmouth, NH: Heinemann.

3

A Sociocultural Perspective on Scientific Literacy and Learning Science

Troy D. Sadler
University of Florida

A reasonable place to begin a discussion of the relationships between science and language arts is an exploration of scientific literacy. In this volume's first chapter, Akerson and Young introduce scientific literacy and primarily rely on four accounts (Bybee, 1997; Lemke, 2004; NRC, 1996; Yore, 2004) to operationalize the construct. Bybee problematizes scientific literacy by describing the complex and multifarious nature of the term and adopts a very broad definition that subsumes multiple understandings of the "natural and defined world" (p. 86) with the intent of accommodating the widest range of students. While still broad, Yore's account of scientific literacy focuses more specifically on cognitive activities associated with science as a way of knowing including "critical thinking, cognitive and metacognitive abilities, and habits of mind to construct understanding in the specific disciplines" (p. 83). Whereas Yore stresses cognitive processes, the *National Science Education Standards* (at least in the portion highlighted by Akerson and Young; NRC, 1996) emphasize cognitive products in the form of well-developed understandings of subject matter, inquiry, nature of science, and interactions between science and society. Finally, Lemke conceptualizes a form of scientific literacy that highlights literacy and the communicative and representational forms of the languages employed in science. Lemke construes literacy in science contexts to include not just written and verbal text but also mathematical expressions, graphs, and other diagrams.

Even in this exceptionally restricted survey of literature, it quickly becomes apparent that the term *scientific literacy* does not represent a unified concept. I am not trying to suggest that the various forms of scientific literacy presented are necessarily incompatible with one another. Yore's version of scientific literacy, which focuses on cognitive processes, could very well produce the kinds of outcomes envisioned by the NRC's scientific literacy goals. However, we have to recognize that educators and authors consistently use the term in very different ways. Lemke's language-based account of scientific literacy differs substantially from the NRC's product-based account. This phenomenon is certainly not a recent development. Since the term's introduction in 1958, educators have continually reinvented its meaning and used it to promote a variety of reform initiatives (DeBoer, 2000).

One of the chief challenges for negotiating scientific literacy as a conceptual resource is the varied senses in which the term "literacy" is applied. Literacy can be positioned in both fundamental and derived senses (Norris & Phillips, 2003). In the fundamental sense, literacy refers to the use of language as in reading and writing. In the derived sense, literacy is more broadly construed to denote knowledgeability, learning, and education. In terms of scientific literacy, the fundamental sense refers to use of language in science contexts; whereas, the derived sense deals with understandings or abilities relative to science. In the four accounts of scientific literacy discussed thus far, Lemke's description is the only one that reflects literacy in a fundamental sense. The other descriptions, like most discussions of the construct throughout science education literature, focus on scientific literacy in a derived sense. With few exceptions (e.g., Fang, 2004), scientific literacy has come to exclusively represent what students should know, understand, or be able to do relative to science (Laugksch, 2000). The construct is typically invoked to characterize the goals of science education; that is, educators define scientific literacy in terms of the normative goals they have for science instruction.

With the remainder of this chapter, I intend to show that literacy, in its fundamental sense, is significant for articulations of scientific literacy. To make this case, I explore two unique approaches for conceptualizing literacy in the fundamental sense. I draw from Norris and Phillips' (2003) discussion of "simple" and "expanded" views of fundamental literacy. I will argue that the expanded view is a more appropriate framework for literacy and that literacy as conceptualized with the expanded perspective is central to science practice. The chapter will also explore scientific literacy in the derived sense and how the construct differs when adopting cognitive versus sociocultural epistemological perspectives. Ultimately, I will advocate a version of scientific literacy based on a sociocultural perspective. This view of scientific literacy is consistent with an expanded fundamental sense of literacy and actually blurs the distinctions between fundamental and derived senses of literacy. It is within this sociocultural framework for science teaching and learning that interdisciplinary investigations of science and literacy can be maximized.

THE FUNDAMENTAL SENSE OF SCIENTIFIC LITERACY

Scientific literacy in its fundamental sense has generally not been prioritized by science educators (Norris & Phillips, 2003; Wellington & Osborne, 2001). In fact, text and reading have been actively excluded in many science learning contexts (Yore, Craig, & Maguire, 1998). Norris and Phillips (2003) suggest that this orientation, which deemphasizes language use, is based on a "simple" view of reading and literacy. The simple view, which certainly transcends the boundaries of science education, equates reading to text decoding. "Even today, there is strong reason to believe that teachers are unwittingly fostering this simple view of reading, despite over five decades of research showing that skilled word recognition is not reading" (Norris & Phillips, 2003, p. 227). An expanded view of literacy, more consistent with current trends in reading education research (e.g., Pressley & Wharton-McDonald, 1997), positions reading as inferring meaning from text. In the excerpt below, Norris and Phillips (2003) explicate the processes involved in inferring meaning and distance this view of literacy from those that correspond to simple decoding.

> Inferring meaning from text involves the integration of text information and the reader's knowledge. Through this integration, something new, over and above the text and the reader's knowledge, is created—an interpretation of the text. It is crucial to understanding in this view to recognize that interpretations go beyond what is in the text, what was the author's intent, and what was in the reader's mind before reading it. Also crucial is the stance that not all interpretations of a text are equally good, but usually there can be more than one good interpretation. (p. 228)

Text, used in this sense, represents an assortment of inscriptions including not only words but also graphs, charts, equations, figures, maps, and diagrams.

Whereas simple fundamental literacy highlights the recognition of vocabulary, the expanded sense of fundamental literacy invokes broader processes of constructing meaning relative to a variety of texts. A substantial difference exists between knowing what specialized terms mean and actively interpreting those terms within larger contexts. These varying perspectives on literacy have important implications for the relationship between language and science. When literacy is cast simply, language bears a merely functional relationship with science. Language is simply a tool for science; however, an expanded view of literacy frames the relationship between language and science as constitutive. Language is a constituent, a fundamental element, of science. When language is positioned as a tool of science, science itself can be construed independent of language. In contrast, if language shares a constitutive relationship with science, then literate practice is essential to science. That is, science cannot be independent of language; without language, there is no science (Norris & Phillips, 2003). This does not necessarily imply that science is synonymous with language use in a comprehensive sense; there are elements of science that do not involve literacy in its fundamental sense. Using instruments such as microscopes or telescopes certainly falls in the realm of science; and yet, it does not involve language. However, it is difficult to consider how the results of a microscopic or telescopic investigation might be used, transmitted, or stored in any meaningful way without language. Adopting an expanded view of literacy in its fundamental sense casts serious doubt on efforts to dilute the significance of language in science education; in fact, it underscores the need for prioritizing language use in science instruction.

THE DERIVED SENSE OF SCIENTIFIC LITERACY

As mentioned earlier in this chapter, discussions of scientific literacy in the science education community are typically framed in terms of the derived sense of literacy. That is, scientific literacy usually represents the desired outcomes of science that may or may not relate meaningfully to language or text. In fact, most articulations of scientific literacy make little or no reference to literacy in its fundamental sense. Derived forms of scientific literacy have come to represent many different goals for science education ranging from appreciation of the nature and aims of science to understanding science concepts and principles to the ability to make informed decisions in increasingly technological societies (Hurd, 1998; Laugksch, 2000). The diverse array of meanings for scientific literacy has lead some to conclude that the construct is useless and impossible for diverse audiences to attain (Shamos, 1996). While this critique may be unnecessarily harsh (Yager, 2004), the ambiguity associated with scientific literacy creates significant impediments for the challenge central to this volume, namely drawing meaningful connections between science and language arts instruction and research. However, progress can be made in this area through the explicit consideration of epistemological perspectives from which scientific literacy (in the derived sense) is framed. My discussion focuses on cognitive and sociocultural perspectives: Cognitive perspectives tend to prioritize cognitive entities such as concepts or attitudes as the intended outcomes of science instruction; whereas, sociocultural perspectives prioritize the appropriation of practice as the intended outcome of science learning experiences. I will argue that cognitive perspectives on scientific literacy encourage the disarticulation of science and language whereas sociocultural perspectives situate language centrally with respect to science practice.

A COGNITIVE PERSPECTIVE

Cognitive perspectives, based on individualistic psychologies, have dominated discussions of education generally and science education more specifically for the past 30 to 40 years (Kirshner & Whitson, 1997). These perspectives undergird much of what exists as the common practices and goals of modern science classrooms. Cognitive perspectives tend to conceptualize the aims of education as the development of cognitive attributes. These attributes may be transmitted or constructed; in either case, the goal of instruction is for learners to come to possess certain knowledge structures or attitudes. Desired knowledge structures may include declarative or conceptual knowledge (i.e., knowing the meaning of target concepts) and procedural knowledge (i.e., knowing how to perform given tasks). Scientific literacy has frequently been defined in terms of these kinds of knowledge and attitudes (Jenkins, 1990). For instance, it would not be uncommon for an elementary teacher to design science instruction with the intent of students developing conceptual understanding of density, the ability to use a graduated cylinder for measuring volume, and positive attitudes toward science. Viewed in this way, learning is synonymous with acquisition of cognitive entities. In science learning, students acquire science concepts, abilities to complete certain tasks often referred to as process skills, and positive attitudes regarding the contributions of science.

This view of learning is implicitly supported and codified by the documents that have become guideposts for American education in the 21st century state standards. This chapter is not meant to be an evaluation of state standards for science across the nation, nor is it an indictment of all standards documents. However, given the demands for accountability as mandated through the federal No Child Left Behind Act, state standards and the resulting testing regimes have become very significant influences on the determination of what is valued in classroom science and, therefore, what should be subject to scrutiny in discussions of scientific literacy as it is actually enacted. As an example of how state standards may reflect or reify a perspective on learning, I present science benchmarks set for two states with which I am most familiar; Florida and Indiana. These provide an interesting comparison because they have been characterized very differently in terms of their quality by independent sources (Gross, 2005). Florida's Sunshine State Standards for science (FLDOE, 1996) define what students should know across several grade level groupings (K–2, 3–5, 6–8, and 9–12) in terms of overarching themes threaded across all grade levels. Following is an example of a specific benchmark for upper-level elementary learners under the theme of force and motion: The student "knows that waves travel at different speeds through different materials" (SC.C.1.2.2). I am not suggesting that there is anything wrong with wanting students to understand something about the properties of waves. However, when the standard is presented in this manner and then assessed through a standardized multiple choice exam such as the Florida Comprehensive Assessment Test (FCAT), the concept becomes an abstract cognitive entity that students are expected to acquire. In assessments of science state standards from across the nation, Florida has received failing marks for the scope, organization, and quality of its standards. In contrast, Indiana's science standards have been judged far more favorably, as one of seven states to receive an "A," based on the same criteria (Gross, 2005). However, although the Indiana standards may be better organized and more thorough, they still cast scientific knowledge in the same abstracted form. Consider the following example of an Indiana science standard (INDOE, 2005) taken from third-grade expectations relative to the physical world: The student should be able to "demonstrate that things that make sound do so by vibrating, such as vocal cords and musical instruments" (3.3.9). As in the previous example from the Florida standards, the goal of science instruction as presented through this benchmark is for students to acquire an abstracted notion of an already determined physical reality.

The state standards just presented and the many others that reflect similar philosophical frameworks position student acquisition of declarative knowledge as the primary goal of science education. Other cognitive articulations of scientific literacy may highlight additional desired ends in the form of other knowledge structures, skills, and attitudes, but ultimately these approaches share an underlying framework that suggests that individuals can and should cognitively receive discrete units of understanding. Much of the debate related to scientific literacy focuses on which and how many of these units students should come to know. When scientific literacy is framed in this manner, the role and significance of language are minimized. Scholars can reasonably argue that conceptual formation or acquisition is mediated by language (i.e., concepts exist only inasmuch as they can be identified or described through language; Munby, 1976), but the real focus of cognitive views on scientific literacy is concept acquisition, not the interactions of learners, ideas, and language. Language becomes a medium through which knowledge can be communicated, and its significance is derived through its utility. This perspective on language use is consistent with the simple view of literacy in its fundamental sense. In fact, adopting a simple view of fundamental literacy enables and encourages a cognitive perspective of scientific literacy in the derived sense. Furthermore, this combination (i.e., simple fundamental literacy and cognitive derived scientific literacy) makes the distinction between the fundamental and derived senses of literacy most pronounced. In essence, conceptualizing fundamental literacy in a simple way promotes a view of derived literacy that prioritizes abstracted cognitive entities. When scientific literacy is articulated in the form of cognitive entities without much attention to language, then it becomes important to draw the distinction between fundamental and derived senses of literacy.

A SOCIOCULTURAL PERSPECTIVE: THE SITUATED NATURE OF KNOWING

Sociocultural epistemology offers a unique framework for conceptualizing the goals of science education, that is, scientific literacy in its derived sense. Whereas the cognitive perspective just elaborated positions knowledge as abstracted entities that ideally can be transmitted to students (or constructed by students), sociocultural perspectives on learning emphasize the significance of context. This shift has important implications for how the goals of science education are framed. Sociocultural perspectives suggest that all learning is situated regardless of the intent or design of the learning experiences (Brown, Collins, & Duguid, 1989). Therefore, even curricula intended to achieve goals consistent with cognitive perspectives, which prioritize learner acquisition of cognitive entities, become situated for the learners. Many science concepts presented in schools are contextually impoverished with respect to what the concepts represent in scientific communities. Ultimately, science concepts become bound to a culture of school science characterized by a disarticulated network of facts that students must reproduce on exams. Even if students correctly respond to typical exam items, we must question what they have actually come to understand. Will the students be able to use science concepts in meaningful ways beyond the confines of formal school settings? Sociocultural perspectives suggest that conceptual understanding will be limited and impoverished without other experiences that connect concepts to meaningful practice. This critique creates serious challenges for cognitive articulations of scientific literacy. If the outcomes of science teaching are bound to school-based experiences, then the significance of scientific literacy as framed by the cognitive perspective is severely minimized.

To illustrate the point being made here, I want to describe an episode from my own experiences as a learner. This is a simple example, and it is not even a direct result of a classroom science learning experiences, but I think it illustrates nicely the situated nature of understanding especially with respect to vocabulary. As an undergraduate student planning to pursue a graduate degree in the biological sciences, I started preparing for the GRE. I purchased a study guide and familiarized myself with the format of the exam. The study guide contained a huge list of vocabulary, which it suggested would be wise to know. I proceeded to make dozens of note cards with terms identified on one side and simple definitions on the other. One of the terms included on a card was "colander." I was a poor college student who ate a lot of noodles so I was very familiar with colanders, but I did not recognize the vocabulary word as representative of the kitchen utensil that I used all the time. I put the term on a card just like many others with which I was unfamiliar and scribbled a dictionary definition. It is important to note that I did this test preparation on my own so I never actually used the word (on the card) in conversation or heard someone else use the word. I had definitely used and heard the word "colander" as representative of the thing in my kitchen but not as the concept that existed on that card. I distinctly remember going through the cards and reading the term as "kō'lǎnd'ər" rather than "kŭl'ən-dər" as if it were meant to refer to an assistant lunar landing device. I attempted to learn this word and the others on my note cards in a decontextualized manner: I just wanted to be able to recognize as many of the recommended terms as I possibly could. In doing so, I did not abstract the vocabulary from context; rather, I learned the terms in a very impoverished context. My understanding was limited to the very contrived context of those cards and the articulation of a formal definition. I could have probably regurgitated a correct definition for "colander," but I was unable to meaningfully connect the term with my lived experiences. "Colander" did not show up on my GRE exam nor did any of the other terms that I had dutifully transcribed and memorized, but several years later as

I stood in a friend's kitchen watching her prepare spaghetti, it dawned on me that the crazy GRE word that seemed so foreign was really just the thing that I had seen and used countless times.

Unfortunately, when we seek to transmit science concepts as the ultimate focus of science instruction, the result can be as dismal as my GRE vocabulary-learning experience. The attempt to abstract scientific knowledge from practice and experience results in contextualizing target concepts in ways that bind them to the classroom and make it unlikely that learners would ever come to meaningfully use the knowledge. I have used a sociocultural perspective to critique cognitive accounts of the derived sense of scientific literacy, but this perspective can also inform an alternative articulation of scientific literacy. In presenting this perspective on scientific literacy, I will highlight two interdependent sociocultural constructs, enculturation and practice, and discuss the implications of framing educational goals via these constructs.

Enculturation

Enculturation refers to processes by which individuals come to be a genuine part of a community. Through these processes, an individual comes to understand, appropriate, and appreciate the values, norms, and practices of the group. Viewed from the sociocultural perspective, learning is enculturation. In their seminal work on the topic, Brown et al., (1989) effectively demonstrate the link between learning as it has been historically conceptualized relative to disciplinary knowledge and culture:

> To talk about academic disciplines, professions, or even manual trades as communities or cultures will perhaps seem strange. Yet communities of practitioners are connected by more than their ostensible tasks. They are bound by intricate, socially constructed webs of belief, which are essential to understanding what they do…The culture and use of a tool act together to determine the way practitioners see the world; and the way the world appears to them determines the culture's understanding of the world and the tools." (p. 33)

When learning goals are abstracted from the culture in which the practice was originally situated, as I have suggested is the case of cognitive articulations of scientific literacy, students do not have access to the broader framework that supplies meaning and significance. If one accepts the argument that all learning is situated, then the abstract learning goal becomes an aspect of the culture of schooling and not of meaningful scientific practice.

In discussing enculturation, I would also like to address what it is not. Enculturation is not meant to refer to learning about culture from an etic, or outsider's perspective. Enculturation is not synonymous with growing to appreciate a culture from afar. Although appreciation for the culture may likely occur, the emphasis is on personally experiencing and participating in the culture. Enculturation is also not synonymous with indoctrination. The process should not imply that individuals have to fully acquiesce to a static collection of values and practices. People can participate in a culture in different ways. Some may fully embrace the mainstream values and standards of a particular community, and others may reject them. In both cases, the individuals are participating in that culture, and most actual cases of participation involve the adoption of complex combinations of accepting and rejecting or modifying the norms of a particular community (Greeno, 1998).

Practice

As suggested in the preceding section, enculturation does not occur at a distance or in the third person. Enculturation occurs by personally engaging in the practices (i.e., the regular activities) of the community (Greeno, 1998). Therefore, if learning is enculturation and practice is an essential aspect of enculturation, then learning must involve practice. This sociocultural perspective on learning, which emphasizes enculturation and learning, draws largely on anthropological studies (e.g., Coy, 1989; Lave & Wenger, 1991) of how individuals come to master trades, crafts, professions, and other activities based in authentic, real-life situations as opposed to formal educational contexts like schools. In fields as diverse as tent making, naval navigation, and midwifery, apprenticeships emerge as a dominant approach to teaching and learning. Through an apprenticeship, a learner works within the community to gain first-hand experiences with the tools, standards, and practices central to participation in that community. The goal of apprenticeship learning is to move the learner from a naïve position beyond the boundaries of a community of practice ever more central to the community. Ideally, the apprentice progresses from an outsider to an active participant. Apprentices do not become immediate experts, nor do they engage in the full spectrum of practices characteristic of the community; learning starts through legitimate peripheral participation (Lave & Wenger, 1991). Participation is legitimate because the apprentice engages in authentic activity, that is, practices that are genuinely significant for the community. Apprentice participation is considered peripheral because the novice does not immediately assume the complex activities most central to the discipline or craft. As apprentices come to understand the knowledge base and practices of the community through peripheral activities, they are prepared to take up more central responsibilities.

Lave (1998) brings the concept of legitimate peripheral participation to life in her discussion of apprentice tailors. The beginners start learning their trade not by cutting and sewing but by ironing finished garments. The practice is a necessary aspect of the craft and simple enough for novices to do well. I would like to draw on my own experiences once again to illustrate the significance of practice and legitimate peripheral participation for learning science. As an undergraduate biology major, I took a job in a population genetics laboratory. Up until that time, I had always excelled in biology and enjoyed the content but understood very little in terms of what it meant to be a biologist or study life science beyond the confines of a textbook or lecture notes. The lab's research focused on predator–prey coevolution using *Daphnia* as a model organism. As a new lab assistant, I spent most of my time washing glassware, tending algal populations, and feeding *Daphnia*. These activities initially seemed quite remote from the activities of more senior members of the lab such as analyzing DNA, designing experiments, and interpreting results. However, my activities served as an initial entry into the culture and practices of this particular laboratory and the field of population genetics more generally. Over time, my tasks and responsibilities were expanded and I assumed increasingly less peripheral participation. My experiences in this lab offered me a very different perspective on biology than that provided by formal coursework. The concepts that I had seen highlighted in text and lectures took on new meaning and significance because they became tools situated in my lab practice rather than abstract ideas to be memorized.

Unfortunately, most science students do not experience apprenticeshiplike learning environments. Although they may participate in school activities, they typically do not engage in practices consistent with the scientific community. "Many of the activities students undertake are simply not the activities of practitioners and would not make sense or be endorsed by the cultures to which they are attributed" (Brown et. al., 1989, p. 34). What then does this mean for classroom science instruction? It is both unreasonable and impractical to expect all students to work in apprenticeships that lead to professional science; however, in order to learn science, students need more than just exposure to abstract concepts. Students need to experience science concepts and tools in authentic practice, where authentic practice represents developmentally appropriate contexts that invoke similar processes as those used in research labs or other settings in which "real science" takes place.

In laying out a cognitive perspective on scientific literacy, I suggested that a likely goal of elementary science teachers would be student development of conceptual understanding of density. There is nothing wrong with having a goal of students understanding this important concept, but the issue is what student knowledge represents. What exactly do students know if they are able to state an appropriate definition of density or even describe it as a ratio of mass and volume? If articulating these truths is all a student can do with the concept, then the value of his or her knowledge must be questioned. Alternatively, students, who are able to engage in scientific practice using density as a conceptual tool to explore how and why objects sink and float, are demonstrating much deeper and significant understandings of a fundamental scientific idea. Additionally, engaging in such practices is not solely focused on achieving a set cognitive outcome. Participating in scientific practice broadens the outcome of learning so that the student comes to understand conceptual tools such as density as they relate to the values, standards, and goals of the scientific community.

Enculturation, Practice, and Language

Given a sociocultural perspective that prioritizes enculturation and practice, the articulation of scientific literacy in its derived sense takes on a new character. The goals of science education shift from the acquisition of cognitive entities, as defined by a cognitive perspective, to becoming a member of a scientific community. As mentioned in the previous section, this is not meant to imply that all learners should ultimately become professional scientists, but the statement reflects the view that learning science involves being engaged in the culture and activities of science.

In some respects, recent emphases on inquiry-based learning experiences have moved the field of science education closer to the desired goal of actively involving students in scientific practice. Inquiry based approaches encourage students to engage in some elements of scientific practice such as manipulation of variables, experimental design, and the confirmation of hypotheses. However, they typically fail to accurately account for the social nature of science or to highlight the significance of discursive practices that enable students to make sense of their findings, apply their understandings of science to personal decision making, and engage in public discourse about issues related to science (Duschl & Osborne, 2002). Language use, broadly construed to include written, spoken, and symbolic discourses, is central to the culture and practices of modern science (Gee, 2005; Lemke, 2004), and attempts to promote sociocultural versions of scientific literacy must attend to this reality. Language use, as it is applied here, refers not to just simple decoding and deciphering vocabulary or sentences. Language use as scientific practice is consistent with the expanded view of literacy in its fundamental sense. Doing science is a social process through which meanings and conclusions are negotiated via written and spoken language. This involves creating and interpreting text and an interplay between authors/speakers, the words and figures they inscribe, and the readers/receivers of the material (Norris & Phillips, 2003).

In the beginning of this chapter, I contrasted the fundamental and derived senses of literacy because the fundamental sense of literacy is central to proposals for interdisciplinary instruction in science and language arts; and yet, discussions of scientific literacy tend to focus on the derived sense of literacy. This contrast is significant particularly when the fundamental sense of literacy is cast simply and the derived sense is framed with a cognitive epistemological framework. These frameworks allow and even encourage the separation of language from science and create situations that marginalize language in science learning contexts. However, when scientific literacy in its fundamental sense is framed with the expansive view and the derived sense of scientific literacy is conceptualized from a sociocultural perspective, the distinctions between the fundamental and derived senses become blurred. Scientific literacy comes to represent the appropriation of authentic scientific practice (i.e., practice meaningful within the culture of science) that, in large part, is defined by the use of language.

APPLICATIONS TO CLASSROOM PRACTICE

The sociocultural perspective on scientific literacy, which subsumes both the fundamental and derived senses of literacy, highlights the critical need for interdisciplinary instruction in science and language arts. To understand science, learners must be engaged in the culture of science that requires that they have opportunities to read, write, debate, create graphic displays, interpret charts, among other literate practices (Yore, 2004). One avenue for achieving these goals is to shift the focus of some of the activities already completed in elementary classrooms. Inquiry-based activities can provide authentic opportunities for students to experience the culture of science, but the goals and enactment of such activities have to be more broadly construed than simply promoting student interest through "hands-on" activity or the acquisition of predetermined facts. In order for inquiry-based activities to be successful from a sociocultural perspective, teachers and students need to capitalize on discourse opportunities naturally embedded within inquiry. Meaningful inquiry experiences necessarily involve opportunities for investigators to negotiate text and use language to construct and share meaning. These situations present ideal settings for the integration of science and language arts instruction.

An example of this kind of approach is presented by Barab, Sadler, Heiselt, Hickey, and Zuiker (in press). This case study presents a 10-day unit during which a fourth-grade class explores a water pollution crisis. A central element of the unit is a multiuser virtual environment (MUVE) that students can navigate with personalizable avatars. The MUVE, which is supported by the same kinds of technologies seen in many popula, commercial gaming products, provides opportunities for students to explore a virtual stream with declining fish populations. Students conducted virtual water tests on parameters such as pH, turbidity, acidity, and dissolved oxygen as well as interacting with other players and non-player characters representing varied interests. Whereas the MUVE provided a context for the inquiry focus, much of the actual class time was spent away from the computer lab interrogating documents and figures (taken from within the MUVE), interpreting data, building a shared sense of understanding, and creating artifacts to support the investigation (e.g., scientific reports regarding water quality test results and letters to the managers of the area surrounding the virtual stream). Throughout the experience, students used their emerging understandings of science concepts and literacy practices such as engaging in content-specific discourses, writing contextually relevant letters and reports, and deconstructing scientific inscriptions. By doing so, desired science and language arts outcomes became important tools for students to leverage in the service of their explorations. These activities differed from more traditional learning situations in that the students were immersed in a rich context in which language and literacy practices were central to the science being done.

Another approach for promoting scientific literacy as conceived by the sociocultural perspective makes use of socially relevant issues with conceptual, procedural, or technological associations with science. This general approach has been advocated under the banner of Science-Technology-Society (STS; Yager, 1996) and more recently STSE (STS-Environment) or socioscientific issues (Zeidler, Sadler, Simmons, & Howes, 2005). Socio-scientific issues (SSI) are typically controversial and ill structured, that is, they do not possess simple, straightforward or readily apparent solutions (King & Kitchener, 2004). Examples of SSI that might fit elementary curricula include debate over keeping animals in zoos, alternative sources of energy, pollution, and water quality. One of the advantages of engaging students in explorations of SSI is that the learning experiences become explorations of interrelationships among value systems, data, interpreted text, and discourse. Students and teachers cannot circumvent authentic practice by looking for shortcuts to a "correct answer." Because of their ill-structured and undetermined status, SSI provide opportunities for authentic investigation, and by doing so, offer opportunities to exercise and build literate practices.

The primary focus of this chapter has been an examination of scientific literacy and various approaches to defining this somewhat nebulous construct. I initially differentiate between the fundamental and derived senses of scientific literacy, where fundamental literacy represents the use of language and derived literacy is more broadly construed to denote the intended outcomes of instruction. Most accounts of scientific literacy from within the community of science educators have focused on the derived sense of literacy. Fundamental literacy can be further dissected into simple and expanded views. The simple view of fundamental literacy regards reading as decoding; whereas, the expanded view presents literacy as inferring meaning that assumes an active relationship between a reader, his or her prior experiences, and the text he or she comes to negotiate. The expanded view also implies a constitutive relationship between science and language that makes it central to and necessary for scientific practice. Language is not viewed as a just a tool of science; without language, science fails to exist.

With respect to scientific literacy in the derived sense, the chapter presents competing frameworks for conceptualizing the aims of science instruction. The cognitive perspective prioritizes cognitive entities such as specific concepts and attitudes; whereas, the sociocultural perspective frames learning as enculturation with an emphasis on practice. Because language is an essential aspect of science practice, literacy in the fundamental sense should be featured prominently in learning experiences informed by the sociocultural perspective. In fact the expanded view of fundamental literacy and the sociocultural perspective on derived literacy tend to blur the distinctions between fundamental and derived literacies. It is within this area where the fundamental and derived senses of scientific literacy merge that interdisciplinary science and language arts instruction become most important and most likely to produce successful outcomes.

FOR FURTHER THOUGHT

1. The phrase "scientific literacy" has been used in very different ways by various authors. Given its diverse, often contradictory, interpretations, does it remain a useful concept for educators? Why?
2. What is the culture of science and what is the position of language within that culture?

3. The author of this chapter establishes three important dichotomies; fundamental versus derived literacies, simple versus expanded fundamental literacies, and cognitive versus sociocultural perspectives.
    (a) Characterize the differences captured by each dichotomy.
    (b) Are there problems or inconsistencies with these dichotomies? Would other representational strategies, a continuum for instance, be more appropriate?
4. How would "transfer" be framed differently by cognitive and socio-cultural perspectives?
5. The author discusses the need to engage students in "authentic practice, where authentic practice represents developmentally appropriate contexts that involve similar processes as those used in research labs or other settings in which real science takes place." How does classroom inquiry differ from "real science?" In what ways can classroom practices be shaped to more accurately reflect "real science?"
6. Think of a standard activity used to integrate science and language arts. How could this activity be modified to better account for a sociocultural perspective on science literacy?

REFERENCES

Barab, S. A., Sadler, T. D., Heiselt, C., Hickey, D. T., & Zuiker, S. (in press). Relating narrative, inquiry, and inscriptions: A framework for socio-scientific inquiry. *Cognition and Instruction*.

Brown, J. S., Collins, A., & Duguid, P. (1989). Situated cognition and the culture of learning. *Educational Researcher, 18*(1), 34–41.

Bybee, R. W. (1997). *Achieving scientific literacy: From purposes to practices*. Portsmouth, NH: Heinemann.

Coy, M. (1989). *Anthropological perspectives on apprenticeship*. New York: SUNY Press.

DeBoer, G. E. (2000). Scientific literacy: Another look at its historical and contemporary meanings and its relationship to science education reform. *Journal of Research in Science Teaching, 37*, 582–601.

Duschl, R. A., & Osborne, J. (2002). Supporting and promoting argumentation discourse in science education. *Studies in Science Education, 38*, 39–72.

Fang, Z. (2004). Scientific literacy: A systematic functional linguistics perspective. *Science Education, 89*, 335–347.

FLDOE. (1996). Sunshine State Standards. Retrieved March 13, 2007 from http://www.firn.edu/doe/menu/sss.htm

Gee, J. P. (2005). Language in the science classroom: Academic social languages as the heart of school-based literacy. In R. K. Yerrick & W.-M. Roth (Eds.),

Establishing scientific classroom discourse communities: Multiple voices of teaching and learning research (pp. 19–37). Mahwah, NJ: Lawrence Erlbaum Associates.

Greeno, J. G. (1998). The situativity of knowing, learning, and research. *American Psychologist, 53,* 5– 26.

Gross, P. R. (2005). *The state of state science standards.* Washington, DC: Thomas B. Fordham Institute.

Hurd, P. D. (1998). Scientific literacy: New minds for a changing world. *Science Education, 82,* 407–416.

INDOE. (2005). Indiana accountability system for academic progress [Electronic Version]. Retrieved December 12, 2005 from http://www.doe.state.in.us/asap/welcome.html

Jenkins, E. (1990). Scientific literacy and school science education. *School Science Review, 71,* 43–51.

King, P. M., & Kitchener, K. S. (2004). Reflective judgment: Theory and research on the development of epistemic assumptions through adulthood. *Educational Psychologist, 39,* 5–18.

Kirshner, D., & Whitson, J. A. (Eds.). (1997). *Situated cognition: Social, semiotic, and psychological perspectives.* Mahwah, NJ: Lawrence Erlbaum Associates.

Laugksch, R. C. (2000). Scientific literacy: A conceptual overview. *Science Education, 84,* 71–94.

Lave, J. (1988). *Cognition in practice: Mind, mathematics, and culture in everyday life.* Boston, MA: Cambridge University Press.

Lave, J., & Wenger, E. (1991). *Situated learning: Legitimate peripheral participation.* Cambridge, England: Cambridge University Press.

Lemke, J. L. (2004). The literacies of science. In E. W. Saul (Ed.), *Crossing borders in literacy and science instruction* (pp. 33–47). Newark, DE: International Reading Association.

Munby, A. H. (1976). Some implications of language in science education. *Science Education, 60,* 115–124.

Norris, S. P., & Phillips, L. M. (2003). How literacy in its fundamental sense is central to scientific literacy. *Science Education, 87,* 224–240.

NRC. (1996). *National science education standards.* Washington, DC: National Academy Press.

Pressley, M., & Wharton-McDonald, R. (1997). Skilled comprehension and its development through instruction. *School Psychology Review, 26,* 448–467.

Shamos, M. H. (1996). The myth of scientific literacy. *Liberal Education, 82*(3), 12–16.

Wellington, J., & Osborne, J. (2001). *Language and literacy in science education.* Buckingham, England: Open University Press.

Yager, R. E. (Ed.). (1996). *Science/technology/society as reform in science education.* Albany, NY: SUNY Press.

Yager, R. E. (2004). Science is not written, but it can be written about. In E. W. Saul (Ed.), *Crossing borders in literacy and science instruction* (pp. 95–122). Newark, DE: International Reading Association.

Yore, L. D. (2004). Why do future scientists need to study the language arts? In E. W. Saul (Ed.), *Crossing borders in literacy and science instruction* (pp. 71–94). Newark, DE: International Reading association.

Yore, L. D., Craig, M. T., & Maguire, T. O. (1998). Index of science reading awareness: An interactive constructive model, text verification, and grades 4–8 results. *Journal of Research in Science Teaching, 35,* 27–51.

Zeidler, D. L., Sadler, T. D., Simmons, M. L., & Howes, E. V. (2005). Beyond STS: A research-based framework for socioscientific issues education. *Science Education, 89,* 357–377.

Part II

THE INFLUENCE OF INTERDISCIPLINARY SCIENCE AND LANGUAGE ARTS INSTRUCTION ON CHILDREN'S LEARNING

What can elementary students learn from interdisciplinary science and language arts teaching? How will we know what these students gain from such instruction? The reports in this section aim to describe the influences of interdisciplinary science and language arts instruction on students' learning, as well as approaches that teachers can use to assess their students' understandings of science and language arts content. For example, in Chapter 4, Morrison explores teachers' use of science notebooks as assessment tools for their students' understandings of science content. Crowther and Canon describe and provide evidence for the usefulness of an innovative strategy called *THC* in Chapter 5. Their approach to interdisciplinary science and language arts instruction promises to engage students in scientific inquiry, allowing them to share their understandings through science notebooking in a way that is consistent with current views of nature of science.

Building on the use of science notebooking in the previous chapters, Powell and Aram describe children publishing their work as evidence of a way of knowing about science in Chapter 6. They describe a balanced model of language arts and science instruction. In Chapter 7, Crowther, Robinson, Edmundson, and Colburn describe the learning that English language learners can undertake in classrooms that use interdisciplinary language arts and science instruction. They further describe methods for adapting lessons to reinforce conceptual learning for ELL students. Finally, providing many actual writing examples from primary students,

Giles shares the influence of interdisciplinary language arts instruction in an inquiry curriculum on students' understandings in a multiage first and second grade classroom in Chapter 8.

4

Teachers' Use of Science Notebooks to Assess Understanding of Science Concepts

Judith A. Morrison
Washington State University

Over recent years, many standards-based curricula (i.e., STC, FOSS) have begun recommending the use of science notebooks as a strategy for elementary teachers to use in developing students' science understanding. Research (Glynn & Muth, 1994; Hand, Prain, & Yore, 2001; Rivard, 1994) has shown that writing-to-learn in science has enhanced students' learning when teachers attend to curricular goals, learners' metacognitive knowledge, and the instructional environment. Therefore, if students are encouraged to communicate their understanding of concepts in science notebook writings, these notebooks can be an effective strategy to help students learn science (Audet, Hickman, & Dobrynina, 1996; Fellows, 1994; Shepardson & Britsch, 1997). Science notebooks also allow teachers to "assess students' understanding and provide the feedback students need for improving their performance" (Ruiz-Primo, Li, & Shavelson, 2002, p. 24).

Science notebooks can be a valuable tool for both teachers and students to use to determine (a) prior knowledge and existing science ideas, (b) how conceptual understanding is being built, (c) procedural understanding, (d) mastery of curriculum goals, and (e) the ability to apply/transfer ideas to new context (Volkmann & Abell, 2003). Science notebooks may be described as a place where students record their questions, predictions, observations, and descriptions of procedures, and, most importantly, what they have learned. Science notebooks may incorporate diagrams, drawings, graphs, and tables (Campbell & Fulton, 2003). Science notebooks contain information about the students' classroom experiences and "they imitate the journals that actual scientists use as they explore the world" (Hargrove & Nesbit, 2003).

In an effort to improve the science literacy of all students, the *National Science Education Standards* [National Research Council (NRC), 1996] have stressed that teachers must continually assess their students' understanding of science concepts. This assessment should cover students' reasoning and their achievement as well as their opportunity to learn science. Teachers should specifically plan for opportunities where their students can discuss and display science understanding (NRC, 2001b). By using these opportunities to gather information about students' learning and then using that information to modify and adjust instruction, the teacher will be able to more effectively impact student achievement (Bell & Cowie, 2001). Traditional classroom science writing may often simply be communicating what the student knows to the teacher by filling in blanks, by producing short responses to teacher-generated questions, or by recording observations and information (Applebee, 1984). In order to move toward classroom science writing where students communicate more in-depth understanding, teachers are encouraged to ask students to write about their ideas and experiences in science notebooks (Ruiz-Primo, Li, Ayala, & Shavelson, 1999).

According to Klentschy and Molina-DeLa Torre (2004), students' science notebook writing may be a way for students to strengthen their language skills as they develop an understanding of the world around them.

> The student science notebook serves as an important link between science and literacy when it is utilized in the classroom as a knowledge-transforming form of writing that provides an appropriate opportunity for students to develop voice in the process of constructing meaning from their experiences with the science phenomena. This, coupled with appropriate and timely feedback from the classroom teacher, has strong potential to provide the improvement in student achievement across the curriculum that educators are seeking. (p. 352)

THE PROJECT

This project explored the use of science notebooks by teachers in their classrooms and tracked the changes the teachers underwent as they moved toward using the notebooks to find out their students' understanding of science concepts and processes. Teachers were introduced to the use of science notebooks as a tool and then they employed science notebooks in their classrooms for 2 years. The teachers' use of notebooks was documented throughout the project as well as their beliefs about student learning and assessment of students' knowledge and understanding about science. The participating teachers were asked to implement strategies of notebook use that would motivate students to communicate their science understanding through writing in science notebooks. Initial strategies were suggested to teachers at their first meeting and then, throughout the project, other strategies were designed by the teachers themselves, implemented in their classrooms, and shared with all participants.

It is important for teachers to be encouraged to use science notebooks to gather information on students' understanding; Baxter, Bass, and Glaser (2001) found that the focus of science notebooks in fifth-grade classrooms was strictly limited to "those aspects of inquiry that teachers attended to" (p. 138). If teachers are only looking at whether the students can follow directions, copy procedures, and complete the activities, all the students will put in their notebooks are data recordings or procedure descriptions. Often, students may understand what has happened in an investigation but will not be able to put their thoughts into words; recording thinking is not an easy task. Without encouragement and training to communicate their understanding of science concepts, students will not automatically write about their learning.

Five experienced (at least 5 years of experience) teachers participated in 2 years of exploration surrounding the use of science notebooks, employing science notebooks in their classrooms, and reflecting on this use. These teachers taught science at either the fourth- or fifth-grade level, either daily or for an extended block (i.e., Friday morning) once each week. This project was set up to explore how science teachers begin to use notebooks and how this use may change over time as teachers reflect on assessing their students' understanding of science concepts. Data were collected from a variety of sources in order to answer the research question: How do teachers use science notebooks to assess their students' understanding. A combination of pre and postquestionnaires, pre and postinterviews, classroom observations, and large group meeting discussions were employed to gain a picture of how these teachers developed in their use of science notebooks.

At the beginning of the project, the teachers outlined a plan for their use of science notebooks for the upcoming school year and described what they hoped to accomplish by implementing science notebooks in their classrooms. The teachers were encouraged to try a variety of strategies when using the science notebooks and to share and discuss these strategies with others in the group. During the next 2 years, the teachers used science notebooks in their classrooms. The teachers met with the researcher as a large group at the university five times during the first year and three times during the second year. During these group meetings, the teachers were asked to share any strategies they were using involving science notebooks, to discuss concerns and frustrations they had with science notebook use, and to bring their students' notebooks to show the group. There was no formal instruction provided after the first group session, although two or three guiding questions were used to elicit conversation at each meeting. These guiding questions were: (a) What new strategies are being used in your notebooks, (b) what concerns or problems are you encountering with notebook use, (c) how are you able to find out students' understanding of concepts from their notebooks, and (d) what evidence do teachers have that science notebooks are valuable. After 2 years of using science notebooks, the teachers' use of science notebooks as an assessment tool was compared to their initial use.

FINDINGS

Data from the questionnaires, interviews, large group meetings, and student work were used to describe the teachers' development in their use of science notebooks to assess students' understanding of science concepts. The problems, concerns, and successes these teachers encountered as they implemented science notebooks were also documented.

Teachers' Development in Their Use of Science Notebooks

What Is in the Notebooks.   Early in the project, these teachers were asked about how they used science notebooks in their classrooms. The majority of these teachers said they used the notebooks as a place for students to take notes, record data, or answer worksheet or book questions. Some of the characteristic answers to this question were: "I have my students write entry tasks, class notes," "They fill in worksheets and paste them in the notebook," and "Used mainly for collection and organization of material." Another teacher said that the use of science notebooks entailed: "Organized collection of writing and data, drawing, charts, etc., written observations and vocabulary." At this beginning point in the study, there was one teacher who used the notebooks as a place for students to reflect on their learning. Her response to the question of how notebooks are used was: "Student work, ideas, prethinking, reflections on inquiry activities, notes from discussions." Generally, little mention of using notebooks as a place for students to reflect on their learning or as a place to write down their own thoughts and ideas was made.

Later in the project, at the end of the first year, the teachers were again asked about how they used science notebooks. The majority of the teachers did mention that they had started to include students' reflections on learning and discussion of conclusions in their notebooks. One of the teachers said:

> The students take notes and write reflections daily. The students use their notebooks to help refresh their memory of what was discussed and what they learned in the class that day. The students use the notebooks to write their personal feelings on how the information related to them.

Another teacher mentioned that the "students keep all of their science material in their notebooks. Assignments, notes, reflections, and handouts. It is a students' reference book." The teachers seemed to have moved closer to using the notebooks as a place for students to reflect on their work, yet many of the teachers said that their goals for the second year included trying to use the notebooks for more student reflection on learning. "Next year the notebooks won't include general assignments, i.e., cut/paste worksheets. It will contain more reflections, news articles, and photos of projects," and "I plan to use it for reflection and observation and not paste worksheets." It was seen that these teachers began to realize that the notebook could be used for much more than a place to have students paste worksheets. They set goals to move away from the restrictions of using notebooks only as a place for students to record work and to move towards attempting to find out students' thinking and reflections. For example, one teacher set a goal of paying more attention to students' writing skills: "Focus more on the writing piece of the journal to develop better writing/communication skills." Another teacher set a goal of having a specific side of the notebook pages for reflections: "[On the] left side will be reflections/metacognition, right side will be procedures/experiments/discoveries." One teacher reflected on how she moved away from using notebooks as a place to keep work to a strategy used to help students organize their thoughts about doing science:

Notebooks two years ago were a cutsy way to keep students' science paperwork, now it's the way my students do science. We test, research, support, discuss, take notes, think, graph, make drawings, photos, articles, others comments, think again [in the notebooks].

Student Writing in Notebooks.   The teachers were asked to describe their general view of a science notebook and the early and later responses to this question were compared. Specifically, teachers' responses that addressed student writing were selected. In the first questionnaire, the majority of the teachers did not mention students' writing in the notebook as an essential element. On the midproject questionnaire (end of the first year) and on the final questionnaire and in the final interview, the teachers' responses showed that they had begun to see that students' writing had to be an essential component of the notebooks. One teacher made the following comment about students' writing: "The students need to write their background knowledge and what they learned and assess what their next steps are." Another teacher talked about how student writing in the science notebooks is a good way to incorporate writing in science:

The children came away from the end of each unit with these [notebooks] that had all the records, their ownership, all the records of everything they had done or thought about. It was very significant to them and evidence when you talk about writing [with the students] and the non-fiction writing that is done is valuable.

[I have the students] explain why they did what they did or describe in detail or give other examples of how else this could be used. "When have you seen something similar to this before?" "How else would this be valuable (what other ways) to you?"

Less and less emphasis has been placed on the students about the perfection of their notebook. More emphasis [is placed] on their thought process and more pictures, graphs, articles, and others [are put] in notebooks.

One teacher commented on the final questionnaire how the notebooks provide more personal information about the student: "They [science notebooks] get me away from having to correct answers on worksheets and tests. To open a notebook is more enjoyable and it is like looking into their [students'] heads."

Problems, Concerns, and Successes Encountered With Science Notebook Use

Problems and Concerns.   Some of the concerns expressed at the beginning of the project regarding using science notebooks were that the notebooks were hard for some students to keep up with, that many students but especially special education students needed a large amount of time to write information into the notebooks. Also, the frustration of teachers about putting worksheets into the notebooks was evident in one teacher's quote about the problem with using science notebooks: "Getting things glued, taped, stapled in can be a problem—time consuming."

When asked on the midproject and final questionnaire, teachers voiced a broader variety of concerns with science notebook use. Some quotes from these questionnaires in response to what aspects of using science notebooks they found problematic or difficult were: "Getting students to use them and keep them. They sometimes figure if there is no grade, why bother," and "The students would rather do activities than have to write stuff down," and "I always wish I had the luxury of going through all of them every night."

Successes.   The teachers discussed a variety of benefits of using science notebooks throughout the project. The most commonly voiced benefit at the beginning of the project was that student work was organized, all in one place; students had access to their science work at all times, and students could be held accountable for past work more easily. Another benefit discussed by a number of these teachers was that they felt the notebooks made their students feel more like they were doing science, that they were more like scientists. During the middle and end of the project, the teachers mentioned the successes they had seen with low achieving students when using science notebooks:

> I realize they are an important resource. I saw firsthand that growth was being made. The growth was not from whom I would have expected. Many of the lower performing students, some who struggle with understanding did much better with the use of notebooks throughout the year.

The teachers reflected on the value of science notebooks and reported the following comments on the end of the project questionnaire: "To a teacher it [notebook] is a permanent record showing their understanding and growth in your class," and "It's most valuable to the teacher in that at a glance you can usually check for understanding—do they use proper terms—is inquiry giving them the right data."

CONCLUSION

The teachers that participated in this 2-year project underwent important growth in their use of science notebooks. When they started the project, they asked their students to put worksheets and vocabulary into their notebooks and there was little emphasis on students' reflections or communication of learning. As the project progressed, the teachers realized that in order to assess students' understanding of science concepts, they would need to require their students to include reflections, summaries, thoughts, and ideas in the notebooks.

The teachers in this study commented that they found the notebooks to be valuable tools to assess all levels of learners. As they began to use the notebooks to assess students' understanding toward the end of the first year and into the second, the teachers saw that the individualization of the science notebooks was important. They relaxed their criteria for what had to be in the notebooks, leaving this more to the students to determine, and they saw that the notebooks became a better reflection of the individual student, a first step in assessment.

When the teachers were asked at the end of the project to list strategies they felt were important to successful science notebook use, they stressed that teachers need to ask their students to write "as much as possible" and to "write as they think." Another general recommendation the project teachers made was that students need to know that the main purpose of the science notebook is a place for them to communicate their understanding and then teachers must use it for that purpose. The teachers participating in this project identified time to write in science notebooks as a crucial component of finding out students' understanding. If teachers are planning ahead for science notebook writing time at the beginning, during , and at the end of science investigations, then their students will soon become used to writing about prior knowledge and experiences, making predictions, proposing explanations of phenomena, and communicating new understandings.

As teachers are requested by the National Science Education Standards (NRC, 1996) to assess their students' understanding of science concepts, it is clear that teachers must first be trained to recognize that students need to be required to communicate their ideas in writing. If teachers only require their students to complete worksheets and place these in their notebooks without any attention to writing about understanding or reflecting on learning, then it will be difficult to assess understanding. One of the recommendations made by the NRC (2001a) is that "teachers need to understand how to use tools that can yield valid inferences about student understanding and thinking, as well as methods of interpreting data derived from assessments" (p. 309).

APPLICATIONS TO CLASSROOM PRACTICE

Requiring students to write about their understanding in science notebooks is a tool that teachers can use regularly and successfully. The teachers in this project were asked to focus on strategies that they could use themselves in their own classrooms. Initially they were given basic science notebook guidelines but each teacher adapted these to his or her own individual teaching style. The teachers found that they needed to try out different ways to have their students communicate understanding; some strategies worked and others did not. The teachers compiled a list of recommended physical aspects and strategies for teachers and students to use with science notebooks. This list is included in Appendix A. Teachers need to keep in mind the idea that unless students are asked to communicate their comprehension on a science topic, they will simply record observations or state what they did without reflecting on meaning. If students are only asked to make records of their experiments and list their results, the teacher will be unable to access their understanding. "Simply logging the results and listing the experiments limits students in the construction of the true meaning of the phenomena and reduces the experience to knowledge and transmission of recalled information" (Klentschy & Molina-De La Torre, 2004, p. 348).

FOR FURTHER THOUGHT

1. List some prompts that you might use to motivate your students to write about their understanding of a specific science topic.
2. Design a rubric that you could use to assess students' understanding communicated in a science notebook.
3. List the components that you would like to have your students include in their science notebooks for each science investigation.

4. How do your instructional practices affect students' use of science notebooks?
5. Discuss strategies that could be implemented in your classroom in order to provide ample time for student science notebook writing.

REFERENCES

Applebee, A. N. (1984). Writing and reasoning. *Review of Educational Research*, *54*(4), 577–596.

Audet, R. H., Hickman, P., & Dobrynina, G. (1996). Learning logs: A classroom practice for enhancing scientific sense making. *Journal of Research in Science Teaching*, *33*, 205–222.

Baxter, G. P., Bass, K. M., & Glaser, R. (2001). Notebook writing in three fifth–grade science classrooms. *The Elementary Science Journal*, *102*(2), 123–140.

Bell, B., & Cowie, B. (2001). The characteristics of formative assessment in science education. *Science Education*, *85*(5), 536–553.

Campbell, B., & Fulton, L. (2003). *Science notebooks*. Portsmouth, NH: Heinemann.

Fellows, N. (1994). A window into thinking: Using student writing to understand conceptual change in science learning. *Journal of Research in Science Teaching*, *31*, 985–1001.

Glynn, S. M., & Muth, K. D. (1994). Reading and writing to learn science: Achieving scientific literacy. *Journal of Research in Science Teaching*, *31*(9), 1057–1073.

Hand, B., Prain, V., & Yore, L. (2001). Sequential writing tasks' influence on science learning. In G. Rijlaarsdam (Series Ed.), P. Tynjala, L Mason, & K. Lonka (Vol. Eds.), *Studies in writing: Vol. 7. Writing as a learning tool: Integrating theory into practice* (PP. 105–129). Netherlands: Kluwer.

Hargrove, T. Y., & Nesbit, C. (2003). *Science notebooks: Tools for increasing achievement across the curriculum*. Columbus, OH: ERIC Clearinghouse for Science Mathematics and Environmental Education. (ERIC Document Reproduction Service No. ED482720)

Klentschy, M. P., & Molina-De La Torre, E. (2004). Students' science notebooks and the inquiry process. In E. W. Saul (Ed.), *Crossing borders in literacy and science instruction* (pp. 340–354). Newark, DE: International Reading Association.

National Research Council. (1996). *National science education standards*. Washington, DC: National Academy Press.

National Research Council. (2001a). *Knowing what students know: The science and design of educational assessment*. Washington, DC: National Academy Press.

National Research Council. (2001b). *Classroom assessment and the national science education standards*. Washington, DC: National Academy Press.

Rivard, L. P. (1994). A review of writing to learn in science: Implications for practice and research. *Journal of Research in Science Teaching*, *31*(9), 969–983.

Ruiz-Primo, M. A., Li, M., Ayala, C., & Shavelson, R. J. (1999). *Student science journals and the evidence they provide: Classroom learning and opportunity to learn.* Paper presented at the annual NARST meeting, Boston, MA.

Ruiz-Primo, M. A., Li, M., & Shavelson, R. J. (2002). Looking into students' science notebooks: What do teachers do with them? (CSE Technical Report 562). Los Angeles, CA: University of California, Center for the Study of Evaluation. (ED465806)

Shepardson, D. P., & Britsch, S. J. (1997). Children's science journals: What can students' science journals tell us about what they are learning? *Science and Children, 37*(6), 39–43.

Volkmann, M. J., & Abell, S. K. (2003). Seamless assessment. *Science & Children, 40*(8), 41–45.

5

Using the THC Model of Science Investigation and Science Notebooking in Elementary and Middle-Level Science Classrooms

David T. Crowther
University of Nevada

John R. Cannon
University of Nevada

It seems that everywhere one turns, whether it be an administrator, a parent, or a state or federal legislator, the determining factor about what should be taught in the elementary classroom is the increase in the teaching of language arts and mathematics content. What message does this send to the elementary teacher about the importance of teaching science? The reality is clear. Science is getting less emphasis and instructional time in elementary schools across the nation (Lemonick, 2006).

We believe this does not need to remain commonplace. When a child is reading, after all, they are reading about something in the same sense as when a child is manipulating objects in math, often times, they are counting. To be sure, reading and mathematics content instruction is important for the ultimate success of students from all classrooms, public, private, or home-schooled, in our great United States. These subjects, however, are not autonomous, even to the highest elected official in the land. President George W. Bush, in a February 2006 speech, announced that contemporary students need "a firm grounding in areas such as math and science" (Murray, 2006, p. 1). He continued by noting that:

> [T]o keep America competitive, one commitment is necessary above all: We must continue to lead the world in human talent and creativity. Our greatest advantage in the world has always been our educated, hard-working, ambitious people, and we are going to keep that edge. (p. 1)

President Bush's challenge is analogous to those of other Presidents before him dating back to Franklin Delano Roosevelt. During his administration, another Bush, that being Vannevar Bush, scientist and advisor to President Roosevelt, drafted a document in 1945 entitled "Science—The Endless Frontier." The document defined the significance of continued support for scientific research after the war effort. Bush called for a national research entity that "should develop and promote a national policy for scientific research and scientific education..." (Bush, 1945, p. 28). His challenges for the future were never totally realized; however, in 1950, the National Science Foundation (NSF) was created.

Presently, the National Science Education Standards (NSES) continue to promote contemporary science teaching. "Inquiry into authentic questions generated from student experiences" as noted in the Standards, "is the central strategy for teaching science" (NRC, 1996, p. 31). Other professional groups have added to the chorus in this time of educational reform. The International Reading Association (IRA), the National Council of Teachers of English (NCTE), along with the NSES, encourage the purposeful use of language, such as the use of language skills, reading, writing, thinking, and oral expression of ideas, in the exploration and study of science. The IRA and NCTE support the use of intensive language in all content areas. They state "No matter what the subject, the people who read it, write it, and talk it are the ones who learn it best" (Learning Through Language, 2002, p. 1).

Reading and science are a natural connection. The obvious connection in the elementary classroom is through children's literature. However, many teachers believe if their science instruction includes a children's book on the topic, then the language arts connection has been met. Although this is a good start and great introduction to a hands-on science lesson, reading a children's book alone is not teaching science nor is it truly integrating literature into a child's science lesson. The integration of children's literature into a science lesson, however, is a natural hook or engagement for children that allows an introduction of the concept or topic to be taught. This literature also activates the background knowledge the learner possesses.

Utilizing reading and writing strategies, and their corresponding skills in a science lesson allows for purposeful learning. The students have a reason to read and a reason to write or communicate through different media. This is especially important when including the English as a Second Language (ESL) or English Language Learners (ELL) students in the classroom. According to the National Science Teachers Association publication, *Learning Science and the Science of Learning* (Bybee, 2002), literacy skills and language development "cannot be disconnected from the substance of the reading and writing" (p. 40).

Others have also suggested that second-language acquisition is most successful when the focus of instruction is on substance rather than on form, and there is sufficient opportunity to engage in meaningful use of that language (Krashen, 1982; Baker & Saul, 1994; Crandall, 1994; Gallas, 1995). The benefits of this train of thought benefit the second language learner as well as all learners in science. Shymansky, Marberry, and Jorgensen (1977) suggest that "As students communicate, they learn to clarify, refine, and consolidate their thinking." They continue stating, "When students have to explain, argue, and reflect on their work rather than simply select responses, answer questions, and complete standard form assignments, both their writing and inquiry skills are enhanced" (p. 4).

The contributors published in *Science for English Language Learners: K–12 Classroom Strategies* (Fathman & Crowther, 2006) cite many helpful methods promoting the essential and purposeful use of language in learning science. Short and Thier (2006) caution, however, that "It is important...for science educators to realize that English language learners are studying new, challenging curricula in and through a new language" (p. 206).

Peterson (2002) recounts early research discoveries during the development of the Science Curriculum Improvement Study (SCIS). The project took place in the late 1960s in and around the San Francisco Bay Area, which at the time, was experiencing an ever-growing English Language Learner (ELL) population in the local schools. She reports:

> During the development and trial stages of SCIS, two elementary schools in a rural town south of the San Francisco Bay Area decided to assess the impact of SCIS on the advancement of spoken and written English among primary school children who spoke Spanish as a primary language. [They]...reported finding significantly greater (in a statistical sense) advances in English speaking and writing among primary school children in the schools where SCIS was being used. (p. 17–18)

Peterson concludes by noting that the results of this controlled experiment suggest "early evidence of the importance of hands-on experience with materials for improving second language acquisition" (p.18). "Through scientific inquiry," Trueba, Guthrie, and Au (1981) report "students have opportunities to use language in the context of solving meaningful problems, and as a result, engage in the kind of purposeful communicative interactions that promote genuine language use" (p. 76).

For the past few decades, the integration of literacy instruction along with reading and general literacy strategies have influenced the teaching of science in the elementary classroom. One of the more common literacy strategies found in elementary science lessons is the K-W-L model for active reading of expository text. The K-W-L was first published in *The Reading Teacher* by Donna Ogle in 1986. The teaching model was promoted as a means to activate children's background knowledge about what they previously knew about a topic they were about to read. The step K represents what we know, and provides a mental framework in preparation for reading an article. This step is followed by the step W, representing what we want to find out, concluding with the step L, what we learned and still need to learn. Ogle (1987) went on to develop the K-W-L Plus that added mapping (i.e., concept mapping) and summarizing what was learned in the (L) part of the K-W-L.

In our observations in classrooms around the country, we've noticed that the K-W-L used in an elementary inquiry science lesson is more commonly used as a brainstorming activity preceding an activity, not necessarily for preparation for an expository reading assignment. Clearly, the K-W-L has shown a great deal of efficacy in preparing children to ready themselves for reading expository text.

The National Reading Panel (NRP; 2000), in its report "Teaching Children to Read," mandated by the U.S. Congress in 1997, summarizes a review of the existing scientific research related to effective reading instruction. The NRP states that comprehension is, and should be, both purposeful and active. With strategies such as K-W-L, students have a purpose for reading and learning. Students must also be encouraged to become active readers in order to achieve their purpose, to get the very most from a text, and this can be accomplished by teaching children specific strategies demonstrated to increase comprehension (Armbruster, Lehr, & Osborn, 2000; Harvey & Goudvis, 2000; Snow, 2000). Einstein reports (2003) "The National Reading Panel outlines the most important of these scientifically-proven strategies, including:

- comprehension monitoring
- summarizing

- question answering
- question generating." (p. 2)

That said, we believe the spirit behind the K-W-L can be transferred and modified to better suit an inquiry science lesson rather than employing a strategy developed primarily for a content reading.

THE THC MODEL OF WRITING SCIENCE

Akerson's (2001) article "Teaching Science when your Principal says teach Language Arts" proposed modifying the K-W-L model, replacing the K (What do we know?) with a T (What do you think about…) resulting as a new "technique"; the T-W-L (p. 44). This somewhat simple, yet powerful change, opens the cognitive door to inquiry and investigation. With this modification, children can state problems, discuss their thoughts relating to the problem, and, perhaps even evolve their discussions into something analogous to a working hypothesis. This step is followed by the W that allows for questions, or a line of inquiry, to ensue. The L completes the activity. Either model allows for students to further examine and question their thoughts and begin the writing process as they begin a science activity or unit of study.

The next generation of the K-W-L model we propose here is the THC (Crowther & Cannon, 2004). It moves the existing thinking–writing mental process to a higher level of mentation by further engaging the learner in not only questioning, but also designing quasiexperimental science investigations, collecting and analyzing data, and reporting conclusions based on the data from the investigations. The model is summarized below:

- T—What do you Think about…
- H — How might we figure this out…Naturally, once we have our ideas on paper of what we think, it is only natural to proceed on to this next step; and finally…
- C— Conclusions…What do we conclude. This step completes the model when the investigation from the H is completed and conclusions are reported.

The *T* is the very first step to beginning a science investigation or project. By understanding the nature of science, we come to the reality that people don't truly know much, but rather continue to develop hypotheses and theories until such notions become consistent over time and can represent a grand theory in science. The laws of science are known, but can still be proved wrong as knowledge and technology of the world develop and become better refined. For instance, *Scientific American* reported in September, 2004, of Einstein's theory of relativity being seriously challenged due to new information unavailable during his lifetime. We suggest that to begin a science lesson with "What do you think about..." not only supports the nature of science, but it also gives children permission to admit not knowing something, and to risk listing what they think. This can also lead to hypothesis development and even a prediction.

One must create a plan, or employ the H to substantiate information they thought was indeed correct. Whether using open-ended inquiry or more guided inquiry, the How step actually leads the teacher through its proper function. In more guided inquiry, materials, prompts, and even a guiding question could be given to the children. In turn, they would write a procedure section for "How." In a more open-ended inquiry, the teacher would leave questions, materials, and procedures as part of what the children would accomplish in the H step. Note that this can be done individually or even more effectively as a group. The H step could be the outcome of the Engagement phase of a learning cycle leading on to the Exploration phase realized through a hands-on investigation before reading text or through an inquiry activity.

The final step of the THC is just that—What do we conclude? What comes naturally at the end of a scientific investigation or experiment? The Conclusion. When scientists do science, they come to natural conclusions based on the data and on experiences. Conclusions are drawn from both qualitative and quantitative sources. By utilizing the "C" at the end of the lesson, this helps students bring the activity, investigation, or experiment together. The C step can be part or parcel of the Explanation phase of a learning cycle or even as the Evaluation phase depending on how the teacher structures the learning situation. As an Explanation, the teacher could ask questions of the students based on their H experiences guiding them to certain conclusions that make sense from their classroom experience. Additionally, the teacher can use this step of the THC as part of the Evaluation phase of a learning cycle utilizing both formal and informal (summative and formative) assessment plans.

THE THC AND ITS RELATION TO LEARNING AND
THE HISTORY OF SCIENCE EDUCATION

In *How People Learn: Brain, Mind, Experience, and School*, Bransford, Brown, and Cocking (2000) report another connection between the THC and recent research in learning. They state:

> Children are both problem solvers and problem generators: Children attempt to solve problems presented to them, and they also seek novel challenges. They refine and improve their problem-solving strategies, not only in the face of failure, but also by building on prior success. They persist because success and understanding are motivating in their own right. (p. 112)

Through continued practice of the THC model, children can learn to become more skilled and refined problem solvers as Bransford et al. suggest. This practice, however, can only be effective with skilled teachers.

Teachers play a pivotal role in helping children develop these skills. Bransford et al. (2000) highlight this construct by noting:

> Children...exhibit capacities that are shaped by environmental experiences and the individuals who care for them. Caregivers provide supports, such as directing children's attention to critical aspects of events, commenting on features that should be noticed, and in many other ways providing structure to the information. Structure is critical for learning and for moving toward understanding information. (p. 112)

One does not need to look long or hard for the lineage from the intellectual history of science education and the THC model proposed within. Jerome Bruner (1960) reported about the 1959 Woods Hole Conference where "some thirty-five scientists, scholars, and educators" came together to "discuss how science education might be improved in our primary and secondary schools" (p. xvii). One conjecture from that meeting was reported as, "The first object of any act of learning, over and beyond the pleasure it may give, is that it should serve us in the future. Learning should not only take us somewhere; it should allow us later to go further more easily" (p. 17). The THC model allows learners to go as far as they wish in search of answers.

The THC lineage can also be traced to one of the first formal evaluations and reporting of the status of the 72 year-young U.S. public school system in 1893 by J. M. Rice (as cited in DeBoer, 1991). In one of his primary classroom observations in Indianapolis, Indiana, Rice wrote:

> I entered one of the rooms containing the youngest children at the time of the opening exercises. The scene I encountered was a glimpse of fairyland. I was in a room full of bright and happy children, whose eyes were directed toward the teacher...She understood them, sympathized with and loved them, and did all in her power to make them happy. The window-sills were filled with plants, and plants were scattered here and there throughout the room...After the children had sung a few little songs the first lesson of the day was in order. This was a lesson in science; its

subject was a flower. It began with the recitation of a poem. The object of introducing these poems into the plant and animal lessons is to inspire the child with love for the beautiful, with love for nature, and with sympathy for all living things...Before the teacher endeavored to bring out the points to which she desired to direct the special attention of the class, the children were urged to make their own unaided observations and to express them. As each child was anxious to tell what he had observed in relation to the plant itself, what he otherwise knew of it, how it grew, where it grew, and, perhaps some little incident that the flower recalled to him, the class was full of life and enthusiasm...The teacher...by her careful questioning, led the children to observe the particular things to which she had decided to call their attention that morning. Her questions were not put to individual children, but to the whole class, so that every question might serve to set every pupil observing and thinking. (DeBoer, 1991, pp. 36–37)

This primary teacher from Indianapolis knew little about the THC model by name at the time, but truly held it in high esteem as was witnessed in her teaching. She understood and demonstrated the importance of questioning and divergent thinking by getting children to simply tell stories about flowers. Even though Rice's evaluation did not specifically mention any classroom narration devoted to "How might we find out about...," it would not be a stretch of the imagination to speculate that this teacher would be asking her school children to devise, conduct, and report on investigations undertaken at school.

THE THC MODEL AND SCIENCE NOTEBOOKING

It is clear that models such as the K-W-L, T-W-L, or THC have roots deep within effective teaching and learning histories. Although other publications have discussed the importance of the science-writing connection, we believe that the THC model is especially suited for use in conjunction with science notebooking.

Children learn to read and write through the continuing practice of reading and writing. Much research has been performed on the use of notebooks and integration of reading and writing in the science classroom. Every level of learner, from kindergarten to college, is represented in this body of research. Most studies have revolved around writing, in order to document what form of writing instruction is carried out in the classroom. Other areas of research have focused on writing as a way of thinking and learning about science, helping students to implement their own critical thinking in science and not merely repeat definitions and words.

Many researchers who study the writing process in science have noted that student writing in science must be improved if students are to improve their scientific literacy (Atkinson, 1999; Hilgers, Hussey, & Stitt-Bergh, 1999; Holliday, Yore, & Alvermann, 1994). The content of science notebooks, and their success or failure at assisting a child's understanding of science, has been shown to be greatly influenced by the teacher (Baxter, Bass, & Glaser, 2001). If the teacher focuses on procedure and results, the student will focus on this as well. Baxter et al., (2001) declare that "Consideration must be given to how notebooks might be conceptualized, implemented, and assessed in a manner that most effectively integrates the doing of science with writing about it" (p. 132). Currently, no clear model exists of what makes a good science writer (Yore, Hand, & Prain, 1999). Due to a lack of direction, few teachers are willing to use writing as a form of assessment in measuring student progress in science. The science notebook then, sadly and simply, becomes a stark repository where students record terms and definitions (Ruiz-Primo, Li, & Shavelson, 2002).

Good scientific writing promotes and allows for critical thinking to take place. This category of cognitive and metacognitive thinking would not happen if classroom teachers merely had students complete the activity and fill out a worksheet. Several completed studies, and some that are currently underway, are investigating the question of whether using science notebooks enrich teaching practices and student success in both science and writing (Baxter et al., 2001; Keys, Hand, Prian, & Collins, 1999; Rowell & Ebbers, 2004; Ruiz-Primo et al., 2002). The real question here is whether it is the use of the scientific notebook itself that improves student understanding or the use of a specific science writing strategy that improves a student's scientific comprehension.

The Theoretical Perspective of Science Notebooking

According to the National Research Council's (1996) National Science Education Standards (NSES), the emphasis on students' conceptual understanding of science concepts and scientific inquiry is at odds with the nationwide focus on accountability in literacy. Teachers from school districts all across the United States have been forced to relinquish precious instructional time devoted to science in order to concentrate on the demands of English language learners (ELL) and of impoverished students. Consequently, many of these same teachers have begun using science notebooks during science class time in an effort to somehow integrate literacy and science.

Notebooking, as presented here, refers to the practice of students writing down all of the information needed to produce a product, including using the THC model as the context for investigations, rather than merely filling in the blanks of a worksheet. We propose this form of notebooking is better suited to scientific investigation because it asks the student to think about a problem or concept, how to figure it out, and what conclusion they and their group came to about the problem.

"Writing," according to Young (2003), "is one of the ways that children learn in science." The experience of science notebooking, as presented here, requires students to clarify their thoughts, sort through ideas, and illustrate an understanding of the subject at hand. Notebooks can offer data confirming student improvement or lack of progress. They can also be used not solely as the final product, but more as an ongoing resource to determine a child's development of a science concept. Current evidence argues that writing in science assists students in generating meaning from data, making connections between procedures and conclusions, and helps engage them in metacognition. A comment made by White and Welford (1988) notes that few students actually write during science instruction and that "learning how to use language well in all areas of the curriculum becomes, at best, a matter of osmosis; at worst, something that fails to happen" (p. 34). Guidelines set forth in Canada (AAAS, 1993; Council for Ministers of Education Canada, 1997; National Research Council, 1996) state that school science should give students the chance to engage in practices that model those employed in the scientific community. Shepardson and Britsch (1997) write "…giving children the opportunity to write about what they already know enables them to solidify their under-standings and provides a base from which the investigation can confirm or challenge their existing ideas and questions" (p. 89). Language usage has been a recent focus by a number of researchers in science education (Aikenhead, 1998; Ediger, 2001; Hildebrand, 1998; Keys, 1999; Prain & Hand, 1999; Wellington & Osborne, 2001). Many of them state that jour-nals are an effective way for students to communicate the science cur-riculum. Science notebooks help students develop their writing skills while engaging them in the scientific approach to questions and hypoth-esis. Holliday et al., (1994) suggest that developing writing skills that emphasizes problem solving, decision making, and discovery is some-thing that must be promoted.

It is necessary for teachers to use science notebooks in a trenchant way, not merely as an assessment tool. Notebooks can be used to observe what scien-tific knowledge children construct through drawing and writing (Doris, 1991). Shepardson and Britsch (1997) suggest that student writing used as the end product offers little prospect for students to develop their thinking and writing as it provides little understanding of a child's science understanding and focuses on factual knowledge. A better approach would be to use notebooks, including the THC method, to provide an organizational framework for guiding the child's thinking. This approach allows notebooks to be used as a tool or resource for the student's growing knowledge.

APPLICATIONS TO CLASSROOM PRACTICE

The THC model of thinking, doing, and concluding assists in using the notebooks as more than just an assessment tool (Crowther & Cannon, 2004). Students performing an investigation must first identify a problem, frame that problem within a context, decide how to solve it, and finally, discover the real answer. Students must determine what they think, why they think it, and how they will find out if they are right.

The science notebooks of contemporary students should be used for "evaluating evidence and constructing arguments of their own, presenting their ideas in written and oral form and defending their conclusions...," state Millar, Osborne and Nott (1998). "Such work would recognize the central role of writing as a means of learning ideas in science, not solely as a means of producing a record of work" (p. 23).

Two arguments emerge from the literature concerning writing in science. One focuses on students learning primarily to understand and reproduce conventional written dialogue of the scientific community (Halliday & Martin, 1993; Kelly & Chen, 1999; Unsworth, 1997, 2000, 2001; Veel, 1996). Proponents of conventional writing in science, "advocate that writing for learning in science should focus on traditional school science genres because (a) these genres represent the enduring specific representational practices of the science community, (b) science literacy entails proficiency in using accurately the language and discursive forms of science, which are seen as incommensurable with everyday language and discourse, (c) such an approach does not disadvantage any social or cultural group of learners, and (d) such genres focus strongly on the referential or instrumental capacities of language, and are therefore appropriate for developing students' explicit knowledge of the meaning of science terms and practices" (Prain, 2003, p. 4).

The other focus considers that students should use many types of writing skills to develop science literacy and knowledge of scientific inquiry (Boscolo & Mason, 2001; Hanrahan, 1999; Hildebrand, 1998, 1999; Prain & Hand, 1999; Stadler, Benke, & Duit, 2001; Sutton, 1992, 1996). Prain (2003) notes that "Writing here is viewed as a resource to enable the learners to understand science concepts, scientific method, and practices beyond the classroom." (p. 4). Hildebrand (1999) states the case by arguing that conventional science writing that has its focus in factual, rational, and objective knowledge fails to liberate the splendor of scientific research writing. "This general orientation," writes Prain (2003) "aims to encourage students to see writing in science as a resource for communication, argument, justification and clarification of viewpoint, as a tool for learning as well as for displaying or organizing knowledge...students learn when they engage successfully with the demands of communicating to actual readerships, including themselves, for meaningful and varied purposes" (p. 8). Both of these viewpoints agree that language can be viewed as both a method for considering predetermined meanings and for conversational intentions, but each draws a different deduction about the functions of language in capable writing for learning in science.

Hildebrand (1999), Lemke (2001), Sutton (1992), and others advocated the use of the diversified writing approach and suggest that students should brainstorm reasons "why," predict, and speculate about causes of "why," justify and explain their reasoning, and modify their views after seeing additional evidence. Cobern, Gibson, and Underwood (1995) suggest that a person who is scientifically educated must be able to apply basic scientific ideas to everyday circumstances. There are several teaching models that help achieve this outcome. Shepardson and Britsch (1997) developed a four-phase investigative process that involves explaining existing ideas, reflecting on those ideas while recording observations, proposing new questions, and communicating the findings to others. In addition, the THC model allows the student to work on communicating their current thinking, to design experiments to test their ideas, and finally, to draw a conclusion, thereby improving their understanding of a concept. This, indeed, is one of the most important features of the model as it permits the student to cultivate the skills needed to become a scientifically literate person (Crowther & Cannon, 2004).

FOR FURTHER THOUGHT

Science notebooking is, in truth, nothing new. Trying to demonstrate, or model, what an effective science notebook might look like is as easy as visiting your local bookstore or library. Check out some of the books that have reproduced the many and varied notebooks of Leonardo DaVinci. DaVinci was a master at taking meticulous notes accompanied by very detailed drawings. As an extra bonus, be sure to show the students examples of DaVinci's work from the array of topics he studied including life studies, science, and architecture.

Here's a riddle for your students. Why were all of DaVinci's notes written backward in his many notebooks? He did this so that only someone smart enough to realize that the notes were, in fact, written in this way, could read them. His sketches continue to be studied. DaVinci's drawings have helped doctors to better understand the complete layout of the muscle and bone structures of the human body. In short, DaVinci could be considered one of the world's earliest and finest science notebookers.

The Internet has many sites devoted to the writings and drawings of DaVinci. Try a Google™ search yourself, or visit any of the sites listed later. Science notebooks do have a rich past and a promising future for students across the world.

Go to:
The WebMuseum of Paris:
http://www.ibiblio.org/wm/paint/auth/vinci/sketch/
The Milan Science Museum:
http://www.museoscienza.org/english/
The Museum of Science in Boston, MA:
http://www.mos.org/leonardo/

1. Using a traditional lesson that you have already planned, what modifications could be made to include the THC model? What question prompts would you use for the T, H, and C?
2. Take some samples of student notebooks and analyze them for content and process knowledge through the different mediums represented in the student work. What themes emerge and what information does this give you about your use of science notebooks in your teaching the lesson?
3. Thinking about technology and its use in the classroom, how could you design a Web quest to include the THC?
4. Given the notion that "No matter what the subject, the people who read it, write it, and talk it are the ones who learn it best" (Learning Through Language, 1993), how would you add the reading, writing, and communication component to your science curriculum?
5. How would you communicate this information to your colleagues?

REFERENCES

Aikenhead, G. S. (1998). Boarder crossing: Culture, school science, and assimilation of students. In D. A. Roberts & L. Ostman (Eds.), *Problems of meaning in science curriculum* (pp. 86–100). New York: Teachers College Press.

Akerson, V. (2001). Teaching science when your principal says "Teach language arts." *Science and Children, 38*(7), 42–47.

American Association for the Advancement of Science. (1990). *Science for all Americans*. New York: Oxford University Press.

Armbruster, B., Lehr, E., & Osborn, J. (2001). *Put reading first: The research building blocks for teaching children to read*. Jessup, MD: National Institute for Literacy.

Atkinson, D. (1999). *Scientific discourse in sociohistorical context: The philosophical transactions of the Royal Society of London, 1675–1975*. Mahwah, NJ: Lawrence Erlbaum Associates.

Baker, L., & Saul, W. (1994). Considering science and language arts connections: A study of teacher cognition. *Journal of Research in Science Teaching, 31*(9), 1023–1037.

Baxter, G. P., Bass, K. M., & Glaser, R. (2001). Notebook writing in three fifth-grade science classrooms. *Elementary School Journal, 102*(2), 123–140.

Boscolo, P., & Mason, L. (2001). Writing to learn, writing to transfer. In P. Tynjala, L. Mason, & K. Lonka (Eds.), *Writing as a learning tool*. (pp. 83–104) Amsterdam: Kluwer.

Bransford, J. D., Brown, A. L., & Cocking, R. R. (Eds.). (2000). How people learn: Brain, mind, experience, and school. Washington, DC: National Academy Press.

Bruner, J. (1960). *The process of education*. Cambridge, MA: Harvard University Press.

Bybee, R. (Ed.). (2002). *Learning science and the science of learning: Science educators' essay collection*. Arlington, VA: NSTA Press.

Bush, V. (1945) *Science—The endless frontier*. Washington, DC: United States Government Printing Office.

Council of Ministers of Education of Canada. (CMEC). (1997). *Common framework of science learning outcomes*. Ottawa, Canada: Author.

Cobern, W. W., Gibson, A. T., & Underwood, S. A. (1995). Valuing scientific literacy. *Science Teacher, 62*(9), 28–31.

Crandall, J. (1994). Content-centered language learning. *ERIC Digest*. ERIC Clearinghouse on Languages and Linguistics. Retrieved March 8, 2006 from www.cal.org/ericcll/digest/cranda01.html

Crowther, D. T., & Cannon, J. (2004). Strategy makeover. *Science and Children, 42*(1), pp. 42–44.

DeBoer, G. E. (1991). *A history of ideas in science education: Implications for practice*. New York: Teachers College Press

Doris, E. (1991). *Doing what scientists do: Children learn to investigate their world*. Portsmouth, NH: Heinemann.

Ediger, M. (2001). Student journal writing in science. (ERIC Document Reproduction Service No. ED 448462)

Einstein, C. (2003). Activating comprehension: Non-fiction in the classroom. [Online] Available http://www.epsbooks.com/downloads/articles/Non-Fiction.pdf

Fathman, A., & Crowther, D. (Eds.). (2006). Science for English language learners: K–12 classroom strategies. Arlington, VA: NSTA Press.

Gallas, K. (1995). *Talking their way into science*. New York: Teacher's College Press.

Halliday, M., & Martin, J. (1993). *Writing science: Literacy and discursive power.* London: Falmer.

Hanrahan, M. (1999). Rethinking science literacy: Enhancing communication and participation in school science through affirmational dialogue journal writing. *Journal of Research in Science Teaching, 36*(3), 699–718.

Harvey, S., & Goudvis, A. (2000). *Strategies that work: Teaching comprehension to enhance understanding.* Portland, ME: Stenhouse Publishers.

Hildebrand, G. (1998). Disrupting hegemonic writing practices in school science: Contesting the right way to write. *Journal of Research in Science Teaching, 35*(4), 345–362.

Hildebrand, G. (1999, April). *Breaking the pedagogical contract: Teachers' and students' voices.* Paper presented at the Annual Meeting of the National Association for Research in Science Teaching, Boston, MA.

Hilgers, T., Hussey, E., & Stitt-Berg, M. (1999). As you're writing, you have these epiphanies: What college students say about writing and learning in their majors. *Written Communication, 16,* 317–352.

Holliday, W. G., Yore, L. D., & Alvermann, D. E. (1994). The reading–science learning–writing connection. *Journal of Research in Science Teaching, 31*(9), 877–893.

Kelly, G., & Chen, C. (1999). The sound of music: Constructing science as sociocultural practices through oral and written discourse. *Journal of Research in Science Teaching, 36,* 883–915.

Keys, C. (1999). Revitalizing instruction in scientific genres: Connection knowledge production in writing to learn in science. *Science Education, 83,* 115–130.

Keys, C., Hand, B., Prain, V., & Collins, S. (1999). Using the science writing heuristic as a tool for learning from laboratory investigations in secondary school. *Journal of Research in Science Teaching, 36*(10), 1065–1084.

Krashen, S. D. (1982). *Principles and practice in second language acquisition.* Oxford, England: Pergamon Institute of English.

Lemke, J. (2001) Articulating communities: Sociocultural perspectives on science education. *Journal of Research in Science Teaching, 38*(3), 296–316.

Lemonick, M. D. (2006). Is America flunking science? *Time,* (167)7, 22–38.

Millar, R., Osborne, J., & Nott, M (1998). Science education for the future. *School Science Review, 80*(291), 19–25.

Murray, C. (2006) *Bush: Boost math and science 'America's Competitiveness Initiative' aims to keep U.S. at forefront of world economy.* [online] Retrieved March 11, 2006, from www.eschoolnews.com/news/showStory.cfm?ArticleID=6098

National Council of Teachers. (n.d.). *Learning through language:A call for action in all disciplines* Prepared by the National Council of Teachers of English Language and Learning Across the Curriculum Committee. Retrieved March 9, 2006 from http://www.ncte.org/about/over/positions/level/gen/107630.htm

National Reading Panel. (2000). *Report of the National Reading Panel: Teaching children to read: An evidence-based assessment of the scientific research literature on reading and its implications for reading instruction.* Washington, DC: National Institute of Child Health and Human Development; National Institutes of

Health. Retrieved March 13, 2006 from http://www.nationalreadingpanel.org/Publications/subgroups.htm

National Research Council. (1996). *National science education standards*. Washington, DC: National Academy Press.

Ogle, D. (1986). K-W-L: A teaching model that develops active reading of expository text. *The Reading Teacher, 39*(6), 564–570.

Ogle, D. (1987). K-W-L Plus: A strategy for comprehension and summarization. *Journal of Reading, 30*(7), 626–631.

Peterson, R. W. (2002). A love of discovery. In R. G. Fuller (Ed.), *A love of discovery: Science education—The second career of Robert Karplus*. (pp. 7–9). New York: Kluwer.

Prain, V. (2003) *Learning from writing in secondary science: Some theoretical implications*. La Trobe University, Australia [Online] Retrieved March 11, 2006 from http:// unr.edu/homepage/jcannon/prain.html

Prain, V. & Hand, B. (1996). Writing and learning in secondary science: Rethinking practices. *Teaching and Teacher Edcuation, 12*, 609–626.

Prain, V., & Hand, B. (1999). Students' perceptions of writing for learning in secondary school science. *Science Education, 83*, 151–162.

Rowell, P., & Ebbers, M. (2004). Shaping school science: Competing discourses in an inquiry-based elementary program. *International Journal of Science Education, 26*(8), 915–934.

Ruiz-Primo, M. A., Li, M., & Shavelson, R. (2002). Looking into students' science notebooks: What do teacher's do with them? [CSE Tech. Rep. 562]. CRESST/Stanford University. Retrieved March 10, 2006 from http://www.cresst.org/Reports/TR562.pdf

Shepardson, D. P., & Britsch, S. J. (1997). Children's science journals: Tools for teaching, learning, and assessing, *Science and Children, 34*(5), 12–17, 46–47.

Short, D. J., & Thier, M. (2006). Perspectives on teaching and integrating English as a second language and science. In A. Fathman & D. Crowther (Eds.) *Science for English language learners: K–12 classroom strategies*. Arlington, VA: NSTA Press.

Shymansky, J. A., Marberry, C. A., & Jorgensen, M. A. (1977). Science and mathematics are spoken and written here. In. D. Holdzkolm & P. B. Lut (Eds.), *Reform in math and science education: Issues for the classroom* (pp. 42–56). Columbus, OH: Eisenhauer National Clearinghouse.

Snow, C. (2002). *Reading for understanding: Toward an R&D program in reading comprehension*. Santa Monica, CA: RAND Reading Study Group.

Stadler, H., Benke, G., & Duit, R. (2001). How do boys and girls use language in physics classes? In H. Behrendt, H. Dahncke, R. Duit, W. Graber, M. Komorek, A. Kross P. Reiska, (Eds.) *Research in Science Education—Past, Present, and Future*. Dordrecht, Boston, London: Kluwer Academic publishers.

Sutton, C. (1992). *Words, science and learning*. Buckingham, UK: Open University Press.

Sutton, C. (1996). Beliefs about science and beliefs about language. *International Journal of Science Education, 18*, 1–18.

Trueba, H. T., Guthrie, G., & Au, K. (Eds.). (1981). Culture and the bilingual classroom: Studies in classroom ethnography. Rowley, MA: Newbury House.

Unsworth, L. (1997). Explaining explanations: Enhancing science learning and literacy development. *Australian Science Teachers Journal, 43*(1), 34–49.

Unsworth, L. (2000). Investigating subject-specific literacies in school learning. *Researching language in schools and communities: Functional linguistic perspectives.* London, Cassell: 245–274.

Unsworth, L. (2001). *Teaching multiliteracies across the curriculum: Changing contexts of text and image in classroom practice.* Buckingham, England: Open University Press.

Veel, R. (1997). Learning how to mean—scientifically speaking: Apprenticeship into scientific discourse in the secondary school. In F. Christie, J. R. Martin (Eds.) *Genres and institutions: Social processes in the workplace and school* (pp. 161–195). London: Cassell Academic.

Wellington, J., & Osborne, J. (2001). *Language and literacy in science education.* Buckingham, England: Open University Press.

White, J., & Welford, G. (1988). *The language of science.* London: Assessment of Performance Unit, Department of Education and Science.

Young, J. (2003). Science interactive notebooks in the classroom. *Science Scope, 26*(4), 44–47.

Yore, L. D., Hand, B., & Prain, V. (1999, January). *Writing-to-learn science: Breakthroughs, barriers, and promises.* Paper presented at the International Conference of the Association for Educating Teachers in Science, Austin, TX.

6

Children Publish in Science as a Way of Knowing

Deborah A. Powell
Missouri State University

Roberta J. Aram
Missouri State University

A dramatic shift in thinking concerning the role of language in science learning is occurring in science education. In the past, many science educators were skeptical of integrating reading and writing with hands-on science inquiry because of the likelihood that doing science would morph into reading about science or writing a fiction story about a science-related topic. The danger that investigative science will shift to language arts lessons using science examples is as real at present as it was in the past. Elementary teachers are confronted in the No Child Left Behind (2001) era with daily pressures to increase reading and mathematics instruction as a way to improve student achievement, often at the expense of science and social studies. If science is going to be taught at all, some teachers, particularly primary teachers, believe it is necessary to integrate it with other areas of the curriculum. Science and language educators are now researching and developing methods of harnessing the power of integrating reading and writing as tools for expanding children's science thinking and conceptual development within the context of inquiry learning experiences. (Fellows, 1994; Holliday, Yore, & Alvermann, 1994; McKee & Ogle, 2005; Pearson & Barber, 2005; Thier, 2002) Children engaging in guided hands-on inquiries can authentically apply reading and writing skills at each stage of their investigation, as scientists do, while they develop their science knowledge and communication skills. The use of science notebooks and nonfiction science literature has begun rebalancing science and language learning.

The classroom teacher is a critical gatekeeper in implementing a curriculum that balances science learning with reading and writing. For elementary classroom teachers to effectively enhance children's science inquiry with reading and writing, they must first (1) embrace the value of building their own science content background, (2) know how to engage children in hands-on, guided or open inquiry, and (3) value science education enough to devote time to planning and teaching science. Teachers must also (4) value using quality nonfiction or informational texts in their classroom, (5) trust that children can read and write and will write for authentic purposes and audiences, and (6) believe that reading and writing content strategies must be purposefully taught. Under the time constraints in this No Child Left Behind (2001) era it is tempting for primary teachers, in particular, to teach science by reading about it. Most basal reading series now have ancillary sets of nonfiction books with suggestions in the teachers' notes for integrating science. Whereas these books are often artfully illustrated with graphics that may have scientific relevance, they are often written for the purpose of teaching children to read nonfiction text, rather than for the purposes for which scientists write. This chapter examines a model for authentically integrating hands-on inquiry of substantive science content with reading and writing factual texts. We suggest increasing the substance on both sides of the literacy balance by identifying the scientific purposes and genre in children's nonfiction literature and using them as templates for children writing about their developing science content knowledge.

READING AND WRITING IN SCIENCE LIKE REAL SCIENTISTS

For children to learn like scientists, they need to investigate, to read, and to write like scientists. The learning cycle investigative model clearly simulates many of the thinking and activity patterns in which scientists engage as they carry out their work. For scientists and children alike, inquiries are initiated by a question, problem, or puzzling observation. Data is collected; explanations are formulated, expanded, and eventually communicated to an authentic audience for a specific purpose.

For children to learn to write like writers, they must recognize that topics come from what we know about, care about, and have experienced.

Balancing Language and Science Instruction

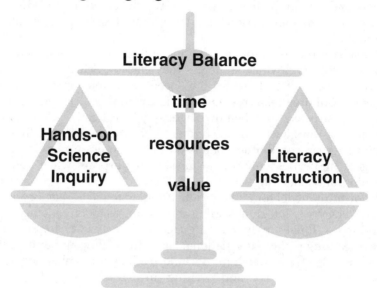

Figure 6.1   Balancing language and science instruction.

Science notebooks allow scientists to record observations, notes, sketches, and other data as well as jot down thoughts, ideas, and memories (Campbell & Fulton, 2003) that can later be incorporated into pieces written purposefully for an authentic audience (Calkins, 1998). Writers take a small kernel of information and build and layer it with meaning. It is through the revision process that writers seek more information, verify facts, make ideas more thorough yet crisp and concise, organize information into structures that fit their purpose, work to weave their big idea or theme through the piece and, of course, attend to the conventions of our language such as spelling, punctuation, and grammar.

For children to read text with comprehension, particularly science texts, they must possess a large store of conceptual knowledge about the world from which to draw while reading. The reader's prior knowledge and meaningful science learning experiences provide a memory bank of ideas with which the reader can identify and connect ideas encountered in the text. That's why it is essential for all children to have opportunities to learn science content deeply through inquiry.

When readers read with comprehension, they actively employ reading strategies such as predicting, confirming, inferring, evaluating, referring to another source, and self-monitoring (Maxim & Five, 1997). When readers understand the text structure in which content is embedded, the concepts become more accessible (Meyer, Brandt, & Bluth, 1980; Stein & Glenn, 1979).

A reader's purposes for reading and interest in the topic determine how they read and which strategies they employ. Science investigation can be the catalyst that creates the "need" to employ various reading strategies. Children read in science to clarify, confirm, or extend an idea they've constructed from their own hands-on investigations. They read to answer their questions and satisfy their curiosity about topics that can't easily be researched through hands-on investigation (e.g., volcanoes or moons of Jupiter). Scientists read for similar purposes when initiating, executing, and extending scientific inquiries.

A powerful model for authentically bringing together science and language literacy is to integrate reading and writing as tools of inquiry as real scientists do. Interestingly, the language skills necessary for successful science learning replicate the national and state reading and writing literacy standards. These standards include reading comprehension strategies, writing to learn, and writing in various nonfiction genre (NCTE/IRA, 1996).

Curiosity and the "need to know" about a science topic can motivate children to read and write to learn. However, frustration can occur when children do not have the literacy strategies needed to comprehend. Only after a strategy is part of a reader's repertoire should it be applied to comprehend new science content. As a result, it isn't possible for a teacher to give equal emphasis to teaching children all of the tools of inquiry in science, writing, and reading simultaneously.

Instead, reading and writing strategies can be taught during the time allotted for language arts using the familiar science topic children have been studying, children's questions and notebook, and science factual literature. Children are more engaged in learning the language arts strategies when these approaches are being applied to their important questions and interests in science.

A MODEL FOR USING TOOLS OF SCIENCE AND LANGUAGE INQUIRY

In the previous chapter, Crowther and Cannon explored how students use science notebooks as a way to increase their science conceptual knowledge. Children use notebooks to record verbal and graphic accounts of their emerging understandings throughout every stage of their inquiry.

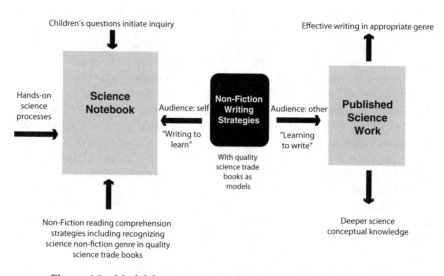

Figure 6.2   Model for using tools of science and language inquiry.

So, how can notebooks extend children's learning after the materials are put away? We propose a model in which notebooks remain the vehicle for recording children's questions, ideas, and research, including the research for questions that couldn't be answered during the hands-on investigations. We extend the power of the notebook by incorporating the recursive nature of the writing process that causes children to rethink and reflect on the content they know.

The notebook begins as a repository of children's research from hands-on investigations. Its life is extended when children reflect on and develop in writing the ideas being formed in their notebooks. Concurrently, children can choose an authentic audience and purpose for whom to communicate through "publishing" their ideas. Content from the notebook is the foundation of the piece. Through the iterative process of revision, children realize the need to clarify, complete, or otherwise deepen their science conceptual understanding by reading nonfiction texts and by consulting other experts. Additional notes from and reflections on these sources are added to the notebook and incorporated into the published piece. Figure 6.2 illustrates a model for using the tools of science and language inquiry.

Children's questions initiate inquiry. Science process skills are used as children record questions, procedures, and data in a notebook. Explanations, based on observations as evidence and written in the notebook, can stimulate a need to read about the science topic. Some teachers ask children to draw a "line of learning," under which they write to explain, describe, report, or discuss findings in their notebooks. This may reveal gaps in understanding and ideas that aren't fully formed. Children can be encouraged to formulate and verbalize their ideas through oral discussion based on shared excerpts and information from their science notebooks. They may then further clarify and expand their tentative understandings by comparing them to those of authors of science literature. Children's questions become the base from which teachers guide them into trade books to extend their learning, verify their facts, and to elaborate and embellish their vocabulary for new concepts they are constructing.

At this point in students' inquiry, they are highly motivated to learn more. They approach text with the motivation to get deeply involved, even when the text appears challenging. They critically read and evaluate text, comparing ideas from several texts to what they have learned in their own investigations. Children are likely to apply reading comprehension strategies learned during reading instruction when interesting resources are introduced at this point in a lesson, causing children to both extend science conceptual knowledge and become familiar with the structures authors use in presenting nonfiction information. Teachers will need to model and encourage children to keep writing in their notebooks recording notes, summaries, comparisons of text, and new questions. Children may also continue to add information to their notebooks from expert sources gained through interviews, e-mails, and notes from guest speakers. Science notebooks may include drawings, diagrams, tables, digital photos, and even doodles. There may be random phrases, questions, and thoughts posted to remind the author of an idea too important to forget. The science notebook is a repository of ideas written for the audience of self. The purpose of the writing is to learn.

The notebook, however, can be a tool for children to write future scientific pieces about their topic. The literature sources that children use to verify information included in notebooks can be models or blueprints for later pieces of scientific writing. Children will often naturally find an authentic reason to write for an audience other than the teacher or themselves. This is what we refer to as "publishing."

Just as scientists publish their findings, children in elementary classrooms can also publish their work. They can write letters to the editor or create factual books for other students in their class or future classes. They can publish in a schoolwide or classroom "science journal or magazine," create museum displays for the classroom science museum, or write scientific reports for the local science fair. Teacher and students negotiate which purpose (or purposes) has a best fit with the topic being studied (Stead, 2002).

When children discover real purposes and real audiences for their writing, the teacher has the opportunity to encourage revision. Through revision, authors revisit their notebooks to mull over their ideas, they reread their references (in this case children's literature and internet sources, to mention two), they talk to others about their ideas, and they write and rewrite what they know. In order for children to organize their written draft to convey their purpose, they need to develop frames or structures that fit other text such as children's literature in which authors are writing for similar purposes. Not only is this exemplary of the writing process, but it is also an opportunity to further extend and ground their science conceptual knowledge. An added benefit is that readers develop the structures that support their comprehension of future texts. We hope our readers have concluded that the model of integrating reading and writing into significant science content learning discussed here is not the same model as thematic units, interdisciplinary units, reading about science, or creative writing in science. Leading with science rather than literacy situates literacy as it is in life (Pearson & Barber, 2005).

Identifiable Scientific Purposes in Quality Children's Science Literature

Society's demands for literacy skills and science conceptual knowledge are high and sharply increasing. In addition to using notebooks as a vehicle to teach science and language strategies that emulate the way scientists work, we make the case that elementary teachers should also include recognizing using various types of nonfiction literature within the science investigative experience to enhance science content reading and writing.

Quality children's science literature is written for the same purposes that scientists write text for their audiences—to describe, recount, report, explain, teach, persuade, and argue, and occasionally to entertain. We emphasize quality science literature because we're not certain that all of the little science "text sets" included in reading series are written with these purposes clearly in mind. Choosing literature from National Science Teaching Association's (NSTA) "Outstanding Science Trade Books for Students K–12" or from American Association for the Advancement of Science's (AAAS) "Best Science Books for Children" is one method of selecting quality science literature. Science educators and librarians can assure the use of quality science literature selections by evaluating children's informational texts using the criteria for selecting children's factual literature (see Fig. 6.3).

Quality children's science literature is organized around recognizable organizational structures that uniquely fit the purpose of the writing.

- Content and language are engaging
- Content contributes to a big idea
- Content and graphics are accurate
- Text is comprehensible to readers
- Illustrations and graphics enhance the text
- Written by a qualified author
- Has qualities of an effective reference aid

Figure 6.3   Criteria for selecting children's factual literature.

A text is organized on several levels. On one level, each paragraph has a structure frequently referred to as "text structures" that follow particular language patterns related to the purpose; description, concept/definition, main idea/supporting detail, compare/contrast, cause/effect, problem/ solution, sequence, and proposition/support (Armbruster, Anderson, & Ostertag, 1987; Richgels, McGee, Lomax, & Sheard, 1987). At the next level, each piece of writing has an overall structure. Not only are the over-all structures predictable, but there are predictable language features, common words that signal the structure, and types of graphics that are best suited to the purpose. We refer to these organizational patterns as *genre.* Genre means the overall text organization that authors use to best express their ideas and purpose.

Charles Bazerman (1988) points out that genres are more than a simi-larity of common characteristics among a number of texts. "A genre pro-vides a writer with a way of formulating responses in certain circumstances and a reader a way of recognizing the kind of message being transmitted" (p. 62). Informational genres are "the types of writing needed for life" (Collerson, 1988, p. 11). By integrating the reading of sci-ence and the writing of science with learning hands-on science, we can begin teaching the range of these genres in the elementary grades. The most common informational genre are explained in Figure 6.4. These include recount, report, explanation, procedure, persuasion; argument and discussion, description, poetry, informational narrative, transac-tional, and mixed (Christie, 1986; Derewianka, 1990; Martin, 1985; Wing Jan, 1991).

Recount.   One narrative form of factual science information is called the recount genre. The purpose of a recount is to retell events and to inform. Recounts frequently appear as naturalists' journals, biographies of famous scientists, and accounts of historical science events. Some

Figure 6.4

Genre: Purpose	Examples	Language/ Features	Frame or Structure
Recount: To retell events or what happened	Journal, travel log, diary, methodology section of a research report	• Use of nouns to identify people, animals & things • Action verbs • Past tense • Signal words convey time sequence; examples: first, after, during, next, soon, meanwhile, initially, afterward, finally • Graphics: photos or illustrations, timeline	• Orientation (who, where, when) • Series of events • Personal comment or ending
Report: To organize and report information about a phenomenon or class of things	Many nonfiction books about one class (e.g., Koalas, Force and Motion, Oceans), research report, task force report	• Uses impersonal objective language • Timeless present tense unless about a phenomena from the past • Signal words indicate generalizations; examples: therefore, generally, additionally, because of • Signal words indicate description: looks like, appears to be, as in, such as • Graphics may be photos or illustrations, diagrams, maps, close-ups, charts or tables	• Begins with general classification identifying the subject • Information and description of qualities, parts & functions, habits, behaviors or uses are sectioned off • Often ends with a summary or connection to reader
Explanation: To explain how things work or came to be	Science non-fiction books written to explain how, Magazine article in *Popular Science* about how a phenomenon works	• Present tense verbs • Signal Words indicate: cause / effect or problem/solution; examples: therefore, because, thus, if…then, hence, since, as a result of	• Begins with a general statement about what is to be explained or a question • Often a series of logical steps explaining how or why something occurs

(Continued)

Figure 6.4 (Continued)

Genre: Purpose	Examples	Language/ Features	Frame or Structure
		• Ending indicates a conclusion such as hence, in conclusion, therefore, consequently. • Graphics are diagrams, drawings, tables, chart, graphs	• May be cause and effect or problem and solution structures • Ends with a final conclusion
Persuasive Argument: To argue or persuade Discussion: To discuss differing, unbiase viewpoints	Editorial, written debate Magazine article discussing an issue such as *Missouri Conservation* article on hunting Black Bear	• Verb tense is usually present • Signal words indicate compare and contrast in discussions (examples: even though, however, on the other hand, similarly) or they indicate statement/restatement in arguments (example: therefore, in conclusion, in short) • Graphics are comparison tables, graphs, side-by-side photos for comparison.	• Begins with a thesis or position statement • Presents the arguments point by point, often with elaboration on each point to counter the other viewpoint. • In a discussion, the two sides are presented without bias. • Ends with a summary and reiteration of the thesis in an argument
Procedural: To tell how to do or make something	Recipe, directions for a game, assembly directions, science experiment	• Verb tense is imperative, present • Signal words indicate chronological sequence (Examples: first, after, during, next) • Usually includes measurements and sizes • Graphics: Numbered diagram, photo of completed project, symbols	• Begin with materials and tools needed • Presents steps in order. • Usually ends with a summary statement
	Wine bottle label, brochure for a new automobile, naturalist's notebook	• May describe a single organism or a phenomena, but doesn't attempt to chunk information as in a report	• Usually begins with a general statement

Figure 6.4 (Continued)

Genre: Purpose	Examples	Language/ Features	Frame or Structure
Description: To provide details of how a phenomena looks, feels, sounds, or tastes	Wine bottle label, brochure for a new automobile, naturalist's notebook	• May describe a single organism or a phenomena, but doesn't attempt to chunk information as in a report • Uses sensory words • Tense may be present or past • Signal words indicate comparison and contrast (examples: although, compared with, similarly), examples or illustrations (examples: for example, for instance) • Graphics usually photos or illustrations	• Usually begins with a general statement • Details follow describing what it looks like, feels like, sounds like, tastes like, or smells like, or more generally how it is • Ends with a summary statement
Informational Narrative to provide factual information in a story form to teach while entertaining	Children's books such as Joanna Cole's *Magic School Bus* series, legends	• Use of descriptive language including action verbs • May have dialogue • 1st or 3rd person • Past tense when in 3rd person; past, present, and some future in 1st person • May use foreshadowing or flashbacks • Contains a theme or moral woven throughout • Voice usually less formal • Signal words indicate chronological order	• Begins with introduction to characters and setting including time and place • Main character has a goal usually indicated in an initiating event • Events are relayed in chronological order except for foreshadowing or flashbacks • Events present problems for the character to achieve goal • Events come to a climax • Resolution • Ending my hint at future

(Continued)

Figure 6.4 (Continued)

Genre: Purpose	Examples	Language/ Features	Frame or Structure
Transactional: to communicate information and feelings, to make a request, or to maintain a relationship	Informal: letters, postcards; Formal: memos, letters	• Language is endearing in informal and friendly in formal • Description and recount are structure of informal; explanation, description, recount, or procedure may make up the body of the formal text • Language indicates a relationship has been established or is attempting to be established in formal • Verb tense is past or present, or present imperative	• May begins with contact information such as addresses of sender or sender and receiver • Date written • Greeting • Body begins with establishing or reestablishing relationship or a clear statement of information to be conveyed • Information to be conveyed is detailed • Relationship is further developed or summary is provided • Closing • Salutation may be included • Signature
Mixed: to convey information for a variety of purposes	Textbooks, many nonfiction books with sidebars		

Figure 6.4 Informational genre.

Adapted from: Christie, 1986; Martin, 1985; Derewianka, 1990; Wing Jan, 1991.

language arts curricula refer to this form as personal narrative, but not all recounts are personal. The recount structure, like the story genre, is temporal and usually begins with a setting of a scene—who, when, and where. A sequence of events follows but unlike a story, there is no problem, climax, or resolution. A recount ends in a closing statement. The signal words indicate a chronological sequence, for example, first, after, during, meanwhile, long after, and finally. The tense is almost always past written in first or third person. The graphics are usually photographs, maps, time line or illustrations. An excellent example of a recount is award-winning author Jim Murphy's (2003) *An American Plague: The True and Terrifying Story of the Yellow Fever Epidemic of 1793*, an historical account of a devastating plague that swept the city of Philadelphia. Peter Busby (2003) recalls the early years, flight years, and end of life years of Wilbur and Orville Wright in *First to Fly: How Wilbur & Orville Wright Invented the Airplane*.

Report. Report, a nonnarrative genre, describes the way something is or was and usually focuses on one phenomenon. Reports are not organized chronologically. They often begin with a general classification or description of the common attributes of the phenomenon. Reports are then subdivided into sections that describe or explain the qualities, parts and functions, habits, and behaviors or uses. The genre ends with a brief summary. The signal words indicate either generalizations (e.g., therefore, generally, additionally, because of, however, and on the other hand) or description (e.g., looks like, appears to be, as in, on top of, and such as). The tense is usually present unless it is about a phenomenon from the past. The graphics are photos or illustrations, diagrams, maps, close-ups, charts, and tables.

For example, Cathryn Sill's *About Arachnids: A Guide for Children* (2003) is subdivided, as one would expect, into the following parts; arachnids' body parts, where they live, what they eat, how they catch their food and protect themselves, how they travel, how they take care of their young, their size, and their danger to humans. *About Arachnids* ends with, "but most are helpful and should be protected" (p. 30).

Explanation. Explanations tell how or why something works as well as the processes involved in a phenomenon. The structure begins with a general statement about the process or phenomena. This deductive discourse often describes causal relationships and solutions to problems. Explanations provide logical steps for explaining how or why something occurs. To accomplish this purpose, compare/contrast or concept/example structures may be employed by the author. The text is usually present tense with signal words indicating cause/effect or problem/solution such as therefore, because, thus, if...then, hence, since, as a result of, consequently, and is caused by. Conclusions are signaled by words such as accordingly, as a result, as a consequence, for this reason, hence, in conclusion, therefore, and consequently. The graphics include graphs, tables, charts, diagrams and drawings. *Why Does Lightning Strike? Questions Children Ask About the Weather* (Martin, 1996) is a typical example of the explanation genre.

Procedure.   Procedures describe how something is accomplished through a series of steps. They begin with a statement of what is to be achieved and a list of required materials and instruments. The series of sequenced steps for carrying out a plan usually written in the imperative, present tense makes this genre unique. Because chronology is imperative to explaining a process, the signal words indicate temporal relationships such as first, after, during, next, meanwhile, secondly, then, or 15 minutes. Visual representations frequently include a diagram or a photo of the completed project. Symbols are sometimes substituted for words to simplify the text for the purpose of providing easy-to-follow directions.

A replicable experiment is a procedure and is included in many children's science books, both literature and educational textbooks. *Fantastic Feats and Failures* (Editors of YES Mag, 2004) includes a procedure on building and testing a bridge (p. 31). Knowing how to write a procedure can enhance writing scientific reports, although procedures are frequently void of concepts and less sophisticated than the traditional scientific research report that includes an introduction, methods, results, conclusions, and discussions.

Persuasion: Argument.   Persuasion, an argument on paper, is critical to science. Of the seven functions of language identified by Halliday (1975) in his seminal work *Learning How to Mean,* "regulatory" or persuasion appears early in a child's language development. Typically, however, this form of written discourse is not introduced to children until postelementary grades. Children's books reflect this dearth of persuasion or argumentation. Consequently, the most common sources of children's understanding of persuasion are literature promoting the care of the environment, advertisements, and newspaper editorials.

Persuasion usually begins with a thesis or position statement. The author presents arguments point by point, often with elaboration to counter another viewpoint. The piece usually ends with a restatement of the thesis or a rhetorical statement to lead critics to the author's conclusions. Persuasive pieces are usually written in present tense and use compare/contrast signal words (e.g., even though, however, on the other hand, similarly, and although) and statement/restatement cues (e.g., therefore, in conclusion, hence, to summarize, and in short). Comparison tables, graphs, or side-by-side comparative photos usually comprise the graphics used to support the argument.

Persuasion: Discussion. Discussion texts inform readers by providing differing viewpoints on an issue. This unbiased assessment of a topic begins with an introduction that may outline the various viewpoints to be discussed. The information and evidence for each viewpoint follow. The author summarizes the different viewpoints often ending with an unbiased conclusion concerning the various arguments. Discussions are usually written in present tense with cause/effect, main idea/supporting details, and compare/contrast structures. Sample signal words are therefore, because, thus, consequently, for example, although, compared with, similarly, and otherwise. Scientists present discussions using evidence and scientific background knowledge. Good discussions are based on evidence from investigations and include a review of and questions about the results of other scientists' work.

Description. Description isn't always discussed as a genre, but a review of children's science trade books clearly indicates that some books are written for the purpose of describing. The genre appears to be similar to a report but rather than being subdivided into various aspects of a single phenomenon, a description is a broader topic subdivided into examples. Descriptions illustrate how something is or appears rather than the explanation that tells how something works or why it works. Main idea and supporting details and compare/contrast are common text structures. Signal words include for example, although, compared with, similarly, and otherwise. The tense may be present or past. Metaphors, similes, and sensory words are common. There is attention to precise use of nouns and powerful verbs, adjectives, and adverbs. Visual graphics are usually photographs or illustrations. The table of contents of *Bugs: A Closer Look at the World's Tiny Creatures* (Johnson, 1995) reveals this structure; Mantids, Wasps, Scorpions, Beetles, Mosquitoes, Glossary, and Index. There is no introduction into the general classification. Another example is *Night Creatures* by Susanne Santoro Whayne (1993). One subtopic is "The Neighborhood," which is further subdivided into Cats, Toad, Deer Mouse, Raccoon, Skunk, Opossum, and Red Fox.

Poetry. Another genre found in children's science literature is poetry. *Aska's Sea Creatures* (Day, 1994) and *Echoes for the Eye: Poems to Celebrate Patterns in Nature* (Esbensen, 1996) are examples of poetry related to

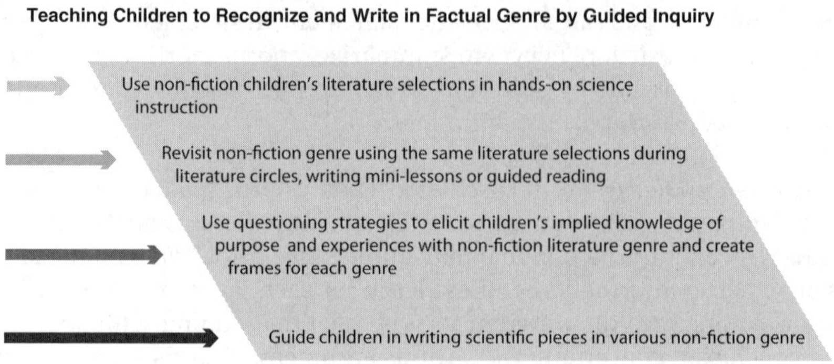

Teaching Children to Recognize and Write in Factual Genre by Guided Inquiry

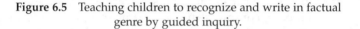

Use non-fiction children's literature selections in hands-on science instruction

Revisit non-fiction genre using the same literature selections during literature circles, writing mini-lessons or guided reading

Use questioning strategies to elicit children's implied knowledge of purpose and experiences with non-fiction literature genre and create frames for each genre

Guide children in writing scientific pieces in various non-fiction genre

Figure 6.5   Teaching children to recognize and write in factual genre by guided inquiry.

science. Our greatest caution is to be certain that poems used as writing models actually convey science concepts accurately. Poetry may be structured in free verse, repetitive patterns, rhyming, narrative, forms such as haiku and cinquain, and concrete and shape poems. Metaphors, similes, sensory words, alliteration, personification, and onomatopoeia are prevalent in poetry. Most poetry has rhythm and many poets use rhyme. Poets rely on the senses by using powerful and carefully selected words to show rather than tell. Although the content value of much science-related poetry may be minimal, children find free verse an effective way to communicate their newly learned science concepts with minimal words. "Stars and Constellations" in Myra Cohn Livingston's *Space Songs* (1988) is an effective example of a free verse science poem. As students inquire about patterns, systems, and interactions in science, poetry may be another way to express their discoveries.

Informational Narrative.   Children will find narrative a useful structure for communicating their ideas about science. Narrative or story structure begins with the setting, characters, and a problem. A plot emerges with a sequence of events building tension to a climax. The story ends with the resolution of the problem and the closing. Signal words such as first, after, during, next, soon, meanwhile, afterward, not long after, eventually, and finally indicate a temporal structure. Stories are written in first or third person, present or past tense. The graphics are usually photos or illustrations. Because children are familiar with writing fictional stories, it is not a good idea to begin with the informational narrative. It is a much more sophisticated form of story than what they are accustomed to writing and most teachers are disappointed with the results when assessing for content. As children learn to base their writing on facts, they will be able to be more successful with the genre. *Arrowhawk* (Schaefer, 2001) is an informational narrative based on a real event. This beautiful picture book concludes with a photograph of the actual hawk, a recount of the tragic event, and an argument for learning more about preserving hawks' natural habitat.

Transactional. When teachers ask children to write for an audience, an obvious purpose becomes writing a letter to someone they know. Transactional writing such as letters, post cards, memorandums, and personal notes communicate information and feelings, are used to make requests, or are used to maintain a relationship. Children are generally familiar with friendly letters to people they know, but may need to be introduced to formal or business letters to people they don't know. Examining examples of friendly and business letters, children will quickly be able to pick out salient features such as the addresses, date, greeting, body, salutation, and signature. A comparison will yield the language features of formal and informal writing; use of colloquialisms, contractions, and often incomplete sentences and other lack of attention to formal rules of language versus the formal vocabulary and grammar children may associate with nonfiction books.

Mixed Genre. Robert Veel (2000) refers to genre as having distinct parts that work together to build meaning. Within any particular genre, unique text structures will emerge. Within a published children's book, occasionally more than one genre can be identified. We refer to these selections as mixed genre. There are no categorical rules by which children's authors structure their texts, but the commonalities described previously are useful for both teachers and children to recognize and incorporate into their own writing about science. An example of a mixed genre, *Eureka! Great Inventions and How They Happened* (Platt, 2003) combines recounts of inventors' lives, descriptions of their inventions, and explanations to how they discovered their invention and how it works.

TEACHING SCIENCE-FACTUAL GENRE BY GUIDED INQUIRY

Teachers infuse quality trade books into their lessons generally after the hands-on materials are put away. As children use nonfiction literature and as teachers read aloud from nonfiction books on the topic, children begin to look for schemata for texts associated with different purposes. Children frequently develop implied knowledge of text genre long before their teacher purposefully introduces a particular genre.

During read aloud, literature circles (Daniels, 2001), guided reading (Fountas & Pinnell, 1996), and writing mini lessons (Atwell, 1998; Calkins, 1998) teachers use guided inquiry to help children construct an under- standing of the unique purposes, features, and structures of each genre. The teacher asks questions designed to scaffold children's construction of the understanding of the genre. The following are examples of "teacher questions."

- What makes a report a report?
- What is the purpose of a report?
- Why do authors write reports? Besides the reports we've examined in children's literature, do you know of any other examples of reports?
- What information does the author provide in the beginning of this report? Are all the reports like that?
- What are some of the things that are included in the middle of a report? In the end?

A guided inquiry approach to teaching genre to children is most effective when each child has a different example in front of them and they are guided in identifying and comparing the commonalities of selections through discussion. As children share their thinking about "What makes a report a report?" the teacher records their ideas in a graphic organizer on chart paper making the genre structure explicit to the children. This structural outline or frame will serve as a model and possibly a reference for children as they are writing their own reports. Because the children have created the frame, most won't need to refer to it; they will already own it.

The writing process, like the learning cycle is recursive. As with all learning, writers weave in and out of these phases with the piece only being complete most often because of the time constraints.

Engage: Rehearsal for Writing

Children thumb through their science notebooks to discover possible authentic audiences. The teacher guides children's decision making by asking, "Who needs to know about this information? How will you convey it to that audience in an appropriate way?" In this way, the teacher assists children in deciding their purpose and genre.

Explore: Drafting and Rereading; Explain: Rewriting and Revisioning

Children take a nugget of information that's important to them and build on it in their writing to address their purpose. Teachers and peers conference with writers for support. Children pour through their notebooks and other texts, reading and rereading. Through their explorations, they may see their text from a new perspective. Don Murray says that authors draft to explore, read to discover, revise for meaning, revise for audience, revise for evidence, and revise for voice (1991). Students struggle with accurate content, organized text, purposeful writing, and rich use of language.

Teachers who value the resultant learning provide opportunities and time along with a healthy dose of encouragement and feedback. Teachers learn to ask questions that move students forward in their writing. They trust that students can write and will write when they take ownership over the process.

Elaborate: Edit and Publish

Students use children's literature not only as reference materials and models of the genres, but also as demonstrations for layout and design. Children take as much responsibility as they can for their writing. They work with peers to assist them in editing and producing their text. The teacher, parent, or volunteer serves as publisher to help with final editing and production.

Evaluate: Response for Audience

Children will self-evaluate based on the response from their audiences. Teachers use conferences, observation, and often rubrics to evaluate both students' content knowledge and their writing skills.

CONCLUSION

This model of integrating reading and writing into significant science content learning is not the same as teaching thematic units, interdisciplinary units, reading about science, or creative writing in science. Instead, this model leads with science rather than literacy, situating literacy as it is in life (Pearson & Barber, 2005).

Science literature is an important resource for helping children learn to investigate, read, and write like scientists. Reading to verify and reading to clarify are two important purposes for using children's literature. As part of their existing reading program, wise teachers will remind children of the various frames and text structures they have studied as one way to retrieve information from texts and answer their questions. To prepare children for "writing for life," teachers must model and nudge children into writing in the informational genres of explanation, persuasion, discussion, reports, descriptions, and procedures. Inquiry science experiences provide content and purpose for this writing.

As children gain control over a range of genre, they widen their choices for how to best present their emerging understandings. As they draft and revise, children commit to paper what they know, mull it over and clarify it, and finally share their knowledge with others in the learning community. Thus, process writing in science turns tentative learning into student-owned learning. Integrating high quality children's science literature, authentic science writing and inquiry just makes sense.

APPLICATIONS TO CLASSROOM PRACTICE

The following classroom applications are a composite of several teachers. First, we describe a preservice teacher who learns that a teacher can't simultaneously introduce new content in science, and writing and reading. Instead, she uses familiar writing and reading strategies as students learn new science content, then introduces the "report" genre as a structure by which students produce a book that also serves as an assessment product. In another case, an experienced teacher engages students' in authentic science inquiry through informational children's literature. Authentic writing opportunities emerge as students grapple with real-life applications of historical science phenomena.

Miss Gordon, a preservice teacher, wanted her fourth graders to write an informational piece about light and color. Students were finishing a 3-week unit in which they had investigated white light, mixing pigments, additive color mixing, subtractive color mixing, color images, and uses of colored light. Her students had not published a lot, but did write in science and social studies. The students had kept a science notebook documenting experiments, field notes from a field trip conducted by a lighting expert at a local auditorium, and writing reflective conclusions about their learning. She decided that in the interest of time, she would introduce the children to the report genre by providing a purpose, "You are to write a report on light and color," and by posing a series of questions (e.g., "Think of the lessons we have done; what would be the most important topics you should report on? What would be the best way to organize these topics?"). As she examined the list the children produced, she realized that the class had created a table of contents from which they could each develop their own books. The children copied the table of contents, wrote their books, and published them at home. Miss Gordon was now able to use the published books as a form of assessment for the science content. From a writing perspective, however, the children likely went from first draft, to editing, and then to publishing. They had no models from which to revise the report structure. Their published pieces were limited by the children's lack of knowledge about writing and genre.

As an alternative strategy, Miss Gordon could set the purpose for writing and guide the students in brainstorming the table of contents in one session. As children begin writing their first drafts, it is ideal to introduce the genre structure and elements during reading or writing time using examples of children's informational trade books written in the report genre. After Miss Gordon reads a few examples, the children conduct an inquiry on the organization, elements, signal words, and types of graphics used in reports. As the children revisit their science pieces, Miss Gordon guides the children in applying their new information about structure and elements of reports.

If her students had already been introduced to the report genre prior to her lesson, Miss Gordon could refer to that lesson and the list of characteristics of the report genre they had created. Children could apply their knowledge of what makes a report a report from the outset of the task.

In this example, students tended to introduce their report with specific information they had learned from the science experiences. If students had more knowledge of the report genre, their report introductions would have included more general information about light before they examined the specific concepts of white light, mixing pigments, additive color mixing, subtractive color mixing, color images, and uses of colored light. This lesson was a good start in meaningfully integrating writing and science. With thoughtful planning, writing and science goals can both be met. If the children have been taught to recognize the features of various informational genres, Miss Gordon could have given them a choice of writing an explanation, procedure, or report.

As an additional extension, Miss Gordon could assist children in recognizing the genre structures of informational literature that they are reading during dedicated language arts time. She and the children can discuss the various ways in which readers adjust their comprehension strategies as they read different genre. This literacy lesson can be applied to the informational texts children read to clarify and reinforce their understandings of science concepts developed through hands-on explorations and science notebook writing.

Miss Gordon's lesson is intended to illustrate and reinforce the ideas presented in this chapter. It is certainly not the only way to apply the integration of reading, writing, and science. The classroom teacher and Miss Gordon were quite pleased with the results of the children's light and color books. The children included graphs, color wheels, diagrams, and enlargements to illustrate their books. They provided enough information for the teacher to discern if the children understood the major concepts of the unit. Therefore, the lesson was a success, even though we have suggested ways that the lesson could have "added value."

As children interact with more sophisticated texts, they may discover that some are a mix of genre. Mrs. Johnston read Bryn Barnard's *Outbreak: Plagues That Changed History* (2005) to her fifth graders during a unit on health, disease and the organisms that cause them. The book is a recount that combines explanations of various viruses interspersed with persuasive sections concerning strategies for maintaining personal and community wellness.

Before Mrs. Johnston had finished reading the book, many students had chosen topics for individual inquiries. As students delved deeper into their inquiries, they discussed their new understandings about potential threats to the human race today and practical strategies they could take to reduce the threat. Some students wanted to take positive action to share their understandings with a wider audience. Several students thought that they should write letters to the editor of the local newspaper—one student suggested a letter to the President—and many felt they should make the information known to fellow students by reporting in the school newspaper facts about illness-producing microbes. A few students decided that they would develop a campaign designed to convince fellow students of the importance of personal hygiene, cleanliness, and hand washing.

Because the students' purposes were primarily to argue or discuss, Mrs. Johnston planned a lesson on writing persuasive text. She brought in letters to the editor from the local paper where people were debating the pros and cons of current immigration laws. Of special interest to her students was a local high school soccer star who had been jailed and was under threat of deportation. The young man had been stopped for a minor traffic violation and was found to be illegally living in the United States and driving without a driver's license. This situation was familiar to the students and they easily related to the arguments, both pro and con, as they were presented in the media. Using these examples, students analyzed the structure, the language, and how the authors used facts and opinions in these pieces. Additionally, students were able to identify the persuasive sections of the mixed genre text about plagues and the microbes that cause them.

This lesson provided students the scaffolding they needed to write their own persuasive texts about strategies to avert modern threats of microbially spread disease. Having authentic audiences and purposes for their writing sparked students' need for further inquiry into the subject matter. As the students revised their text, Mrs. Johnston was able to assess their ideas about and skill in writing persuasive texts as well as the science content students had acquired.

FOR FURTHER THOUGHT

1. A powerful model for authentically bringing together science and language literacy is to integrate reading and writing as tools of inquiry as real scientists do. What strategies can be employed to avoid frustration in children who do not have the literacy strategies needed to comprehend science text?
2. What kinds of opportunities can be provided for children to construct their own understanding of "nonfiction" or informational writing?
3. How can the information writing genres be explained to children? What are the best kinds of examples to help children construct these concepts?
4. How can you create an opportunity for children to "need" to learn the science content so they can communicate their learning to an authentic audience for a real purpose?
5. What do we mean by saying that leading with science rather than literacy situates literacy as it is in life?
6. How can nonfiction literacy skills be introduced during dedicated language literacy or communication arts instruction to build a foundation for use of these skills during science?

REFERENCES

Armbruster, B. B., Anderson, T. H., & Ostertag, J. (1987). Does text structure/summarization instruction facilitate learning from expository text? *Reading Research Quarterly, 22,* 331–346.

Atwell, N. (1998). *In the middle: New understanding about writing, reading, and learning.* Portsmouth, NH: Heinemann.

Barnard, B. (2005). *Outbreak: Plagues that changed history.* New York: Random House.

Bazerman, C. (1988). *Shaping written knowledge. The genre and activity of the experimental article in science: Rhetoric of the human sciences.* Madison, WI: The University of Wisconsin Press.

Busby, P. (2003*). First to fly: How Wilbur & Orville Wright invented the airplane.* New York: Crown Publishers.

Calkins, L. (1998). *The art of teaching writing* (4th ed.). Portsmouth, NH: Heinemann.

Campbell, B. & Fulton, L. (2003). *Science notebooks: Writing about inquiry.* Postmouth, NH: Heinemann.

Christie, F. (1986). Learning to mean in writing. In N. Stewart-Dore (Ed.), *Writing and reading to learn* (pp 21–34). New South Wales: Primary English Teaching Association.

Collerson, J. (Ed.). (1988). *Writing for life.* Rozelle, Australia: Primary English Teaching Association.

Daniels, H. (2001). *Literature circles: Voice and choice in book clubs and reading groups.* Portland, ME: Stenhouse.

Day, D. (1994). *Aska's Sea Creatures.* New York: Doubleday.

Derewianka, B. (1990). *Exploring how texts work.* Rozelle, Australia: Primary English Teaching Association.

Editors of YES Mag. (2004). Fantastic feats and failures. Toronto, Canada: Kids Can Press.

Esbensen B. J. (1996). *Echoes for the eye: Poems to celebrate patterns in nature.* New York: HarperCollins Children's Books

Fellows, N. J. (1994). A window into thinking: Using student writing to understand conceptual change in science learning. *Journal of Research in Science Teaching,* 31, 985–1001.

Fountas, I. C., & Pinnell, G. S. (1996). *Guided reading: Good first teaching for all children.* Portsmouth, NH: Heinemann.

Fountas, I. C.& & Pinnell, G. S. (2000). *Guided readers and writers (Grades 3–6): Teaching comprehension, genre, and content literacy.* Portsmouth, NH: Heinemann.

Halliday, M. A. K. (1975). *Learning how to mean.* London: Edward Arnold.

Holliday, W. G., Yore, L. D., & Alvermann, D. E. (1994). The reading-science learning-writing connection: Breakthroughs, barriers, and promises. *Journal of Research in Science Teaching,* 31, 877–893.

Johnson, J. (1995). *Bugs: A closer look at the world's tiny creatures.* New York: Reader's Digest Kids.

Livingston, M. C. (1988). *Space songs.* New York: Holiday House.

Martin, J. R. (1985). *Factual writing: Exploring and challenging social reality.* Victoria, Australia: Deakin University.

Martin, T. (Ed.). (1996). *Why does lightning strike? Questions children ask about the weather.* New York: Scholastic.

Maxim, D., & Five, C. L. (1997). The teaching of reading strategies. *School Talk,* 3(1), Urbana, IL: National Council of Teachers of English.

McKee, J., & Ogle, D. (2005). *Integrating instruction: Literacy and science.* New York: Guilford.

Meyer, B. J. F., Brandt, D. M., & Bluth, G. J. (1980). Use of top level structure in text: Key for reading comprehension. *Reading Research Quarterly, 16,* 72–103.

Murphy, J. (2003). *An American plague: The true and terrifying story of the yellow fever epidemic of 1793*. New York: Clarion Books.

Murray, D.M. (1991) *The craft of revision*. Fort Worth, TX: Holt, Rinehart, and Winston, Inc.

National Council of Teachers of English & International Reading Association (1996). *Standards for the English Language Arts*. Urbana, IL: NCTE & IRA.

No Child Left Behind Act, 107 U.S.C (2001).

Pearson, P. D. & Barber, J. (2005, May). *Seeking the right metaphor for the science-literacy connection: reciprocity, isomorphism, or identity?* Paper presented at the International Reading Association Conference, San Antonio, TX.

Platt, R. (2003). *Eureka! Great inventions and how they happened*. Boston, MA: Kingfisher.

Richgels, D. J., McGee, L. M., Lomax, R. G., & Sheard, C. (1987). Awareness of four text structures: Effects in recall of expository text. *Reading Research Quarterly*, 22, 177–196.

Schaefer, L. M. (2004). *Arrowhawk*. New York: Holt.

Sill, C. (2003). *About arachnids: A guide for children*. Atlanta, GA: Peachtree Publishers.

Stead, T. (2002). *Is that a fact? Teaching nonfiction writing K–3*. Portland, ME: Stenhouse.

Stein, N., & Glenn, C. G. (1979). *An analysis of story comprehension in elementary school children*. In R. Freedle (Ed.), New directions in discourse processing (pp. 53–120). Norwood, NJ: Ablex.

Veel, R. (2000). Learning how to mean—scientifically speaking: Apprenticeships into scientific discourse in the secondary school. In F. Christie & J. R. Martin (Eds.), *Genre and institutions: Social processes in the workplace and school* (pp. 161–195). New York: Continuum.

Whayne, S. S. (1993). *Night Creatures*. New York: Simon and Schuster.

Wing Jan, L. (1991). *Write ways: Modeling writing forms*. Melbourne, Australia: Oxford University Press.

7

Preparing English Language Learners in the Science Classroom

David Crowther
University of Nevada

Michael Robinson
University of Nevada

Amy Edmundson
California State University, Long Beach

Alan Colburn
California State University, Long Beach

The diversity in elementary classrooms across the United States is growing at a rapid rate. This diversity, which encompasses different races, cultures, religions, socioeconomic levels, abilities, disabilities, and learning styles, is a celebration of the differences that make up the United States. However, with this increase in diversity also comes the responsibility for classroom teachers to reach more students at a variety of levels. Although literature exists for each of these groups separately, teachers know that good teaching strategies benefit all learners. With that in mind, this chapter will focus on science education literature, instruction, and strategies that are specific to the English language learner (ELL), but when used in regular classroom instruction will benefit all students. Finally, learning science must incorporate the tools of science that include building literacy skills.

As mentioned earlier, the diversity in America's classrooms is growing at a rapid rate. According to the National Center for Educational Statistics (NCES), between 1979 and 2003, the number of ELL students (ages 5–17) grew from 3.8 million to 9.9 million or from 9% to 19% of all school-aged children. In that same period of time, 1979 to 2003, (24 years) the school-aged child population in the United States grew 19%. In contrast, the number of ELL student population grew 161% (NCES, 2005). According to the U.S. Department of Education, during 2002–2003 nearly 10% of K–12 public school enrollment was "limited English proficient." This amounts to more than 4,580,000 students. Of considerable interest is the ages of these students entering the schools. Approximately 44% of English learners are in grades K–3, 35% in grades 4–8, and 19% in grades 9–12 (Kindler, 2002). With nearly 80% of the English language learners entering school in grades K–8 grades, a much better job needs to be done in informing educators at these levels about the literature and strategies that work best for this population of students.

RESEARCH IN SCIENCE EDUCATION AND ENGLISH LANGUAGE LEARNERS

Many studies discuss benefits for English language learners in science instruction in the elementary and middle schools. This literature ranges from general paradigm association such as inquiry-based and hands-on instruction to specific teaching strategies like cooperative learning, word walls, and modifications in reading, writing, and communication while doing science. The literature includes discussion about programs that include training, specific strategies, and lesson formats for teaching science content and working with EL students (e.g., SDAI, SIOP, and GLAD). This section overviews selected literature in these areas.

Research on Inquiry-Based and Hands-On Instruction for English Language Learners

Inquiry-based science can benefit English language learners. Amaral, Garrison, and Klentschy (2002) conducted a 4-year research project in the El Centro Elementary School District in Southern California that measured the achievement of English language learners in science, writing, reading, and mathematics. Teachers used hands-on science kits to teach inquiry-based science instruction. Teachers spent 8 weeks teaching one science kit and taught four kits per year. All instruction was given in English. English language learners in the program were compared with students that spoke only English and compared with students that received traditional textbook instruction.

Amaral, et al. (2002) found consistent improvements by English language learners. They found that the achievement scores of students were higher the longer they were exposed to the inquiry-based program. In addition to finding increased achievement scores, they also discussed additional reasons why inquiry-based science instruction benefits English language learners; (1) the use of real materials to build context, (2) equality of common experiences among students, (3) having access to one's primary language to explore ideas, (4) access to peer assistance through cooperative learning, (5) having comfort that not knowing the answer is accepted, and (6) the creation of a positive attitude toward learning.

Hampton and Rodriquez (2001) implemented a research project in the El Paso, Texas area that was designed to determine the value of teaching inquiry-based science instruction to elementary school students that were developing language skills in their primary and secondary language. College interns from the University of Texas taught students inquiry-based science through the Full Option Science Series (FOSS) curriculum using varying levels of English and Spanish. About half of the students in the study received instruction in English and the other half in Spanish, depending on their language ability. Data was collected for the study through written responses from the college interns, through attitude surveys and through a written assessment from students. The interns observed that inquiry-based science motivated children to participate, regardless of the language in which the instruction took place.

The interns observed that natural language acquisition was taking place. It is interesting to note that the interns who allowed only English to be spoken came across some difficulties. They found it difficult to assess the progress of students and observed that some students struggled with the language that prevented them from the full experience of the lessons. The interns later decided that they needed to let the students use any language to explore scientific processes. Hampton and Rodriguez concluded that their research indicated strong, positive feelings from students about inquiry-based science. Surveys and written assessments supported an increase in student language skills, science content, and science skills.

Teachers often see positive results when inquiry-based science is taught to ELL students in their classrooms. Settlage (2004) implemented a research project in San Juan School, located in Utah, examining the issues in teaching culturally diverse students, especially ELL students. San Juan

School underwent several demographic changes, resulting in 60% of the student population becoming ELL. The study was implemented through the research of two second-grade teachers, with Settlage being a participant/observer. One teacher in the study was in her second year of teaching and had in-depth science methods coursework, whereas the other teacher had taught for 3 years and had superficial science methods coursework. The study was centered on the teachers' experiences teaching a FOSS Air and Weather unit using the learning cycle in a classroom that included numerous ELL students. The teachers began their science lessons by showing the students the materials they would be using and describing the question they would be exploring. After the lesson, the students would come together as a whole class to discuss what they had learned.

The teachers were surprised that it appeared that their students could learn the science concepts without explicit instruction. However, the teachers struggled with the misalignment between teaching strategies they had received for English language learners and inductive teaching in science. The ELL training based on the Sheltered Instruction Observation Protocol (SIOP) (Echevarria, Vogt, & Short, 2004) had teachers explicitly telling students concepts at the beginning of each lesson that varied from the inductive teaching method where concepts are discussed after investigating. The teachers came to prefer the inductive method of teaching because they believed it was more successful in the classroom. Teachers also preferred inductive teaching because the students with different cultural backgrounds were able to gain shared experiences through science that they could bring to a classroom discussion.

A study implemented by Ann Rosebery, Beth Warren, and Faith Conant (2003) supported the conclusion that inquiry-based science builds reasoning and language skills in language minority classrooms. The researchers created the inquiry-based Cheche Konnen project to implement "doing science" in classrooms with Haitian Creole middle and high school English language learners. The project did not follow a set curriculum but rather let science investigations develop through collaborative, student-directed activities. During the school year, one class did a collaborative investigation on the water fountains in the school; the investigation included taste tests and water quality tests. Another classroom did a collaborative investigation on the ecology of the local pond.

Students were given two think-aloud problems, one where they could directly apply what they had learned and one that involved a transfer of knowledge. The interviews were given in September and June. In the September interviews, the students offered few hypotheses for the think-aloud problems. The students attributed the cause of the problem to some anonymous person, attempted to designate items from the story as the cause of the problem, or used personal experiences as evidence for their hypothesis. When given the two think-aloud problems in June, the students generated more testable questions. Most students thought beyond the information that was given in the stories. The students showed improvement on how to think, talk, and understand the processes of science.

Fradd, Lee, Sutman, and Saxton (2001) implemented research projects to promote literacy with ELL students. The Promise project was a study of four inner city fourth-grade classrooms with "focus" teachers who shared their students' language and culture. The study involved two science units that consisted of 10–15 lessons that lasted 2–3 hours each and focused on promoting oral and written communication of science knowledge. All fourth-grade teachers in each of the schools were included in the third year of the study. Through observation and reflective journaling, the researchers saw teachers transition from being traditional caregivers to classroom facilitators who became learners alongside their students; this was a cultural change for many of the teachers. Teachers saw differences between the instructional approaches used in the Promise project and the strategies supported by their school district. Students were assessed through paper-and-pencil pre/postunit science tests. During the first 2 years of the study, the focus teachers used the units developed for the study whereas the nonfocus teachers used the materials used by the school district that covered the same science content. In the second year of the study, students using the Promise project materials achieved higher scores on the posttest assessment than did those in nonfocus classrooms. During the third year, all of the fourth-grade students in the school used the Promise project materials. The focus and nonfocus classrooms had similar scores, both of which were higher than the scores from the second year of the study.

Insights from the Promise project led Fradd et al. to develop the Science for All project. This project was extended to seven schools, with a total of approximately 900 fourth-grade students a year for 3 years. Science for All (SFA) promoted science inquiry beginning with explicit instruction. Through scaffolding, the students were guided to student-initiated open inquiry. Literacy and language development was developed through the SFA lessons. Each lesson emphasized a specific language function such as describing, reporting, or explaining. Vocabulary was developed by using only the key words necessary for understanding, rather than a long list of science terms. Drawings, charts, and tables also allowed ELL students multiple formats to represent science understanding. Pre/posttests and researcher observation demonstrated significant growth in understanding science concepts and inquiry from a group of students that had traditionally not achieved well in science.

Bravo and Garcia (2004) did a smaller scale study of the Science for All project. In this study, data was collected from two bilingual fourth-grade classrooms through the collection of writing samples to evaluate ELL students' understanding of the scientific inquiry model and of science report writing. Students participated in two science units (Water Cycle and Weather) with instruction for 2 to 3 hours a week. The Authentic Science Inquiry Literacy Assessment System (ASILAS) was administered in a pre/post manner using a four part rubric to measure students' science inquiry and literacy development through writing. The four categories of the rubric were science inquiry, organization, style, and conventions. After both units, students demonstrated growth in writing like a scientist. At the beginning of the Water Cycle unit, 37% of the students in the study were reaching the grade-level benchmark whereas 75% of the students met the grade-level benchmark at the end of the unit.

Another study implemented by Fradd, Lee, and Sutman (1995) demonstrates how students perform differently on assessments. They investigated the science knowledge, vocabulary, and cognitive strategies of diverse groups of fourth-grade students; monolingual Caucasian, African American, bilingual Spanish, and bilingual Haitian Creole. Each group of students studied the same science topics that followed the same format. The researchers found significant differences between the four groups of students. The ELL students had more difficulty with science knowledge and vocabulary than did the monolingual students. The researchers believed that one reason for this difference related to prior knowledge and experiences. When asked if the students had any personal experiences with the science tasks, all of the monolingual students had experiences whereas only 35% of the bilingual students reported prior experiences in science. During instruction, the monolingual students relied heavily on verbal communication whereas the other groups relied more on nonverbal cues and gestures to supplement verbal communication. The researchers also noted that the science terms used in English may not be used in the same way or as often in other languages. Although some of the second language students produced large quantities of writing, they lacked the vocabulary mastery to be precise in their explanations.

Assessing the knowledge of ELL students is often a challenge because it is difficult to differentiate between language and concept understanding. Students perform differently on assessments and often need alternative methods to demonstrate their content knowledge. In Settlage's (2004) research project implemented at San Juan School, the assessment scores of ELL students in science were raised. The teachers in the study saw writing as a weakness for all the students, not just ELL. Most of the writing students produced was descriptive rather than explanatory. The researcher attributed this to the fact that the students were often not directed to write explanations of their observations during science and knowledge that was expressed by students in the classroom discussion was not necessarily reflected on the assessment. The study found that using drawings, whether provided by the teacher or drawn by the student, allowed students to demonstrate a more complex understanding of what they were learning.

A study implemented by Aguirre (1996) examined ELL student performance on concept development and scientific vocabulary through the use of open-ended questions. Fifth-grade ELLs were divided into two groups. Each group was given the same open-ended question at three assessment periods during the school year. One group was asked to answer the question by writing a paragraph while the other group was asked to answer the question by making a drawing. When being assessed on in-depth concept development, students generally performed better using drawing than writing. The students performed equally well in writing and drawing scientific vocabulary. However, students that were considered to be above average performed better on vocabulary using the writing mode. Below average students performed poorly on the writing mode for vocabulary; but low scores on vocabulary did not reflect low scores in concept development. Most of the students in the drawing group (96%) felt that it was easier to answer the questions by drawing than by writing.

Selected Programs for Teaching English Language Learners

The above studies focus on using inquiry as a means to teach science and the natural integration of language acquisition in the learning of science. Other studies focus on specific strategies to be considered in the teaching of inquiry science to English language learners.

Preparing teachers to work with English language learners has historically been a separate course (or sequence of courses) in teacher training or in-service programs that stood apart from content area instruction. The trend in the past 10 years or so is to include specific strategies of learning for ELL students in conjunction with the specific content areas of instruction. These "sheltered-English programs" address the language proficiency and the content area components using specially modified instruction that links language learning with academic work

Sheltered instructional strategies or specially designed academic instruction in English (SDAIE) strategies include creating instruction that relates to students' prior knowledge, tailoring teacher talk to students' English language proficiency levels, allowing students to process material in a variety of formats, and using assessment methods that allow students to display learning in a variety of ways (Becijos, 1997). Although all of these ideas for working with ELLs may be found in separate content area instruction and are part of almost every other method and model, they have more recently been organized into a unified program model in their own right. This method of instruction requires significant teaching skills in both English language development and subject-specific instruction; clearly defined language and content objectives; modified curriculum, supplementary materials, and alternative assessments (Echevarria & Graves 2003).

One of the researched and nationally successful models is the Sheltered Instruction Observation Protocol (SIOP) (Echevarria et al., 2004) developed as part of a 7-year research project (1996–2003) conducted for the Center for Research on Education, Diversity and Excellence (CREDE) to provide teachers with a well-articulated, practical model of sheltered instruction. There are eight components with a total of 30 features that comprise the SIOP Model. The components reflect what we know about effective subject matter instruction and provide a framework for developing lessons for ELL students. The eight components include; preparation, building background, comprehensible input, strategies, interaction, practice/ application, lesson delivery, and review/assessment. In the SIOP model, each of these eight categories has multiple subcomponents that should be taken into consideration when preparing, teaching, and assessing ELL in content area instruction, but as you will learn, many of these strategies are considered "good teaching" strategies and will benefit all students in learning science.

A second program, with its roots in Northern California is entitled Guided Language Acquisition Design (GLAD) dates back to 1985 when it was developed in Fountain Valley by Marcia Brechtel. GLAD consists of a series of teaching strategies based in language development research brought together for content area instruction (Brechtel, 2001). GLAD uses modeling and practice of content words in the context of the subject being taught to make learning more meaningful. This is done using direct instruction from the teacher in the beginning (poems, chants, narrative input, pictorials, etc.) and evolving into more student-centered instruction (sentence patterning charts, listen and sketch, and the 10/2—10 min of instruction and then 2 min of student interaction) to get students more involved and talking to each other about what they have learned. The GLAD program has grown regionally and even nationally as another way to engage children in meaningful language instruction in the context of the content being taught. Studies are now emerging that describe the effectiveness and success of the program (Conley, 2005; Fountain Valley School District, 2005).

Although there are numerous SDAIE programs available today, the ones described earlier are just examples of successful models that the authors have both observed and used in content area instruction.

Research Review of Strategies for Teaching ELL in Science

Each of the earlier models proposes instructional strategies that help the English language learners better understand, learn, and retain content. This section will review literature that discusses specific strategies for ELLs in science instruction.

Keenan (2004) stated that in order to reach the English language learners in her middle school setting, there were specific strategies that helped with her science instruction. In addition to the use of inquiry, Keenan mentions that the use of cooperative learning during investigations allowed students to communicate with each other and negotiate meaning, often in the student's native language. In addition, Keenan uses lots of visuals in the forms of graphic organizers, charts, pictures, videotapes/DVDs, and real-life objects. Keenan also suggests the use of instructional conversations and science talks prior to and during instruction allows for constructing some of the academic vocabulary that may be necessary in the learning situation. Finally, Keenan suggests that using scaffolding and sequencing are important factors that help her ELL students learn science.

Lincoln and Beller (2004) emphasize that the adaptations to curriculum are important, but that adaptations must be done without compromising the content. Strategies that they support include setting goals before making adaptations to the curriculum, list and repeat lesson objectives and instructions; use simple language, not simple concepts; allow for bilingual tests and assessments so as to test knowledge, not English ability; provide additional vocabulary help; and increase wait time for cognitive processing for ELL students.

Buck (2000) has some general strategies that will help ELLs at the elementary level of instruction. She suggests that the use of the chalk/white board be used more frequently and that step by step directions be written out. Terminology should be printed on large sheets of paper or on the board for reference; we now refer to these as word walls. Rephrasing unclear statements using different words and simpler sentences makes a difference. Also summarizing what has been learned at frequent intervals is important. When students are working, allow collaborative groups and pair nonnative speakers with native speakers, vary instructional delivery, encourage parent participation, actively involve students in peer instruction, and finally, make connections to out of school experiences. When considering learning strategies for students, the use of prior knowledge, question generating, scaffolding, and summarizing are paramount for the EL student.

Colburn and Echevarria (1999) explore sheltered instruction strategies that include activity-based learning, integration of key words and vocabulary in the context of the lesson. They use English by incorporating reading, writing, listening, and speaking into the lesson, encourage lots of interaction—student to student and teacher to student, they allow for group responses rather than just individual responses to questions, the use of lots of supplemental materials, and the use of notebooks to record observations, data, and thoughts.

Hansen (2006) proposes a way to integrate SIOP strategies into the learning cycle. Although this seems like a natural combination, Hansen provides specific strategies to incorporate into each of the phases of the learning cycle. In the engagement phase, the use of language buddies and preassessment are highlighted along with several other SDAIE strategies. In the exploration phase, she suggests cooperative groups and multiple levels of communication. In the concept development phase (explanation phase), Hansen suggests using many strategies for terminology including several GLAD strategies with charts, 10/2, and process grids. Finally, in the assessment and evaluation phases, Hansen suggests multiple avenues of assessment beyond the traditional "test" that allows for students to demonstrate their understanding of the content rather than the command of the English language.

Finally, in the book entitled *Science for the English Language Learner* (Fathman & Crowther, 2005), the authors present a compendium of research and strategies for science instruction for the English language learner. The text is a resource for K–12 teachers and includes chapters written by specialists in both language acquisition and science education. Specifically, in the chapter entitled Strategies for Teaching Science to English Learners (Maata, Dobb, & Ostlund, 2005), the authors propose multiple examples dealing with connecting with students, teacher talk, student talk, academic vocabulary, reading skills, writing skills, collaborative learning, scientific language, and process skills of inquiry. Additionally, there are issues of assessment that are discussed in the chapter entitled Strategies for Assessing Science and Language Learning (Katz & Olson, 2005). These strategies include using multiple assessment types, knowing the strengths and limitations of each assessment type, considering assessment as an ongoing process rather than as summative only, providing language learners options, matching the level of support provided in an assessment with the language proficiency of the student, documenting modifications made for language learners, matching assessment with instruction, and rethinking the role of summative assessment.

As can be seen from the previously discussed research, there are common strategies that run throughout. Cooperative learning allows for multiple uses of communication and cooperation when implemented appropriately. This also allows for dialogue between students, and EL students may be paired with more proficient EL students who may do some interpretation for them. These studies suggest that the more you use visuals or the real thing (realia), the better the EL students will be able to understand what is being taught and to make connections to the real world. Graphic organizers, grids, lists, word walls, and other strategies that allow for the organization and understanding of material in multiple learning modes seem paramount. During instruction, the teacher must use scaffolding as well as using frequent opportunities to repeat, rephrase, and summarize the topics being discussed. Additionally, keeping lecture components short or remembering the 10/2 (10 min lecture to 2 min student interaction) and increasing wait time for calling on people to answer questions will help EL students and all learners in the classroom. Finally, rethinking assessment in terms of what is appropriate for the lesson and the level of the learners along with plenty of alternative assessments (projects, notebooks, role playing, etc.) will help the teacher to better understand what the students have learned, not just the ability to communicate in English. Trying out just a few of these strategies per lesson will allow for greater understanding in science not just for EL students, but for all the students in the classroom.

APPLICATIONS TO CLASSROOM PRACTICE

Learning Cycle, Sheltered Instruction, and Lesson Adaptations

This part of the chapter discusses and carries out the modification of an existing lab activity to better meet the English language and science academic language needs of English language learners. The section begins with some comments about the 5E teaching model and the STS teaching philosophy, both of which are included in the modified science lessons. It continues with a comparison of an existing science activity in life science before and after modification for ELL. The hope is that, after studying this activity before and after modification, a teacher will be able to take the existing curriculum and modify it to better suit the needs of ELL.

The 5E Teaching Model and STS Philosophy.   An effective teaching model that is student centered, stresses inquiry, and can easily incorporate effective learning strategies for ELL is the learning cycle. Atkins and Karplus (1962) are credited with developing the learning cycle with three main phases, exploration, concept/terms development, and application. This is in a sense the activity before content (ABC) model of instruction that is most commonly used with inquiry instruction in science today. The original three-step learning cycle has been modified in several formats, one of the most popular used today is that designed by Roger Bybee now referred to the 5E model. The 5E model proposes the lesson begin with an engagement to get the children interested and engage background knowledge; exploration that is the main portion of the lesson that is hands-on and when children make discoveries of the content being presented; explanation where the content is labeled and key vocabulary is reinforced; elaboration and extension activity that allows for further understanding of the content; and evaluation in terms of both formative and summative assessment (Bybee & Landes, 1990; Trowbridge & Bybee, 1996). When adapted to full class laboratory investigations, the 5E teaching model gives structure to the prelab, lab, and postlab processes but still allows for teacher lab modification to promote student inquiry and emphasize all four communication modes of listening, talking, reading, and writing. In the following, with the use of the 5E model, is a sample of various techniques and/or teaching skills that can be incorporated into a lab activity to make it a better learning tool for ELL.

Engagement.   The first E can be used to go over the objectives and to motivate and preassess students. The teacher might begin by questioning students about connections to real-life experiences and background knowledge. If possible, find a short news article that relates to the topic to use for connections to real life. Students can read and discuss it prior to the lab. During any presentations, the teacher should generally use gestures, slow speech, and visuals that lead to student discussion and to better understanding. Also, a lab-related concrete demonstration prior to the full class investigation can allow the teacher to determine the CALP level of the students for the lab before the students state and write the objectives. This can be done if the teacher will ask the students to first predict what will happen, think about it, and discuss observations made during the actual demonstration. In this scaled-down version of the lab, the teacher may also name and demonstrate the use of new materials that will be used in the full-blown student lab. It is also a good place to go over both content and language objectives. According to Echevarria and Graves (2003), content and language objectives for each lesson should be stated both orally and in writing and the engagement is a good time to do this. The content objectives should be tied to grade-level content standards, and in general, these content objectives should be limited to one or two per lesson. The language objectives may focus on one or more of the following but are not limited to these: vocabulary, reading or writing skills; functional language; or higher order thinking skills.

Exploration. Before students begin the exploration or actual lab, the teacher might prepare them by using vocabulary from the engagement for a word wall consisting of vocabulary they should use during their discussions in the lab and to answer questions that are part of the exploration. The teacher may have three columns, one each for science concepts and terms peculiar to the lab activity, everyday words and additional science words that are more descriptive and appropriate as academic English. As groups of two to four students carry out the lab (exploration), they practice listening, speaking, reading, and writing in one setting. They may even speak in their native language to clarify science terms in English. If the teacher pairs an ELL with a language buddy, one who is both fluent in English and the ELL's native language, new science vocabulary can be explained by the fluent buddy as needed. For these reasons, the exploration is considered by this author to be the most important E for both learning science and promoting language development. Furthermore, during and after the lab, students may be asked to draw and label the lab setup and list vocabulary words with definitions from the word wall for their lab books. In a typical lab, the background information, procedure, focused observations, science materials, and general interaction (in heterogeneous cooperative groups) all facilitate language acquisition. The focused observations should also have questions that address both the content and language objectives. Following the lab, during the third E, explanation, the student talk is extended during discussion of the materials and observations with both the lab groups and the teacher.

Explanation. During this third E, the teacher may take a few minutes to elaborate on any students' naïve conceptions and directly teach new ideas to clarify concepts observed and discussed in the lab. The teacher may even "shelter" lab instruction by demonstrating parts of the lab again to point out and show key science concepts that students did not understand and/or found confusing. The teacher can also use different cooperative activities for language practice. For example, in a "pairs compare" activity, groups of four students can give multiple possible responses about observations, inferences, and answers to the questions from the lab activity. In this activity, shoulder partners use a "rally table" to write answers and keep them secret from the other two shoulder partners. After the teacher calls time, the pairs should compare answers and reach consensus. The teacher can then help students single out erroneous inferences, assumptions, and answers to lab questions to further clarify the lab experiences. Alignment to the standards and objectives might be addressed as well. Vocabulary words entered in the lab books can also be elaborated on. Students should pronounce and use the words in sentences and make any corrections in the definitions they have already written in their lab books. Moreover, instructional technology such as Power Point, DVD, videos, Web sites, and so forth may all be used to reinforce what was learned in the lab and discussion with more concrete examples. Visuals such as these can make the science information more interesting, holding students' attention better, as well as scaffold students for better understanding.

Elaboration.   The fourth E, elaboration is where the third domain of STS fits best. During this part of the activity, students can further practice spoken and written language by applying and connecting the science concepts, observed in the exploration and clarified in the explanation, to society or real-world examples. Students may elaborate on the examples they brought up in the engagement and connect them to the new information learned in the just completed lab. This makes students see science as relevant to their lives. To practice reading the new vocabulary on the lab topic, the teacher may design a handout. "What's Happening" is commercially available in some school districts for this. The fourth E, as well as the third STS domain, are known to promote better student retention of the science knowledge (Yager & Rustum, 1993). Also, teachers who adhere to the STS teaching model encourage student questions throughout the activity. This fits with the fourth domain of the STS model, creativity.

Evaluation.   The evaluation should loop back to the engagement and exploration to assess and reinforce the content and language objectives. In authentic assessment and evaluation, the teacher will require the students to further discuss and write about the lab investigation with the appropriate science concepts and vocabulary that align with the standards and objectives. These should have been discussed and clarified during the third E, explanation. The teacher might have the students do a "talking chips" activity during which each student says something important about what they learned in the activity before putting the chip down and listening to the next group member. A couple of rounds of this might cover all of the important ideas of the investigation. The teacher could close this E with a cloze activity that uses the new science and everyday vocabulary learned and practiced in the investigation. Later, the teacher will read the lab reports to check the vocabulary and questions that should have been answered during the lab and revised during the explanation. When the lab reports are returned, the teacher can further clarify any erroneous information and reinforce the expected learning.

The 5 E teaching model (Bybee & Landes, 1990; Trowbridge & Bybee, 1996) adapted from the original learning cycle (Atkins & Karplus, 1962) will be the instructional model used in the lesson. The science, technology, and society (STS) teaching philosophy (Yager & Rustum, 1993) will also be used as a way of connecting science to society and helping students gain more interest in science through understanding its relevance to everyday events. The STS methodology (Domain 3) allows teachers to apply and connect science to everyday society. It is a good fit with both the 5E teaching model and National Science Education Standards (NSES; NRC, 1996) overarching goals of science literacy and inquiry learning.

With this background information on the 5E model and STS, we are now ready to proceed with the science lesson modification. We will set the stage with some comments about the unmodified, original lesson.

Lesson Modification Example

Comments about the original lesson. Every experienced teacher will generally modify lab activities to meet the needs of different classes. The teacher may also have to substitute materials when all materials suggested in the activity are not available. Modern textbooks generally have suggestions for alignment with the NSES, developing thinking skills, and using a variety of instructional strategies; for example, cooperative learning strategies and instructional technology; to meet individual student needs, for example, ELL. Regarding STS science teaching, many science books have inserted a technology section into each chapter that offers suggestions for applying and connecting science to society. This supports the third domain of STS science teaching, connections and applications. Science texts may not suggest using the 5E model, but the teachers guide may stress the constructivist learning model, which the 5E model supports. The unmodified lab activity used in this example does include societal applications and connections in the induction prior to learning the science concepts and process skills that are part of the activity.

To modify the following lesson to better meet the needs of ELL, the lesson uses the 5E teaching model with an STS approach and incorporates some of the suggestions given in the California Science Project (CSP) publication, "Effective Science Instruction for English Learners" (Dobb, 2004). Ideas from the SIOP model (Echevarria et al., 2004) are also used. The unmodified lesson is taken from a regular life science textbook common to upper elementary grades.

UNMODIFIED ACTIVITY—OBSERVING OSMOSIS

It is difficult to see osmosis occurring in cells because of the small size of most cells. However, there are a few cells that can be seen without the aid of a microscope. Try this activity to see how osmosis occurs in a large cell.

Problem

How does osmosis occur in an egg?

Materials

Raw egg, (2) 500mL containers with covers, 250mL of vinegar, 250mL of corn syrup, 250mL graduated cylinder, 2 labels, A and B

Procedure

1. Copy the data table and use it to record your observations.
2. Measure 250mL of vinegar into container A. Add 250mL of syrup to container B. Place the egg into container A. Cover both containers.
3. Observe the egg for 2 days. Record the appearance of the egg in the data table.
4. At the end of 2 days, use a spoon to remove the egg from container A. Rinse the egg and place it in container B.
5. Observe the egg the next day. Record its appearance.
6. Measure the remaining liquid in containers A and B. Record the amounts.

Analyze

1. What did you observe after 30 minutes?
2. What did you observe after 2 days?
3. What did you observe after 3 days?

Conclude and Apply

1. What caused the movement of water in container A and container B?
2. Calculate the amount of water that moved in containers A and B?
3. Infer what part of the egg controlled what moved into and out of the cell?

Data and Observations			
Time	30 Minutes	Two Days	Three Days
Vinegar Volume			
Observations			
Corn Syrup Volume			
Observations			

MODIFIED ACTIVITY—OBSERVING OSMOSIS

Background

This lab activity continues class work on cell transport and properties of the cell membrane that allow some materials to pass through the membrane but not others. You have already studied diffusion and osmosis and now you will proceed to a concrete example of these concepts with a lab investigation. A large cell, a chicken egg, will be used to demonstrate how osmosis occurs in small cells.

Problem

How does osmosis occur in an egg?

Materials

Raw egg, (2) 500mL containers with covers, 250mL of vinegar, 250mL of corn syrup, 250mL graduated cylinder, 2 labels, A and B

Engagement /Prelab

1. Content objectives—Students will be able to:

    a. Describe and give an example of diffusion.

    b.   Describe and give an example of osmosis.

    c.   Compare and contrast diffusion and osmosis.

2. Language objectives—Students will be able to:

    a.   Compare diffusion and osmosis in small groups.

    b.   Discuss examples of diffusion in everyday life.

    c.   Read the lab and ask questions about any part of it you do not understand.

    d.   Write in your own words definitions for vocabulary in your lab book.

    e.   Write answers to questions from the lab activity in your lab book.

3. Preassessment questions and discussion—Do a place mat activity and have students address the following questions individually and then come to group consensus.

    a.   Describe some everyday examples of diffusion of a gas or liquid.

    b.   Discuss the purpose of a membrane in an animal cell.

    c.   Explain what a solvent and solute are and identify the solvent and solute in a sugar solution and a salt solution.

    d.   Analyze what is meant by a solution that is more concentrated or more dilute using the words solute and solvent.

    e.   In geology, you may have studied soils that allow water to pass through them or stop water from passing. What is a science word for this?

4. Motivation

    a.   Have students write down predictions for what they think will happen when slices of potato are placed in separate beakers, one with a solution of salt water and the other with plain water.

    b.   (Teacher Guided) Carry out the demonstration for students to check at the end of the period. Have prepared beaker samples of the sliced potatoes available that were done earlier so students can compare the results in each beaker.

    c.   Have the students discuss in their lab groups what they observed and write down the observations and explanations for what they think happened to the potato in the salt solution to make it flexible and less rigid than the one in the pure water.

    d.   Have the students observe the results of the new demonstration, after they finish the full class lab activity, to confirm/verify that it is the same as the previously prepared beakers of potato slices in the salt solution and pure water as in (b) above.

e. List any words the students are unfamiliar with on a word wall and discuss explanations for the words. (Although most of the words should already be known, they could include some of the following; diffusion, osmosis, permeable, semi permeable, membrane, equilibrium osmosis, solvent, solute, solution, dilute, concentrated, flexible, rigid and selective. Students should put these words in their lab books in sentences and when possible, with pictures or diagrams to increase concrete understanding. Spanish-speaking students can also look up these words in Spanish dictionaries and single out the ones that have English cognates.)

5. Safety, housekeeping, and management before the lab activity—go over this before the exploration. This should include any safety procedures and instructions about where to store the beakers for later observation and how to get and put away equipment. Also, any other things that will keep the lab safe and make it flow smoothly.

Exploration/Lab Work

(Questions for students to answer before they do the procedure.)
You may discuss them with your lab partner, other students, or the teacher. Write out your answers, predictions, in you lab book.

1. What do you predict will happen to the egg while it is in the vinegar in container A?
2. Predict what will happen to the volume of vinegar while the egg is in it? After 2 days, decide whether your prediction was accurate. Try to determine why what you predicted did or did not happen?
3. Why should you cover the containers?
4. Predict what will happen to the egg after a day or 2 in the corn syrup solution.
5. Predict what will happen to the volume of corn syrup while the egg is in it. Explain why you predicted this.

Procedure (The teacher should emphasize to students that they must focus carefully when making all observations).

1. Copy the data table and use it to record your observations.
2. Measure 250mL of vinegar into container A.
3. Add 250mL of syrup to container B.
4. Place the egg into container A. Cover both containers.
5. Observe the egg for 2 days. Record the appearance of the egg in the data table.

6. At the end of 2 days, use a spoon to carefully remove the egg from container A without damaging it. Rinse the egg and place it in container B.
7. Observe the egg the next day. Record its appearance.
8. Measure the remaining liquid in containers A and B. Record the amounts.

Data and Observations			
Time	30 Minutes	Two Days	Three Days
Vinegar Volume			
Observations			
Corn Syrup Volume			
Observations			

Analyze

1. What did you observe after 30 minutes?
2. What did you observe after 2 days?
3. What did you observe after 3 to 4 days?

Explanation/Postlab

1. Discuss your observations with other groups and the teacher during the full class discussion. (Have groups of four students do the "pairs compare" activity. The teacher should help students arrive at consensus with the expected responses. Erroneous assumptions and inferences may be singled out.)
2. Did you change any of your answers? List those you changed and explain why you changed them.
3. What new concepts did you learn that are part of the content objectives/science standards? List them.
4. What new science and everyday English vocabulary did you learn? (The teacher may elaborate on the new vocabulary words and have students pronounce the words and use them in sentences.)
5. The teacher can use a short power point presentation to reinforce key vocabulary with examples.

Elaboration/PostLab

(For questions 1–6, the teacher can have five numbered posters around the room that groups of four–five students each visit one at a time and alternate to write answers with different colored pens. Afterward, the teacher can further discuss and highlight the best information and students can enter it in their lab books.)

1. Why did the vinegar dissolve the eggshell?
2. What happened to the eggshell? Explain.
3. What happened to volume of the vinegar? Explain.
4. If you would have checked the pH of the vinegar before and after the eggshell disappeared, do you think it would have changed? Explain.
5. When you digest food, are your intestines permeable or selectively permeable membranes. Explain.
6. Why can some people not eat milk products?
7. (Teacher Demonstration) Show students examples of celery, carrots, and radishes that are in water or have been left out in the air. Have them compare them and describe how this relates to osmosis. Discuss why vegetables are "freshened" with water on the produce shelves. Words such as wilted, limp, and firm may come up here and students should discuss them and define them in their own words.
8. Go to a Web site and look up the term reverse osmosis. Describe what it is and what use it has for society.

EVALUATION

Conclude and Apply

1. Describe what caused the movement of water in container A and container B.
2. Calculate the amount of water that moved in containers A and B?
3. Infer what part of the egg controlled what moved into and out of the cell.
4. Explain why we say the egg membrane is semipermeable.
5. If someone opens a bottle of ammonium hydroxide in one part of a room and you soon smell it in another part of the room, what do we call the process involved in the movement of the ammonia molecules in the air?

6. Describe how diffusion and osmosis are similar and different.
7. Describe how you think oxygen and carbon dioxide get in and out of the capillaries in the lungs and how calcium and glucose pass in and out of the cells.

Additional Reinforcement and Application Questions

The teacher should go over these questions and clarify any confusion. The evaluation can finish up with a cloze activity of essential vocabulary learned in the lab.

1. What is meant by a concentrated and a dilute solution? Give an example with sugar water and explain two ways you could distinguish the dilute one from the concentrated one.
2. In a sugar water solution, identify the solvent and the solute.
3. If salt is dissolved in water, which is the solute and which is the solvent?
4. Draw a picture (a model) of glucose molecules passing through a permeable membrane and identify the solution and its relative concentration (dilute or concentrated) on each side of the membrane before and after it reaches equilibrium.

Exploration/The Lab Investigation-Additional Teacher Notes.

Discussion of Lesson Modifications

Because the students are inquiring (exploring) as they carry out the activity, the teacher should make sure the students work in lab groups of at least two students but no more than four students each. Ideally, ELLs will be paired with students who are native English speakers or peer mentors and those students will know beforehand that part of their job in the lab is to help the ELL with his or her English by engaging in discussion and trying to use the vocabulary words common to the activity. They should discuss what they are observing each day and share any experiences during the class discussion that other students may not have had. Their lab books should have a section to write out what they discuss including both their own ideas and the ideas of lab partners or students in other groups. For example, a student may notice the bubbles being given off from the egg shell in the vinegar solution during the first day and other students may not. This should be discussed with possible explanations given for the observation. The teacher might give hand lenses to enable students to make better observations than they would be able to make with the unaided eye.

By the third day, some students will notice an intact membrane and that the shell has completely dissolved. This is the point at which the egg, without the shell, is carefully placed in container B, the corn syrup or a saturated solution of sugar water. After another day, students will observe that the egg has gotten smaller and more rubbery. After each part of the procedure—Step 2 when the egg is covered with vinegar, Step 3 when the egg is observed after the first and second days, Step 4 when the egg is observed and placed in the corn syrup and the last day when the egg is observed after a day in the corn syrup—the teacher should allow time for discussion regarding what was observed before students come to agreement and write down their observations. This cooperation will allow the ELLs to gain more practice using the terminology of the observations. Academic science words and terms such as dissolving, gas production, diffusion, membrane, and permeability should also be used and discussed by the teacher so that the students will use them in their observations if they otherwise do not think of it. When students describe the observations, they should also be encouraged to draw and label diagrams and write out inferences about what they think happened.

The activity has an analyses part (Questions 1–3) but no prompting is given about which vocabulary words should be practiced. To some degree, this teacher prompting, as the teacher prepares them to observe and walks around and listens to what the students are discussing, will reduce the inquiry but this may still be needed if students are to practice key science words throughout the daily observations.

The activity suggests that 5 min each day be allowed to make observations and 30 min to summarize and answer the question on the last day. The 5 min will have to be expanded to at least 10 min, maybe 15 or more, if students are to be able to observe and discuss and write down full sentences with inferences. This is the best time to use "classroom talk" and practice using the "academic science vocabulary" because the students have concrete experiences to which to attach the words.

Explanation. After the students have made all of their observations and recorded their data in the data table, the teacher should have them answer the conclusion and application questions in the activity. More than 30 min may be needed for this. This is the time when the full class has time to discuss what they saw and come to agreement on what they think happened based on the observable evidence and their current knowledge of science. This is also the time when the teacher will clarify misconceptions and have students repeat parts of the activity if they are unconvinced about what happened. The students should be allowed to be as creative as possible in posing questions and explanations until the class, with the teacher's help as needed, agrees on the conclusions. If students understand the concepts behind osmosis, including diffusion through a semipermeable membrane from a more concentrated to a less concentrated area, with teacher scaffolding, they can understand oxygen and carbon dioxide exchange in the capillaries in the lungs and the passing of minerals and nutrients such as calcium and glucose into the cells. It must also be understood that the science teacher needs a thorough grounding in the science concepts or naïve conceptions or misconceptions will be created in students. Words such as concentration, dilute, and equilibrium will also have to be introduced to students for them to explain Question 4. Where there is more water, there is a higher concentration of water and the water is attempting to reach equilibrium by passing through the semipermeable membrane to where the water is less concentrated. The student data will infer that the water in the vinegar passed into the egg because the egg gets larger and the volume of liquid, acetic acid decreases. (The students may also be told that the acetic acid in the vinegar reacted with the eggshell, calcium carbonate, and produced a salt, calcium acetate, and water.)

In Step 5, students will realize that the egg got smaller and the volume of syrup increased. This is complicated for most students because they must understand that in a concentrated sugar solution, there is less water than in a pure water solution of the same volume. Therefore, if the concentration of water is greater in the egg, water will pass into the sugar solution. In the extension, this can be demonstrated further if students are allowed to prepare a saturated solution of sugar water to show that the mass of the solution contains a lot of sugar, not just water, and the sugar solution is denser than an equal volume of pure water.

Students must discuss this idea thoroughly, write down explanations, and draw pictures if they are to really understand it and not just memorize what osmosis is. Teacher assessments and evaluations must ask for explanations, descriptions, and labeled diagrams, and not just use multiple choice, true–false, and matching questions if student are to really understand the terms and be able to use them in oral and written language.

Evaluation.   When the 5E model is used, the information the teacher goes over in the explanation should be the main information on which the students will be evaluated. This must be authentic and should align with the standards. The evaluation should involve a lot of questions that require students to describe what they observed and what inferences and conclusions they drew. Students can also be asked to draw and label diagrams and label teacher diagrams. When teachers grade this work, they must grade the English usage as well as the correct science terms and concepts.

Closure. This section of the chapter addressed how a teacher may modify an existing science activity in whatever science book the class is using, to make the activity more effective for ELL to learn academic science and English language. Depending on the needs of the students and time allocated to the unit, the modifications may vary.

The saying that "Good teaching comes from good preparation" is the overriding philosophy of both sheltered English instruction and the learning cycle. Sheltered instruction with the strategies supported from research provide a framework within which to think about all of the components of a lesson and adaptations that are made to specifically work with ELL students. However, many of those adaptations are good for all students. The learning cycle and 5E model is a sequence of actually teaching an inquiry lesson from a natural and constructivist philosophy based on Piagetian research (meaning that children learn from experience and the primary experience is kinesthetic). These two strategies of "good preparation and good teaching" work together to enhance learning for all students in the science classroom.

Source: Biggs, A., Daniel, L., & Ortteb, E., (1999). *Life Science*. New York: Glencoe McGraw-Hill (pp. 77). Reprinted with Permission.

FOR FURTHER THOUGHT

Many teachers find that the demographics in their classrooms have changed significantly in the last 10 years and find themselves inadequately prepared to deal with the English language learners in their classrooms. The previous literature review and applications to the classroom provide research and strategies that may help. The following questions and tasks may help you adapt your instruction further from the information provided in this chapter.

- Using an existing science lesson plan, consider the modifications that you would use to make the lesson more appropriate for the English language learners in your classroom. Note how these modifications may not be as drastic as it may seem.
- Conduct some interviews of your entire classroom. Try to determine the different learning styles of all the children in the classroom. What

adaptations could you make to the lessons that may cater to different learning styles?

- Consider the 5E inquiry lesson design. What adaptations can you make to each of the phases that would be more EL appropriate?
- Make a list of the EL strategies that you are most interested in, then incorporate one strategy per day during your science lessons. Record your observations about EL learning and regular student learning. Note if there were more responses, more involvement, and more interaction from your strategies.
- Ask other teachers in your building what strategies they are using to accommodate for the ELLs. Note which strategies they are using and compare them to the strategies suggested in this chapter.

REFERENCES

Aguirre, M. (1996, November). Effect of open-ended questions on Spanish-dominant LEP students' ability to demonstrate in-depth science concept development and use scientific vocabulary. *NYSABE Journal*, 46–69.

Amaral, O., Garrison, L., & Klentschy, M. (2002, Summer). Helping English learners increase achievement through inquiry-based science instruction. *Bilingual Research Journal*, 26, 213–239.

Atkins, J. M. & Karplus, R. (1962). Discovery or invention? *The Science Teacher*, 29(5), 45–51.

Becijos, J. (1997). *SDAIE: Strategies for teachers of English learners*. Bonita, CA: Torch Publications.

Bravo, M., & Garcia, G. (2004, April). *Learning to write like scientists: English language learners' science inquiry and writing understandings in responsive learning contexts*. Paper presented at the annual American Educational Researchers Association. April. San Diego, CA.

Brechtel, M. (2001). *Bringing it all together*. San Diego, CA: Dominie Press.

Buck, G. (2000). Teaching science to English-as-second-language learners. *Science and Children*, 38(3), 38–41.

Bybee, R., & Landes, N. M. (1990). Science for life and living: An elementary school science program from biological sciences curriculum study. *The American Biology Teacher*, 52(2), 92–98.

Colburn, A., & Echevarria, J. (1999). Meaningful lessons. *The Science Teacher*, 66(3), 36–39 (March).

Conley, A. (2005). *GLAD's impact on the oral language development of ELL students*. Unpublished master's thesis, University of Nevada, Reno.

Dobb, F. (2004).*Essential elements of effective science instruction for English learners*. Los Angeles, CA: California Science Project.

Echevarria, J., & Graves, A. (2003). *Sheltered content instruction: Teaching English language learners with diverse abilities* (2nd ed.). Boston: Allyn & Bacon.

Echevarria, J., Vogt, M., & Short, D. (2004). *Making content comprehensible for English language learners: The SIOP model.* Boston: Pearson.

Fathman, A., & Crowther, D. (2005). Science for English language learners. Arlington, VA. NSTA Press.

Fradd, S., Lee, O., & Sutman, F. (1995). Science knowledge and cognitive strategy use among culturally and linguistically diverse students. *Journal of Research in Science Teaching, 32*(8), 797–816.

Fradd, S., Lee, O., Sutman, F., & Saxton, M. (2001, Fall). Promoting science literacy with English language learners through instructional materials development: A case study. *Bilingual Research Journal, 25,* 479–501.

Hampton, E., & Rodriguez, R. (2001, Fall). Inquiry science in bilingual classrooms. *Bilingual Research Journal, 25,* 461–478.

Hansen, L. (2006). Strategies for ELL success. *Science and Children, 43*(4), 22–25.

Fountain Valley School District. (2005). *Project GLAD.* Retrieved March 13, 2006 from http://www.fvsd.k12.ca.us/district_office/tstRlts.html

Katz, A., & Olson, J. (2005). Strategies for assessing Science and language learning (pp. 61–75). In A. Fathman & D. Crowther (Eds.), *Science for English language learners.* Arlington, VA: NSTA Press.

Keenan, S. (2004). Reaching English language learners: Strategies for teaching science in diverse classrooms. *Science and Children, 42*(2), 49–51.

Kindler, A. (2002). *Survey of the states' limited English proficient students and available educational programs and services 2000–2001 summary report.* Washington, DC: NCELA.

Lincoln, F., & Beller, C. (2004). English Language learners in the science classroom. *Science Scope,* (28)1, 28–31.

Maata, D., Dobb, F., & Ostlund, K. (2005). Strategies for teaching science to English learners. In A. Fathman & D. Crowther (Eds.), *Science for English language learners.* Arlington, VA: NSTA Press.

National Center for Education Statistics. (NCES). (2005). *Public elementary and secondary students, staff, schools, and school districts: School year 2002–2003* (NCES 2005–314). Retrieved from http://nces.ed.gov/pubsearch/pubs info.asp? pubid=2005314

National Research Council. (1996). National science education standards. Washington, DC: National Academy Press.

Rosebery, A., Warren, B., & Conant, F. (2003, Spring) Appropriating scientific discourse: Findings from language minority classrooms. *California Journal of Science Education, 2,* 69–121.

Settlage, J. (2004, April). *Inquiry for English as second language learners: Challenges and successes.* Paper presented at the annual NARST meeting, Vancouver, British Columbia.

Trowbridge, L., & Bybee, R. (1996). *Teaching secondary school Science.* Columbus, OH: Merrill.

Yager, R. & Rustum, R. (1993). STS: Most pervasive and most radical of reform approaches to "Science" education. From Yager, R. (Ed.). (1993). *The science, technology, society movement.* Washington, DC: National Science Teachers Association.

8

Inquiry Curriculum in the Primary Grades

Carole Gile
William Penn University

> What learners currently know–regardless of how little or how much–
> is the only starting point from which they can learn.
>
> —Harste, 1993, (p. 4)

It was my great fortune to have the opportunity to teach in a first and second grade (multiage) classroom for 3 years following my doctoral education and 6 years of teaching in higher education. The final year of university teaching provided me the chance to study with educators Jerome Harste and Carolyn Burke, both groundbreakers in conceptualizing inquiry as curriculum. The next year, I was helping my husband convalesce from surgery, and in my spare time I volunteered in a local elementary school. The principal and I arranged a visit to the Center for Inquiry Elementary School in Indianapolis, and we invited the principal of a local private school to accompany us. Little did I know that the invitation would lead me back to elementary teaching. In February of that year, a teacher at the private school resigned near the middle of the second semester, and the principal invited me to apply.

During the interview for the multiage classroom position, I was told that the school had just purchased a very expensive, intensive phonics program. My heart sank as I boldly told the principal that I would not teach intensive phonics; however, I would teach the children to use all linguistic and pragmatic cues. Throwing caution away, I added that I would not teach with a basal reading program, although I might use the anthologies as resources. Much to my surprise and delight, I was hired.

I could see that the curriculum was mine to design, and I couldn't wait to implement years of educational study and experience in the primary-age classroom. Moreover, I was more than excited to center the Science and Language Arts curricula on inquiry learning. Often on my mind as I thought about using the language arts to enhance science learning was James A. Van Allen's statement, "I am never as clear about a matter as when I have just finished writing about it" (1979, p. 7). Still, I had many questions: Could first and second graders write, read, and listen well enough to use these language arts to learn about science? Would inquiry carry over to the other disciplines? Could the children flexibly use the sign systems of writing, mathematics, art, and music? Could inquiry sustain the children's natural curiosity and, moreover, develop inquiring minds? Could first and second graders actively participate in such a curriculum? Would it be appropriate for them? Would it provide them with the learning they would need to solidly ground them with knowledge expected of first and second graders? Would they be ready for third grade? These were my own inquiry questions—questions that I had the freedom to investigate.

From the very beginning, the curriculum in the first and second grade multiage classroom evolved as a part of reflection and reflexivity; however, it began with Harste's (1993) insightful principle for understanding how inquiry curriculum is planned; that is, start with what the children know. The first days of each school year brought the upper grade students to my classroom to be interviewers and writers for the first and second graders as they answered questions on interest interviews and the Burke Reading Interview (Goodman, Watson, & Burke, 1987).

The Burke Reading Interview asks questions that provide insight into a child's view of reading including their (1) model of reading, (2) model of a good reader, (3) view of self as a reader, (4) strategies they know and/or know about, (5) how to help a reader with reading, and (6) what he or she would like to do better as a reader. These interviews gave me insight into what would be interesting and motivating to students, and it gave me some ideas about their reading backgrounds. Typical interests the children conveyed included wild animals such as cheetahs and jaguars, their own pets, collections and hobbies, television and reading interests.

Each school year began with a theme cycle—one year, animals; another, oceans; and another, health, nutrition, and physical fitness.

Topics associated with science were popular, and it was easy to relate these to social studies, math, art, music, all the while integrating these with the language arts. The health, nutrition, and physical fitness inquiry is the focus of this writing.

The students and I engaged in conversations that focused on how to stay healthy and what foods contribute to good health. Bulletin boards reflected the topic and included physical fitness posters and a poster of the food pyramid. I gleaned books from the school and public libraries and placed them on tables about the room. Giving the children time to browse through the books and view the posters helped us to learn how we related to the topic. After this immersion in the topic, we began more intensive inquiry by brainstorming questions the children and I had. Unlike strategies that ask students what they already know, I honed in on students' questions in order to first encourage their curiosity. I wanted them to think like scientists. I would learn what students already knew about health, nutrition, and physical fitness as the study progressed. The invitation to focus on their own questions and to share them with others brought about discussions that ranged from where to get information to questioning each other's perceptions about the topic.

The children were then invited to investigate the books further, and to listen to books that caught their interest. Parent volunteers and students from Grades 5, 6, 7, and 8 were invited to our classroom to read to the different groups from the books. The children could choose which book to listen to, thus forming the first semblance of interest groups. The readings were followed by further conversations about the books. About this time, the children were honing in on the questions they wanted answered—their interest was whetted.

The children's conversations centered on something they read, something that was read to them, or something they knew or learned as they talked with other students and their parents about what we were doing at school. This particular year, a parent who is a nurse brought in a book about the human body for the children to use. After reading part of it to them and relating information gained to the care of their own bodies, the students expressed the desire to engage in inquiry into specific body structures including the heart, the brain, the lungs, and the skeleton.

The children were invited to think about which of these they were most interested in learning about and to group themselves with others who shared the same interest. They then sorted out the books available in our classroom library that pertained to their topic, gathered them together and went into different areas of the classroom to review them with their group members. They also added books from their personal libraries.

After a few days of reading, browsing, listening, and talking together, butcher paper was taped to the chalkboards, one large sheet for each topic. Each topic was written in the center of the sheet. The children gathered by whichever topic they chose and, with the help of parent volunteers and/or the older students, they told what they knew about their topic while their ideas were webbed. The helper was invited to contribute, too, both as a model and as encouragement to explore an avenue the children might not know about. One of the topics chosen by several students was the skeleton. The web for skeleton included the following:

- Our bones help us move
- [Bones] Need milk for calcium for strength
- Ligaments hold the bones in place
- Muscles help to control the movement of our body skeleton
- Osteoporosis is a bone problem

One fact contributed is, "The brain is soft. We know because it needs bone around it for protection—the skull." Someone in the group noted that this fact branched over to another groups' web, the brain.

Knowledge the children contributed to the topic the brain included: Our brain helps us to think, [our brain] Needs healthy food to help it work; It is a message center; If you could unfurl the cerebral cortex, it would cover our classroom. In this particular web, the contribution, "Our brain helps us to think" is a probable already known fact, whereas the next two contributions are more likely facts learned from listening and reading, and the last fact concerning the cerebral cortex is obviously a fact remembered from reading or listening.

At this point, *I Wonder...* books (C. Burke, personal communication, October 26, 1995) were distributed, and the students composed their questions about their topic into inquiry questions. These little books were teacher made—folded copy paper with various colored construction paper covers, which the children decorated to go with their topic. Inside, the children listed their questions, already known facts, and facts gleaned from reading and conversations.

As our curriculum emerged, the students formed their own collaborative teams, sometimes a small group, sometimes partners. Occasionally a child would decide to pursue their inquiry on their own. The children

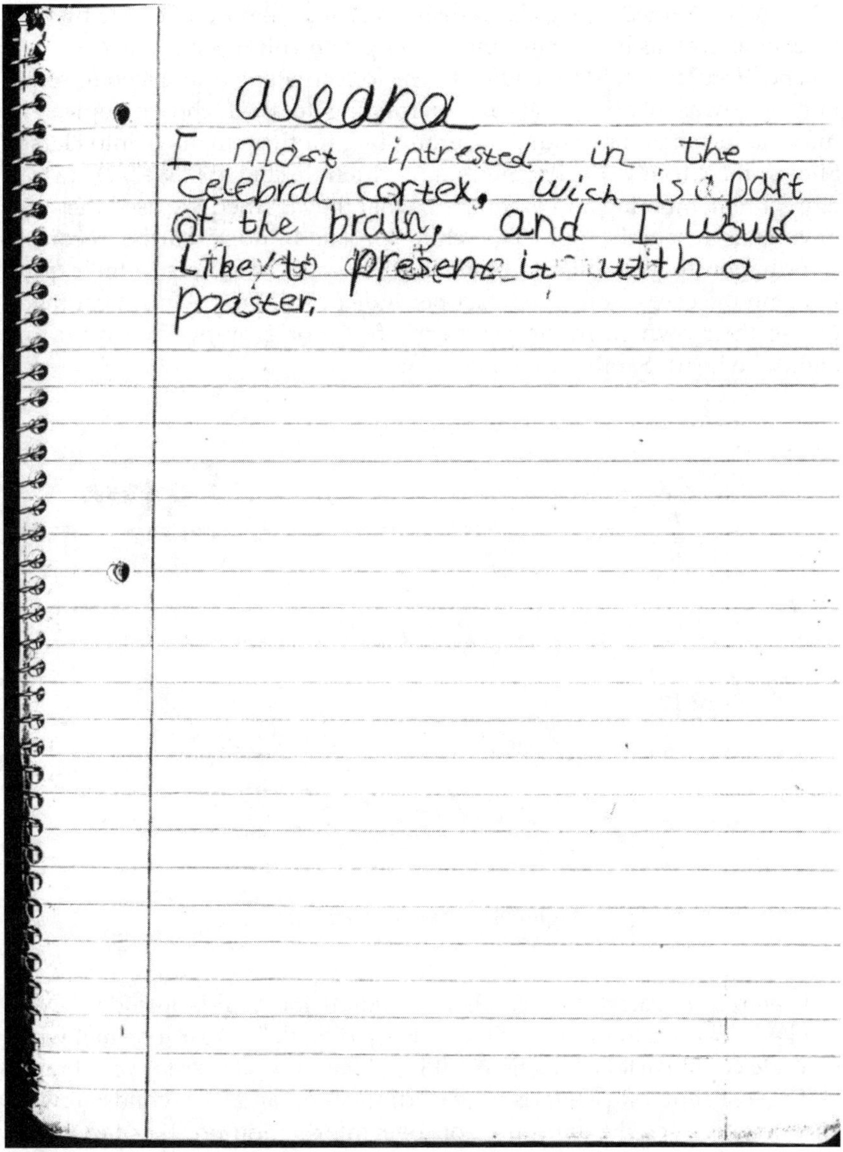

Figure 8.1 Allana chose to write about her inquiry interest in her journal.

read and examined materials on their own, and they were read to by their teacher as well as by parents and upper grade volunteers.

Therefore, the children could choose to read alone or to listen to someone who was reading materials pertaining to their chosen topic. The information shared provided the grounding for them to move into Harste, Short, and Burke's (1988) generating written discourse (268–273), a strategy for remembering and organizing what they learned We used the strategy as a research tool. The children used index cards, recorded information they wanted to remember as well as answers to their questions on the cards—one idea/fact per index card. They were encouraged to use their own words to state each fact. For example, when writing about the heart, Sarah wrote (Fig. 8.2):

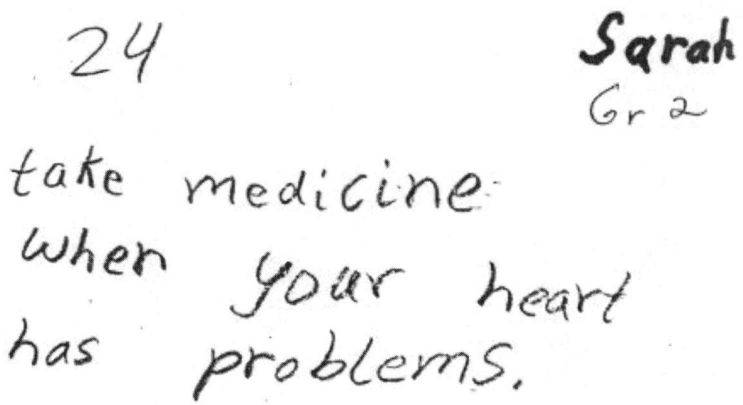

Figure 8.2   Sarah's Fact Card.

Examples of facts other children wrote on their cards include, "Don't smoke," "Eat healthy food," "Drink plenty of milk," "Wear a helmet when you ride your bike for a long time," "Play games. It's exercise for your brain."

The concept of plagiarism was discussed, and the children were encouraged to credit the source of their information on their fact cards. Because the second graders had experienced the strategy the year before, they were instrumental in helping the first graders get started.

The students were invited to look at their topic through a variety of lenses that revolved the topics through as many of the disciplines they could, such as science, anthropology, biology, health, social studies. They were invited to relate their topics and findings back to the umbrella topic and to think about how to show what they learned through the use of multiple sign systems such as language, music, art, mathematics, dance, and/or drama. Most often the students chose to incorporate into a poster writing and art (Fig. 8.1). Allana, though, chose to write a report and present it. In either case, speaking was involved in presenting their research. Allana planned her inquiry in her journal (Fig. 8.3).

When several children in the group were satisfied with the information gathered, they shared their ideas and discussed them. In some cases, the same idea was recorded more than once, even though different resources were used. The students derived that the idea was important; however, in order not to repeat the same information in their collaborated presentation, they decided who should present the idea. They spent time pooling their cards, gleaning out the repetitive ideas and sequencing the ones they kept in an order they thought was best. They discussed the reasons for ordering the cards as they did, which sometimes led to experimenting with other sequences and, finally, they chose the order they thought fit the meaning they were sharing as well as the form the completed project would take.

Some of Allana's cards are fact cards and some are facts stated as questions with the answer also on the card. Samples follow (spelling and punctuation are hers). The numbers she wrote on the cards signify the order she wanted to use to write her report (Figs. 8.4–8.7).

The students were aware that when their inquiry culminated, they would be sharing their project with a larger audience—the whole class and, possibly, parents and/or other classes. Allana organized her cards and used them to write a research report, complete with questions to ask her audience after she shared her report with them (Figs. 8.5, 8.6). This idea caught on with several others who composed questions to go with their presentation of their posters.

The amount of writing and the voice that Allana develops in her piece demonstrates that, given the opportunity to participate using the language arts while correlating them with science and the other disciplines, a second grader can find her voice while learning a great deal about her topic. In the process, I learned so much about what she knows and where she is in her control of her topic, spelling, and so forth. There was a baby brother in her family—possibly an influence on some of the information she reported.

Allana followed her report with a test. She wrote these questions at the end of her report (some of these were also written on her fact cards; Figs. 8.9a, 8.9b):

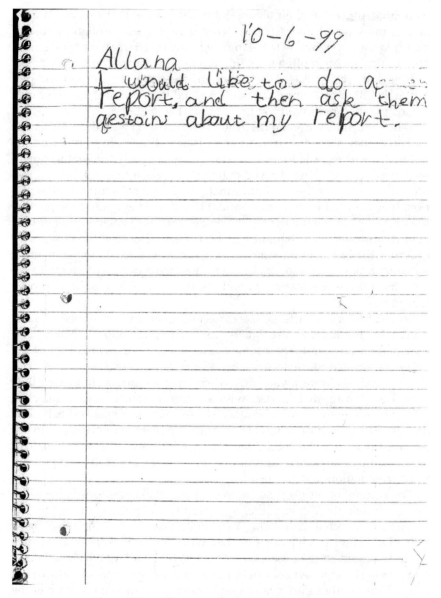

Figure 8.3. Allana continues to plan her inquiry.

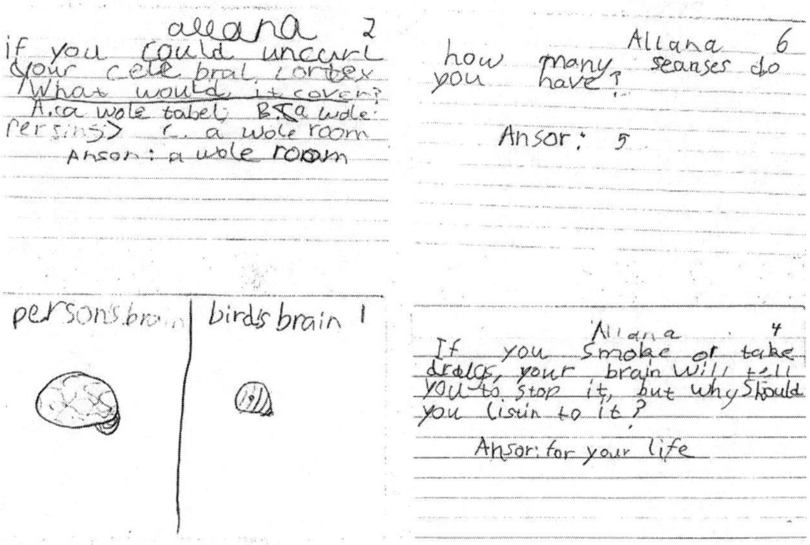

Figure 8.4   Allana's fact cards.

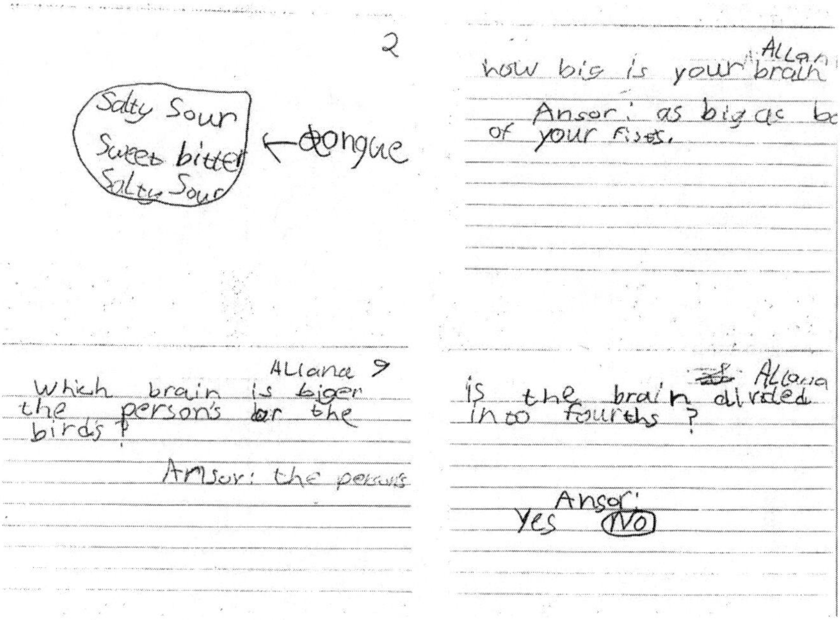

Figure 8.5   Allana's fact and question cards.

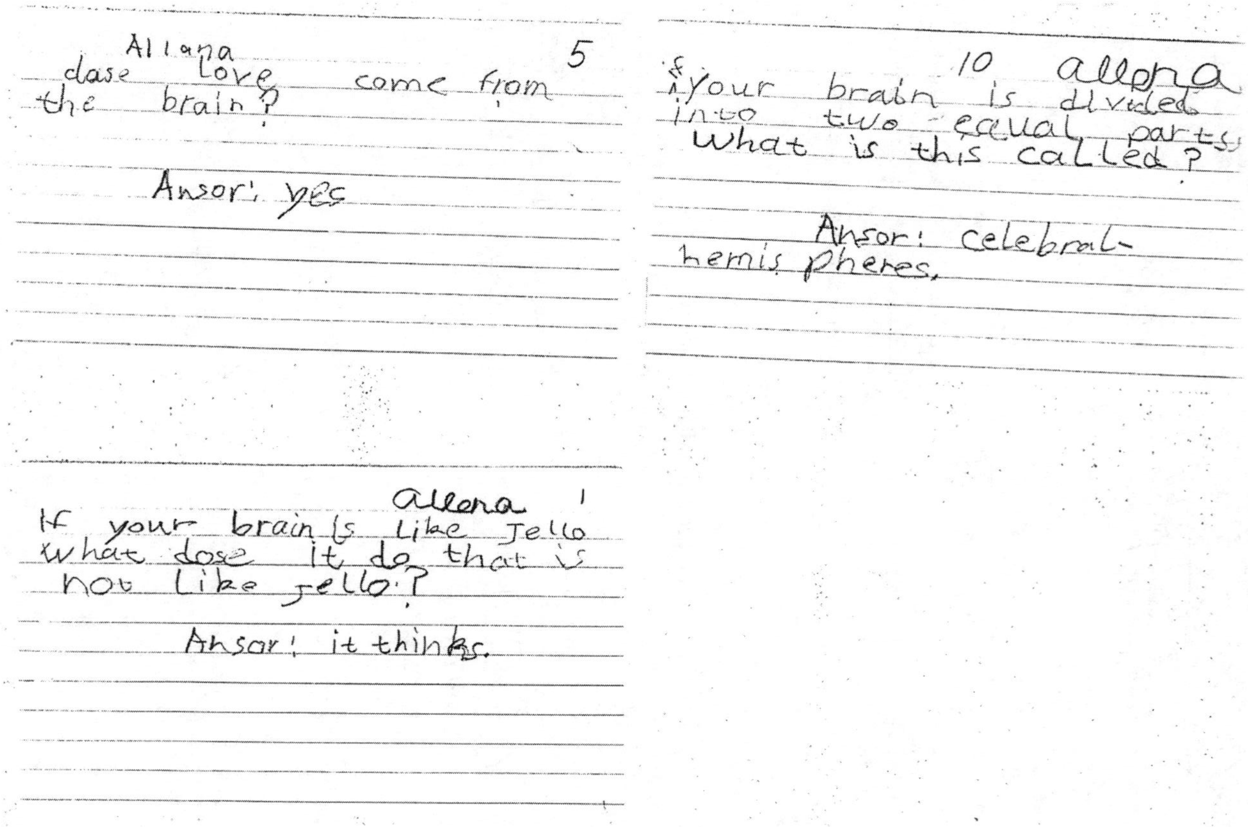

Figure 8.6 Allana's fact card questions.

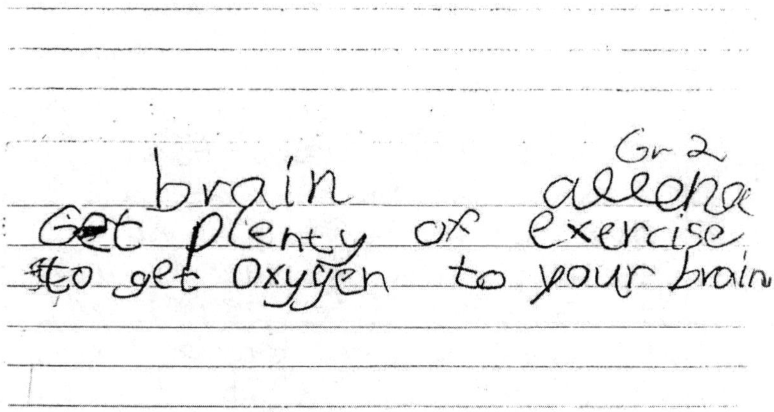

Figure 8.7 Allana's fact card.

I did not interfere with the children's efforts to develop a "test." Their reason for doing this was to encourage their audience to listen closely to their presentations. My reason was that developing questions was a good way for students to gain understanding on how tests are made and how test questions work—including the achievement tests that they would be taking at the beginning of third grade. Notice that in writing the questions, Allana works out the conventional spellings of cerebral and whole.

To celebrate a "pausing point" in their inquiries, students presented their projects to the class. I say "pausing point" because any inquiry can still remain open; indeed, many of the students were just getting enough knowledge of their topic to ask more specific questions, and there was always an open invitation to delve deeper into an inquiry if a student should desire to do so.

There were 22 children to listen to, and it worked well that they sometimes gave group presentations and completed their inquiries at different times. When more than two presentations were ready in one period, we gathered several times a day to listen to each other, rather than sitting through long sessions involving more presenters.

A description of our spelling program is appropriate here. Spellings the children needed were transferred from their temporary spellings to the conventional spellings as they were placed on our word wall. Each new word was written by the appropriate letter of the alphabet and, after a time, we took time to place all of the entries in alphabetical order. This was first done on the chalkboard, and then the words were rewritten in order on our word wall. All of the children participated in figuring out

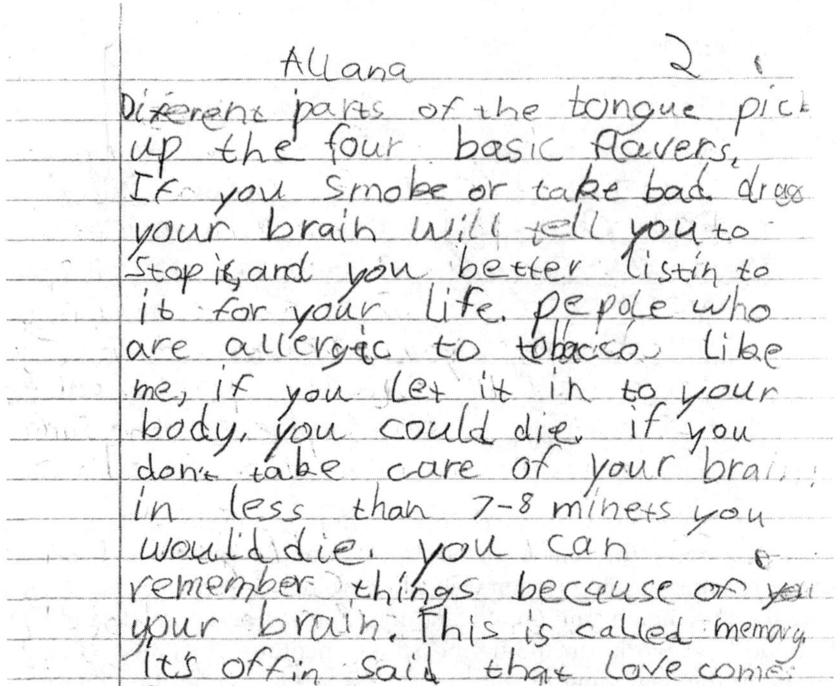

Allana   2

Diferent parts of the tongue pick up the four basic flavers. If you smoke or take bad drugs your brain will tell you to stop it, and you better listin to it for your life. pepole who are allergic to tobacco like me, if you let it in to your body, you could die. if you don't take care of your brain in less than 7-8 minets you would die. you can remember things because of your brain. This is called memory. Its offin said that love comes from the heart, but Realy it comes from the brain becuase you use your memary partly for remembering when you felt loved and Safe. for exampel a baby sucks a pacifier becduse it reminds them of drinking milk in there mother arms. play games to exercise your brain. get plenty of exercise to get oxygen to your brain.

Figure 8.8 Photocopy of Allana's report.

which word came next, and by the end of the year the children could alphabetize any and all words—some to the fourth or fifth letter. The children's personal spelling needs were also the ones they practiced for

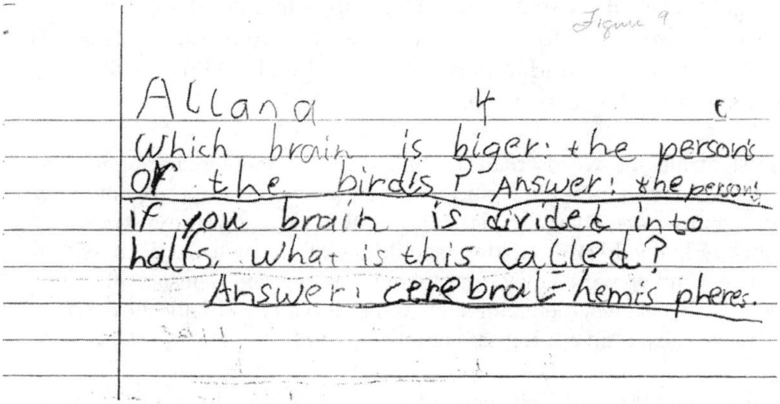

Figure 9

Allana   4   c
Which brain is biger: the person's
or the birds? Answer: the person's
If you brain is divided into
halfs, what is this called?
    Answer: cerebral-hemis pheres.

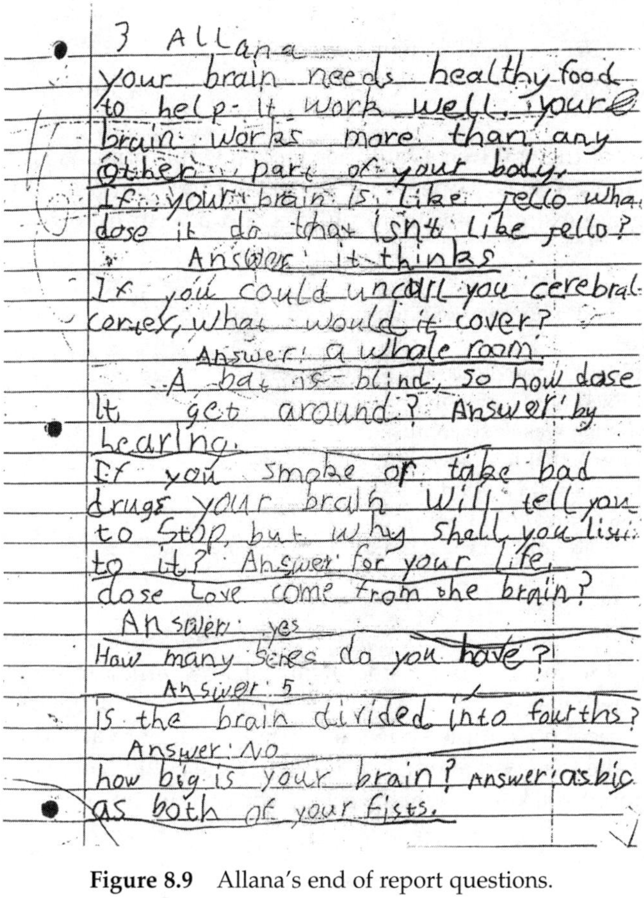

3 Allana
Your brain needs healthy food
to help it work well. Your
brain works more than any
other part of your body.
If your brain is like jello what
dose it do that isn't like jello?
    Answer: it thinks
If you could uncurl you cerebral
cortex, what would it cover?
    Answer: a whole room
A bat is blind, so how dose
it get around? Answer by
hearing.
If you smoke or take bad
drugs your brain will tell you
to stop, but why shall you listen
to it? Answer: for your life.
dose love come from the brain?
    Answer: yes
How many senses do you have?
    Answer: 5
Is the brain divided into fourths?
    Answer: No
how big is your brain? Answer: as big
as both of your fists.

Figure 8.9 Allana's end of report questions.

spelling. Instead of red-marking misspellings in a child's writing, I chose words each child needed, taken from his or her own compositions. These were made into a list and added to the word wall. Wilde's (1992) discussion of spelling served as a guide:

> First of all, the words that children work on memorizing should be unique to each individual since children know and need to know very different words. They also certainly shouldn't have to study words they already know. Ideally, children should pick their own words, based on interest and on words they use a lot but don't yet spell consistently....Five words a week, whether completely self-selected or partially chosen from a teacher list, is an appropriate number. (p. 92)

In this way, the children learned words they needed to use, including language/terminology beyond what would be found in a traditional spelling program.

EVALUATION

Evaluation of the children's inquiries took several forms. A student self-evaluation used was Copenhaver's (1993) three plusses and a wish. Following are examples of three plusses and a wish from two different children.

> Plus: I liked it how I asked questions about my report after it.
> Plus: I liked it how I did something difrent.
> Plus: I liked how I tried my best.
> Wish: I wish wasn't so confused.
> Plus: I think that my facts are good to know.
> Plus: I think I did a good poster.
> Plus: I like how I did my presntion.
> Wish: I wish I did more facts and my poster standed out more.

In the first example, it is possible that this child realizes that the more you know, the more you become aware of how much more there is to know or, perhaps, just how much information is available on any one topic. The second example shows this child's ability to acknowledge not only what she felt good about, but also what she could have done better. I have no doubt she knows what she will work on to improve in the future.

Inquiry Observation Form   Name *Sarah*
Topic *The Heart*   Date *Oct. 28, 1999*

Concepts:		Comments
Draws parallels between the brain, skeleton, heart and health and nutrition		Connects care of the heart with ~~exercise~~, nutrition, and medical care.
Understands that care of the body is related to how the body functions	+	

Processes:		Comments
Formulates interesting questions	+	5 questions in "I Wonder.." book, are based on knowledge gained throu reading on own How the Body Works
Generates appropriate means for answering questions (i.e. books, videos, interviews, etc.)	+	
Spends time reading, listening, constructing, observing, reflecting, etc.	+	Willing, industrious worker
Talks to others to make sense of data		often observed explaining things to others
Explains, shows, helps others to make sense of their data		
Asks thoughtful questions		Asks questions based on facts heard and read
Generates follow-up questions	✓	
Plans, organizes, and carries through on procedures to gain information	+	Good planning, organization

Attitude:		Comments
Is willing to be challenged	+	Enjoys challenge
Is productive and involved during inquiry work periods	+	Excellent engagement
Expresses enjoyment as a result of hard work and learning		Appears to enjoy others' responses to her work
Contributes to group work	+	Helpful collaborator
Displays sensitivity and respect for others	+	Helps others not in her group;

Product:		Comments
Is well developed and organized	+	Excellent organization of facts
Is visually pleasing	+	very Good- Good drawing of heart, nice idea to put facts displayed on hearts
Shows detail	✓	
Effectively communicates students' learning	+	

Presentation:		Comments
Articulates and/or demonstrates ideas clearly	+	Presentation is handled well; projects voice clearly
Is well informed	+	States information gained
Handles questions with authority and control Well done	+	
Gives good examples		not observed

Figure 8.10   Sarah's inquiry observation form. Topic: The heart.

Peer responses and questions during the presentation phase were
more informal forms of evaluation. I used Boyd's (1993) observation
form for inquiry, modifying it somewhat for the topic and age
(Fig. 8.10).

As I compare this type of evaluation to paper–pencil tests, I see the limitations of tests such as achievement tests. The many facets of subject area

and language learning that I could observe as the children worked their way through their inquiries provided so much more information for me to use to set the scene for further teaching and learning. I found this observation form to be useful, although at times some of the children's presentations went quickly, or a child would need my help during his presentation. During such times, I found it difficult to keep up my written observation. This problem could be aided by videotaping the children's presentations and reviewing them later. I would include the children in the reviewing of their presentations, too, much as a student teacher supervisor would involve the student teacher in reviewing his or her teaching.

Evaluation isn't something that happens only during the inquiry cycle—evidence of learning shows up in a variety of ways many times. In fact, evidence of learning can surface much later. Perhaps the most meaningful curriculum evaluation of all is the students' engagement throughout the cycles that naturally occur as they question, research, share, and formulate new questions, and their interest in pursuing one inquiry after another. After finishing her inquiry about the human brain, Allana asked what she could do next. I invited her to think about something she's been wanting to know about. During journal writing time a few days later, I happened to look over Allana's shoulder as she was writing. Her journal entry demonstrates that her learning experiences come together for her use in handling new topics.

Earlier in the inquiry cycle, the class was involved in a discussion using the idea cards they had written. A question, "How many bones does a cat have?" came up. None of us knew, but one of the students knew that the book *All Kinds of Cats* (Harste & Burke, 1983) contained the answer, and she found it and shared the information with the class. At the end of this book, there is a page that invites readers to try the structure the authors used in composing *All Kinds of Cats*. I think Allana (Fig. 8.11) demonstrates how inquiry is a means for using all she has learned to process and express new information as she experiments with writing in her journal:

Observing this incident provided insight into how correlating the language arts and the academic disciplines provided students with the opportunity to see—probably tacitly—curriculum relationships for themselves.

Another means of evaluation during and after an inquiry—or other classroom experience—is an idea I learned from Carolyn Burke (personal communication, Oct. 23, 1995) in which photographs are taken as children are working in the classroom, and they are given the pictures to tell through writing what they were doing at the time the photograph was taken. I took pictures of the children involved in their inquiry experiences.

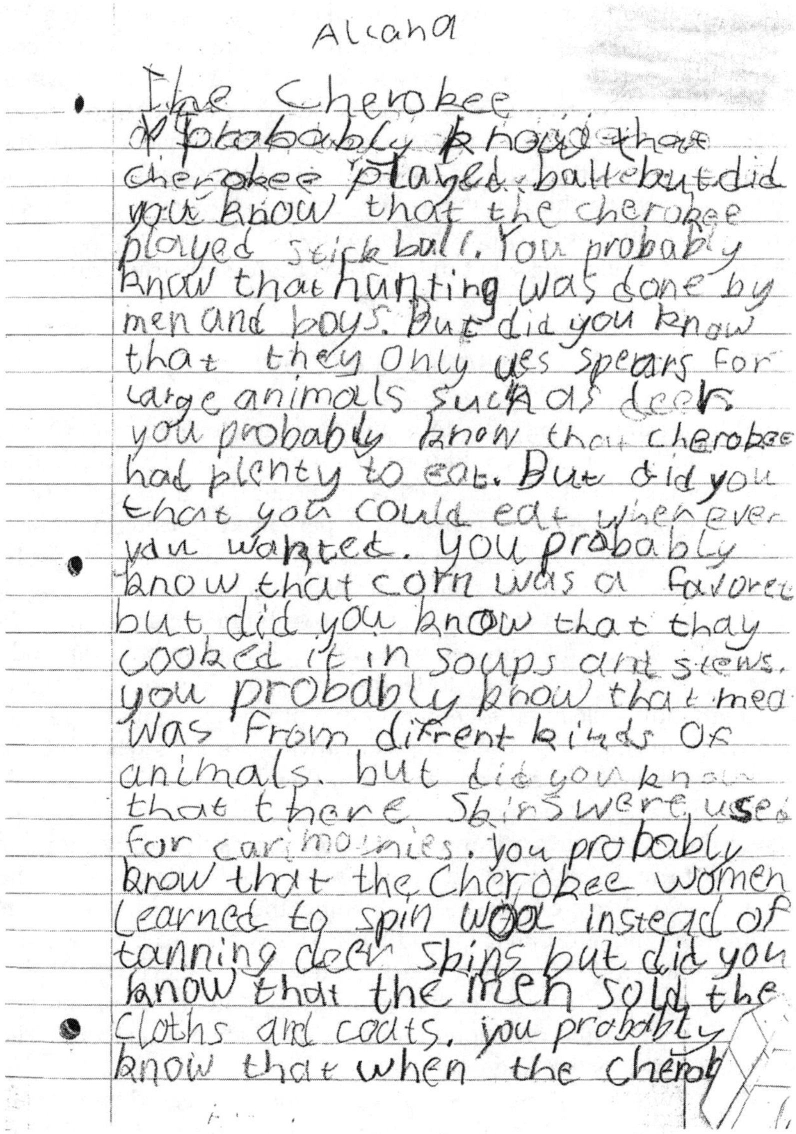

Allana

The Cherokee
probably know that
cherokee played ball but did
you know that the cherokee
played stick ball. You probably
know that hunting was done by
men and boys. But did you know
that they only ues spears for
large animals such as deer.
you probably know that cherokee
had plenty to eat. But did you
that you could eat whenever
you wanted. you probably
know that corn was a favoreit
but did you know that thay
cooked it in soups and stews.
you probably know that mea
was from difrent kinds of
animals. but did you know
that there skins were used
for carimounies. you probably
know that the Cherokee women
learned to spin wool instead of
tanning deer skins but did you
know that the men sold the
cloths and coats. you probably
know that when the cherok

Figure 8.11 Allana's new inquiry found in her journal.

I presented the photographs to the children by putting several at a table, then inviting them to examine them and choose one or more they wanted to write about. The children enjoyed this very much, and they worked through the writing process in order to make a class scrapbook. They later prepared and proofread a final draft of their writings so that our scrapbook would be in top order for the wide audience that viewed it when it was displayed in our classroom. Parents, students in other grades, and visitors enjoyed browsing through the years' events, as evidenced by their conversations with the children as they viewed the scrapbook together. Needless to say, the children themselves enjoyed viewing and reviewing their class scrapbook even more. In fact, as they reviewed their scrapbook, they were also reviewing what they learned through their inquiries.

APPLICATIONS TO CLASSROOM PRACTICE

Mediating an inquiry curriculum is an engaging challenge; however, as students proved that they could use the language arts to learn about science and other subjects, I could see that it encouraged their curiosity and self-motivation. Students who had not experienced working with larger chunks of meaning than filling in blanks on workbook pages or who had little experience working on their own needed demonstration and guidance in order to have a clear idea of the possibilities open to them. For them—and for me—the move into inquiry learning can be compared to riding a bicycle. The best way to learn is to try it. Sometimes the going was rough, but we learned together how to proceed. The multiage classroom was a real help because there were always students who had lived through the experience several times, and they became willing and able peer-demonstrators/teachers.

Over time, the children learned to choose topics that truly interested them and to make decisions throughout the inquiry that pushed their learning beyond my expectations. Opening the curriculum to include their interests and questions piqued their curiosity and led from one question to another—often to deeper questions related to science as well as the other subject areas. Their questions were appropriate for them and often were well beyond the questions found in their science textbook. Their participation was active and ongoing.

My early worries about classroom discipline were eased by the interest the children vested in finding and sharing answers to their questions. The talk that naturally ensued as they helped each other find information, shared reading, listened to each other, constructed their presentations, made decisions about facts to present and, finally, shared their information with the whole class was important talk. If we expect children to truly learn the terminology of a subject, getting it into everyday use is vital. And if it is important for first language learners, think of the benefit to second language learners. Watson (1973) shares a story about a kindergarten classroom in which the children were taking cookies out of a play oven. The student teacher gave them a spatula, telling the children, "Here, use this spatula, so you won't get burned." The word and idea caught on and spread from child to child. This illustration stuck in my mind and served to remind me to set the stage for children in our classroom to experience such opportunities to learn ideas and vocabulary.

Occasionally a child would not immediately show interest in the main topic that other children were investigating. Sometimes the child wanted to sustain investigation of an earlier research question or pick up on a new question that had piqued interest—perhaps through a recent experience such as the arrival of lambs (one lamb visited the classroom one afternoon, with a father's help), or the arrival of snow in late fall. Such events in a child's life are important, and the experiences could be woven into the fabric of learning that sometimes was bridged to the current topic and other times laid a foundation for a future inquiry. Allowing the child the opportunity to explore an interest while the interest was at its height kept the learning/working atmosphere within the classroom going, thus making active learning the means for maintaining discipline.

As I examine and reexamine the artifacts the children produced, I realize that the learning they demonstrate through their inquiry efforts is well worth working through the challenges of curriculum planning and implementation. The inquiry learning literature now available can serve to arm teachers with further descriptions and ideas concerning the creation of inquiry curriculum. Several such resources are suggested in the section "For Further Thought."

I realize as I write this that when the students performed science experiments, they were participating in a form of dramatization, especially when a group would prepare a demonstration and show it to the class. It would have been appropriate to encourage them to dramatize ground breaking science, too, such as important and colorful discoveries as Franklin's discovery of electricity, or Newton's gravity experiment. Often after reading to the children, they would want to act the story or information out. For example, after a variation of *Jack and the Beanstalk* (1989) was read to them, the children wanted to act out the story. When this happened, I encouraged them to do so.

These playwrights reflect Ferreiro's statement (2003):

Reading is a grand theatrical event where we must discover who are the actors, the stage directors, and the authors... Children's fascination with reading and re-reading the same story has to do with this fundamental discovery: writing fixes language, controls it in such a way that the words don't disperse, or vanish or get changed around. (p. 25)

The children knew that writing a script would indeed fix the language for them so that they could move on to acting and staging their production.

Paley (1990) states:

Any approach to language and thought that eliminates dramatic play, and its underlying themes of friendship and safety lost and found, ignores the greatest incentive to the creative process.

Play and its necessary core of storytelling are the primary realities in preschool and kindergarten, and they may well be the prototypes for imaginative endeavors throughout our lives. For younger students, however, it is not too much to claim that play contains the only set of circumstances understandable from beginning to end. (p. 6)

The children would gather, figure out who would be who and what each would say. After they acted out their play, they would often ask if they could invite an audience to watch them perform. Seizing the opportunity, I would ask, "How will you remember what you are to say?" Then the children would scramble for paper and pencils and write down their parts.

Embedded in the writing is the opportunity to tell the story, to make the story their own, to format a play, and to use writing conventions. On the composition draft I would make a check in the margin by a misspelled word and invite the students to find the conventional spelling on our word wall. They proved they could do this, thus editing their own writing. Each week students could also choose to practice one or more bonus words—not necessarily their own word but one they wanted to know—from the word wall.

Further, I typed the children's script writing in order to provide them with a visual experience of the conventional spellings of the words they needed to convey their meaning. The children would read and reread these scripts many times as they practiced their plays through readers' theater or, in this case, a play produced for their families and other classes.

The second graders had experienced the composition and production of plays their first grade year, and when they wrote their parts for *Jack and the Beanstalk*, they included not only their speaking parts in their writing but also stage directions and other script forms, as Maureen, Seth, and Buffy demonstrate (Fig. 8.12).

Paley (1990) states, "You must invent your own literature if you are to connect your ideas to the ideas of others" (p. 18). Think of the potential of making and writing down initial hypotheses and revising these as scientific study progresses–a form of inventing and revising scientific literature. My class once wrote a play based on the Pilgrims—I now would encourage more dramatization of Science information.

Ferreiro (2003) states, "There are children who enter written language through magic (a cognitively challenging magic) and other children who enter written language through training in 'basic abilities.' In general, the first become readers; the others have an uncertain fate" (p. 25). I believe that the inquiry curriculum our first and second grade created provided opportunities for the children not only to become readers, but also to become authors, scientists, mathematicians, sociologists, artists, musicians, actors, and storytellers. They became flexible users of language through the melding of their own curiosity with the disciplines and the language arts. I like to think we created the type of magic of which Ferreiro writes.

FOR FURTHER THOUGHT

1. What are some of the challenges involved in creating curriculum with students that centers on their own questions about a topic?
2. What are some additional ways a teacher could mediate opportunities to help students delve more deeply into science through reading, writing, and sharing?
3. Compare starting curriculum with students' inquiry questions to the traditional scope and sequence of a science textbook. How could inquiry curriculum be useful in meeting standards and mandates?
4. What potential does inquiry curriculum hold for motivating and sustaining students' curiosity?
5. What do you think is meant by *correlated curriculum*? How is correlation illustrated in Allana's writing?

For further discussion and understanding of the potentials of learning through inquiry, investigate the January, 2006, issue of *Language Arts*. This project could become a class investigation, and the articles in the issue could be divided among groups, read and discussed in class discussions and/or shared journals.

OTHER SUGGESTED RESOURCES

Other resources to investigate that tie Language Arts to Science include the following:

Chancer, J. & Rester-Zodrow, G. *Moon Journals: Writing, Art, and Inquiry Through Focused Nature Study*. Portsmouth, NH: Heinemann.

Whitmore, K. & Crowell, C. (1994). *Inventing a Classroom: Life in a Bilingual, Whole Language Learning Community*. New York, Maine: Stenhouse Publishers.

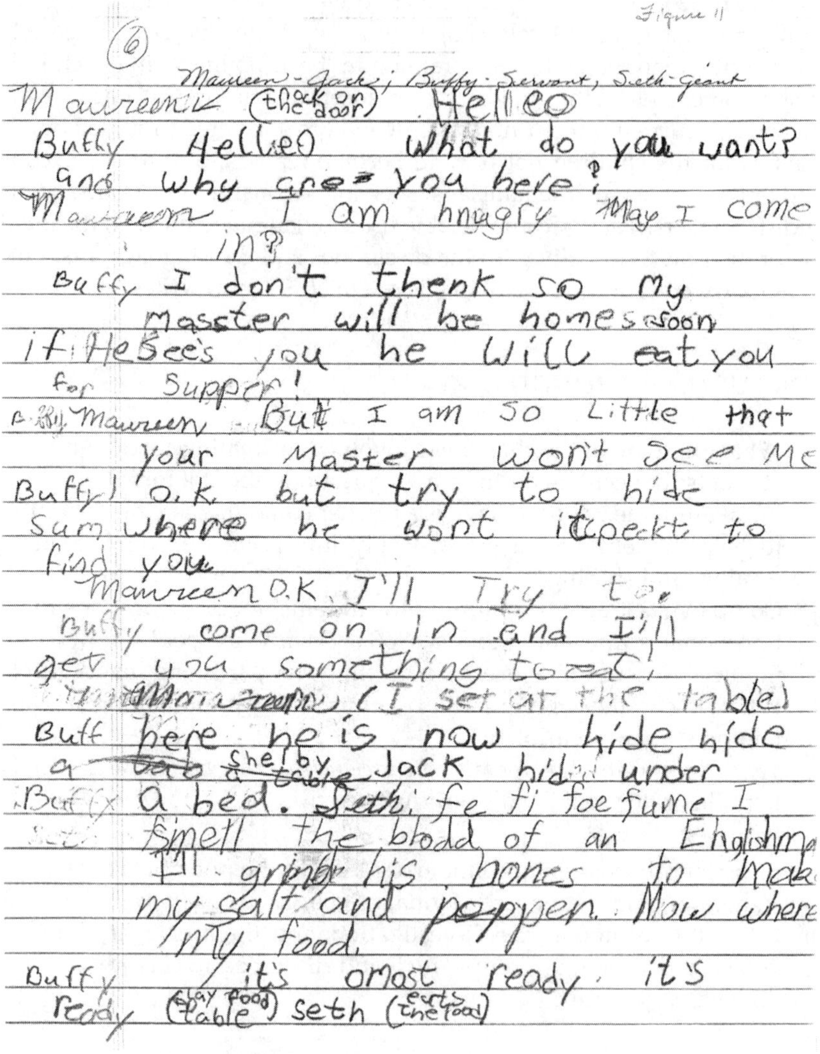

(6)

Figure 11

Maureen-Jack; Buffy-Servant, Seth-giant

Maureen (knock on the door) Hello
Buffy Hello what do you want? and why are you here?
Maureen I am hungry May I come in?
Buffy I don't thenk so my masster will be home soon if He Sees you he will eat you for Supper!
Maureen But I am so Little that your Master won't see me
Buffy o.k. but try to hide sum where he wont itcpekt to find you
Maureen O.K. I'll Try to.
Buffy come on in and I'll get you something to eat!
Maureen (I set at the table)
Buff here he is now hide hide (shelby) Jack hides under a bed. **Seth** fe fi foe fume I smell the blood of an Englishm. I'll grind his bones to make my salt and poppen. Now where my food.
Buffy it's omast ready. it's ready (play food) (table) seth (eats the food)

Figure 8.12 Jack and the Beanstalk play script draft by Maureen, Seth, and Buffy.

REFERENCES

Boyd, C. (1993). *Creating curriculum from children's lives: Primary voices K–6* (Premier Issue). Urbana, IL: National Council of Teachers of English.

Burke, C. Personal Communication. October 26, 1995.

Burke, C., & Harste, J. (1983). *All kinds of cats*. School Book Fairs.

Copenhaver, J. (1993). *Instances of inquiry: Primary voices K-6* (Premier Issue). Urbana, IL: National Council of Teachers of English.

Ferreiro, E. (2003). *Past and present of the verbs to read and to write*. Berkeley, CA: A Groundwood Book/Douglas and McIntyre.

Goodman, Y., Watson, D., & Burke, C. (1987). *Reading miscue inventory: Alternative procedures*. New York: Richard C. Owen Publishers, Inc.

Harste, J. (1993). *Inquiry based instruction: Primary voices K–6* (Premier Issue). Urbana, IL: National Council of Teachers of English.

Harste, J., Short, K., & Burke, C. (1988). *Creating classrooms for authors*. Portsmouth, NH: Heinemann.

Jack and the Beanstalk. (1989). Gerda Muller, Illustrator, London: Treasure Press.

Paley, V. G. (1990). *The boy who would be a helicopter: the uses of storytelling in the classroom*. Cambridge, MA: Harvard University Press.

Van Allen, J. A. (1979, April). Why scientists must know how to write. *Spectator*, p. 7.

Watson, D. J. (1973). *Miscue analysis*: class lecture. September 23, 1982. Permission given by Watson.

Wilde, S. (1992). *You kan red this!* Portsmouth, NH: Heinemann.

Part III

RESEARCH ON PREPARING ELEMENTARY TEACHERS TO USE INTERDISCIPLINARY SCIENCE AND LANGUAGE ARTS INSTRUCTION

Equally important to the influence of interdisciplinary science and language arts instruction on elementary students' understandings is research on best approaches to developing elementary teachers' practice for interdisciplinary language arts and science instruction. This section shares research on the types of methods that are effective in preparing elementary teachers to use effective interdisciplinary language arts and science instruction. In Chapter 9, Bintz and Moore describe their work using literature-based text clusters to teach science, emphasizing science concepts, science processes, nature of science, skills for inquiry, and dispositions toward science. Richards and Shea describe the difficulties and successes associated with preparing preservice teachers to connect science, the arts, and reading in Chapter 10. Chapter 11 finds Morrison describing the use of science notebooks to prepare preservice teachers to understand their use with children, and to improve the preservice teachers' conceptions of formative assessment.

In Chapter 12, Graves and Phillipson describe the use of critical literacy to prepare preservice teachers in science methods courses. Their work is related to the development of current views of nature of science and the use of scientific argumentation and reasoning. Britsch and Shepardson share research on the preparation of practicing teachers to interpret children's science journals in Chapter 13. Their work is important in bridging the gap between approaches used with preservice and inservice teachers. Lu's work with semiotics in Chapter 14 enabled her to integrate geosciences instruction into a literacy program for preservice teachers. Akerson describes how to use action research studies with perservice teachers to encourage them to use evidence-based methods for effective interdisciplinary language arts and science instruction.

9

Using a Literature-Based Text Cluster to Teach Science

William P. Bintz
Kent State University

Sara Delano Moore
ETA/Cuisenaire

> ... [T]rade books have the potential to offer young students an entryway into the wonders of science, history, math, geography, or any of the other content areas.
>
> —Labbo, 1999 (para. 1).

On a recent vacation, we visited Blackwells, a major bookstore in Oxford, England, to browse for high-quality and award-winning literature in the children's book department. Once there, we noticed a group of children huddled on the floor happily reading several books together. After awhile, they all left leaving the pile of books on the carpet. We were curious what books had entertained these children so much so we looked in the pile. One book, *Five Little Fiends* (Dyer, 2002), caught our eye. Like the children we sat on the floor and read the book together. Here is a précis:

> This story describes how each of 5 friends decides to take a "thing" it likes best from their surroundings. One took the sun; one took the sky; one took the sea; one took the moon; one took the land. Each took the thing and admired it as his/her own. They soon realized, however, that the sun could not stay up without the sky; the sea could not flow

without the pull of the moon; the moon could not glow without the light from the sun. In the end they decided to put everything back together as it originally was and once again marvel at their surroundings.

We immediately loved this book, not only for its delightful story but also for its text potentials. The term *text potential* is an important construct in reading education. It posits that any text has unlimited potential for readers to create meaning (Bintz, 1995). Stated differently, a text has no single meaning, but potentials for multiple meanings and layers of meanings. *Five Little Fiends* is a good example. On one level and from a scientific perspective it is a wonderful narrative about five little fiends who learn about the important interrelationship between the sun, sky, sea, moon, and the land. On another level and from a curriculum perspective this story is about the nature of interdisciplinary curriculum.

For example, let's view the five fiends as students and the sun, sky, sea, moon, and land as academic disciplines, say math, science, language arts, social studies, and art. Historically, formal schooling has treated academic disciplines more in isolation than integration. Moreover, individual content areas have been taught in arbitrary blocks of time, for example 55-min class periods, 90-min blocks. Like the five little fiends who learned about the important interrelationship between the sun, sky, sea, moon, and the land, we are learning about the important interrelationship between academic disciplines. In particular, we are learning that integrating content areas is much more powerful than teaching and learning them separately. In this sense, we see *Five Little Fiends* as a potential for developing and implementing interdisciplinary curriculum in the classroom. This chapter describes our recent attempt to do just this.

Specifically, the purpose of this chapter is four-fold; (1) to present a rationale for interdisciplinary curriculum, especially integrating science and literacy, (2) to share a literature-based text cluster designed to teach science as inquiry and comprised of several major strands; scientific inquiry, scientific method, biographies of scientists, and commentaries on being a scientist, (3) to discuss samples of student work based on using the text cluster in a middle grades classroom, and (4) to share some lasting impressions for using literature-based text clusters as a tool to support interdisciplinary teaching and learning in science.

INTEREST IN AND BENEFITS OF
INTERDISCIPLINARY CURRICULUM

Many professional organizations and much professional literature continue to express interest in and document benefits of interdisciplinary curriculum. Here we are particularly interested in the integration of science and literacy. The National Science Teachers Association (NSTA) has often published themed issues in *Science Scope* (see vol. 28, no. 6) on linking science and literacy, as well as numerous individual articles in *The Science Teacher* (Creech & Hale, 2006) and *Science and Children*. In fact, NSTA publishes a regular column on "Teaching (Science) Through Trade Books" in *Science and Children* (see Bintz & Moore, 2005) and organizes a national committee of science educators to annually review, award, and publish a list of *Outstanding Science Trade Books for Students K–12* (www.nsta.org). NSTA also continues to collaborate with other professional organizations, like the International Reading Association (IRA), to copublish major works in the integration of science and literacy (see Saul, 2004).

In addition, much research continues to be conducted and professional literature published on the topic of integrating science and literacy. Recent research has been conducted on the value of using biographies to learn about science and scientists (Monhardt, 2005); using informational literature in the form of trade books to teach science (Saul & Dieckman, 2005); using twin texts, one factual and the other fictional (Camp, 2000; Soalt, 2005) and combined text–picture books (Dean & Grierson, 2005) to teach science; and using science text sets to promote both literacy and inquiry (Ebbers, 2002).

Research such as this continues to document the benefits of interdisciplinary curriculum in terms of time, achievement, and motivation in science and literacy. For example, according to the 2000 National Survey of Science and Mathematics Education, in Grades K–5 there is an average of 105 min per day spent teaching reading/language arts and 23 min on science. Similarly, in Grades 4–6, there is an average of 90 min per day for reading/language arts and 31 min per day for science. Obviously, there is a wide discrepancy in terms of amount of time spent teaching these subjects when they are taught separately. However, according to Romance and Vitale (1992), when instructional time teaching science and reading was combined, student achievement in science was at significantly higher levels than student achievement when the subjects were taught separately. Mechling and Oliver (as cited in Royce & Wiley, 2005) also found that when science and reading are integrated, reading achievement scores improve as well. Clearly, when science and reading are integrated, good things tend to happen.

Literature-Based Text Clusters

Apparently, another good thing is teaching and learning science through literature. According to Casteel and Isom (1994), student motivation increases and science teaching becomes more dynamic when teachers use high-quality and award-winning literature to teach science. Literature-based text clusters can help. A text cluster is a powerful way to organize and use literature to teach science (and any other content area). The concept of text cluster builds on and extends the notion of text sets, an organizational tool long used to provide literature-based reading instruction across the curriculum. Simply stated, text sets are collections of high-quality and award-winning books that are related in some way, such as by theme, topic, or genre. They are designed to invite readers to explore the intertextual connections that exist between and among texts in the set (see Short, Harste, Burke, 1995; see also Harste, Short, Burke, 1988).

Text clusters are essentially an interrelated collection of text sets. Typically, text clusters are based on a specific theme and grounded in national (and state) content and process standards. Here we include a literature-based text cluster designed to support the teaching and learning of science as inquiry with a particular focus on scientific inquiry, scientific method, biographies of scientists, and commentaries on being a scientist (see Fig. 9.1). This cluster is grounded in National Science Education Standards (NSES). These include:

- Understanding of scientific concepts;
- An appreciation of "how we know" what we know in science;
- Understanding of the nature of science;
- Skills necessary to become independent inquirers about the natural world;
- The dispositions to use the skills, abilities, and attitudes associated with science.

Walking Through the Text Cluster

The science as inquiry text cluster consists of four components; scientific inquiry, scientific method, scientists, and nature of science. Scientific inquiry includes texts that address the question, What is inquiry? Each text on the top row addresses this same question but in a very different way. Each illustrates that inquiry involves problem posing, problem solving, generating hypotheses, and making predictions. For example, *Ducky* (Bunting, 1997) is based on a true story and invites young readers and scientists to inquire about how the following true story happened: A crate containing 29,000 plastic bathtub toy animals left on a ship from Hong Kong, China bound for Tacoma, Washington, USA. It was washed overboard in a storm. Hundreds of the toys have since been found on the eastern coast of

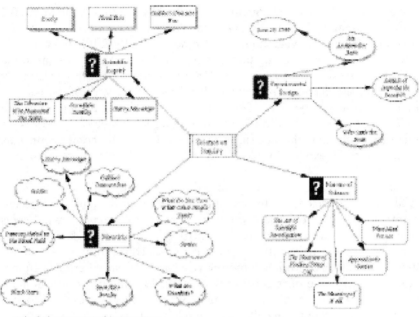

Figure 9.1 Example of text cluster.

the Gulf of Alaska (Bunting, 1997, author's note). How could this happen? Texts on the bottom row continue the same concepts but in more sophisticated and complex ways. For example, *Snowflake Bentley* (Martin, 1998) and *Starry Messenger* (Sis, 1996) use the stories of Wilson Bentley and Galileo to discuss observational inquiry and its place in the scientific community.

The experimental design component moves students more formally into the area of experimental design. For example, *Mr. Archimede's Bath* (Allen, 1980) illustrates a fairly straightforward experimental design in an unusual context. In this story, Mr. Archimedes is frustrated over the fact that his bathtub keeps overflowing. He suspects one of his animal friends is responsible. He systematically measures the water and asks each animal, one by one, to stay out of the bathtub so they can see what happens. He learns that it is not one single animal that is responsible, but that all are responsible. *June 29, 1999* (Wiesner, 1992) takes this idea further by sharing the story of Holly, a young scientist, who, unlike Archimedes, chooses an experiment with variables that she can't control as well.

The scientists component addresses the question, Who are scientists? For example, *What do You Care What Other People Think?* (Feynman, 1988) and *Genius* (Gleick, 1992) introduce students to the life and work of Nobel

Prize winner Richard Feynman. Similarly, *Black Stars* (Sullivan, 2002) provides engaging profiles of 26 African American women of science and invention from early years to modern times, 1849–1967. It is important to note two characteristics of this component. One, it includes multiple books on the same scientist, such as *Galileo* (Fisher, 1992), *Starry Messenger* (Sis, 1996), and *Galileo's Treasure Box* (Brighton, 1987). Multiple books provide multiple perspectives. For instance, each text is a biography but *Galileo's Treasure Box* is told from his daughter's perspective. And two, it includes books that also appear in the scientific inquiry component. This occurs because texts in this cluster have potential both within and across components.

Finally, the nature of science component addresses the question, What is the nature of science? The texts in this section of the cluster represent commentaries on the work of scientists. For example, *Apprentice to Genius* (Kanigel, 1986) talks about the scientific dynasty that worked with the concept of neurotransmitters and receptors. This group of scientists, including Julius Axelrod, Solomon Snyder, and Candace Pert, is well recognized for its line of inquiry—this relationship among scientists is an important element of the nature of the work. Other texts in this group also discuss the importance of collaborative relationships and other aspects of the nature of scientists. They discuss the importance of being able to separate the scientist from his or her work by replicating experimental findings, the importance of knowing the history of the field in which you work, and other critical elements.

Teaching Experimental Design

As teachers and teacher educators ourselves, we developed this literature-based text cluster on science as inquiry to use with teachers and students in the classroom. In this section, we describe one experience in which we did just that.

Recently, we collaborated with a middle school science teacher, math teacher, and content reading specialist to teach an integrated literacy, math, and science unit to a group of 27 sixth-grade students at Morton Middle School in Lexington, Kentucky. Specifically, we wanted to use the scientific method component of the text cluster to help students understand scientific method and experimental design.

We started with an oral reading of *Mr. Archimedes Bath* (Allen, 1980) to help students make connections between the story and scientific method, experimental design, and dependent and independent variables (see previous précis). This story has many layers of meaning and therefore much instructional text potential. It can introduce Archimedes, the famous Greek mathematician and scientist who, according to historical accounts, shouted "Eureka, Eureka!" after discovering what has since become known as the concept of hydrostatics (Dunham, 1990). It can also introduce the concept of displacement and its relationship to buoyancy, as well as the process of formal scientific inquiry and experimental design.

After orally reading the book, we distributed an experimental design sheet to each student (see Fig. 9.2).

We asked students to first flip the sheet over and on the back, spend 10–15 min writing a retelling of the story. Afterward, students shared their retellings with the class. (see Fig. 9.3).

Next, students flipped the sheet back over and spent 15–20 min recording connections between the story and experimental design (see Fig. 9.4).

From here, we went on to complete an integrated unit organized around experimenting with a rubber band cannon. Students collected data about how various features of a shot (rubber band size, pull-back, and angle) impacted the distance the rubber band traveled and then engaged in a target-shooting competition using their data. The experience included the following engagements; demonstrating, organizing, collecting data, analyzing and calculating data, learning about graphs, graphing, interpreting data, applying measures of central tendency, and reflecting (see Bintz, Moore, Hayhurst, Jones, & Tuttle, 2006). In the end, we returned to a discussion of *Mr. Archimedes' Bath* and how it related to the hands-on engagements. One student said:

> This story is just like the rubber band cannon. The animals are like the size of the rubber band, the pull-back, and the angle. They are all independent variables. And the distance the rubber band traveled is like the water going up or down in the story. They are dependent variables.

This experience reinforced our belief (and those of our teacher-collaborators) that these sorts of literary connections give students powerful tools for understanding sophisticated scientific concepts. Students were able to make connections to the story that helped them better understand the concept of controlling variation and independent/dependent variables in experiments. Other texts used in the larger experience provided similar grounding for other elements of the work.

Lasting Impressions

Developing and implementing this, and other literature-based text clusters to teach science has left us with some lasting impressions. But first, it is important to note that one of us is a literacy educator (Bintz) and the

Experimental Design	Mr. Archimedes Bath
Title: Give your experiment an appropriate title	**Title:**
Purpose/Question: What is the purpose of your experiment? What do you want to find out?	**Purpose/Question:**
Materials: List all materials that you will use in your experiment.	**Materials:**
Variables: Identify your independent variables & dependent variables, and the constants. *Independent Variables:* *Dependent Variables:* *Constants:*	**Variables:** *Independent Variables:* *Dependent Variables:* *Constants:*
Hypothesis: What do you think will happen? If the (independent variable) is (increased / decreased), then the (dependent variable) will (increase / decrease).	**Hypothesis:**
Procedure: List the step-by-step plan that you will follow.	**Procedure:**
Findings: Collect your data, record your results, and represent them in charts, graphs, scatter plots, etc.	**Findings:**
Conclusion(s): Does your data support your hypothesis? Why?	**Conclusion(s):**
Reflection: What would you change if you were doing this experiment again? Is more research or experiments needed? What did you learn from doing this experiment?	**Reflection:**

Figure 9.2 Using literature to teach experimental design.

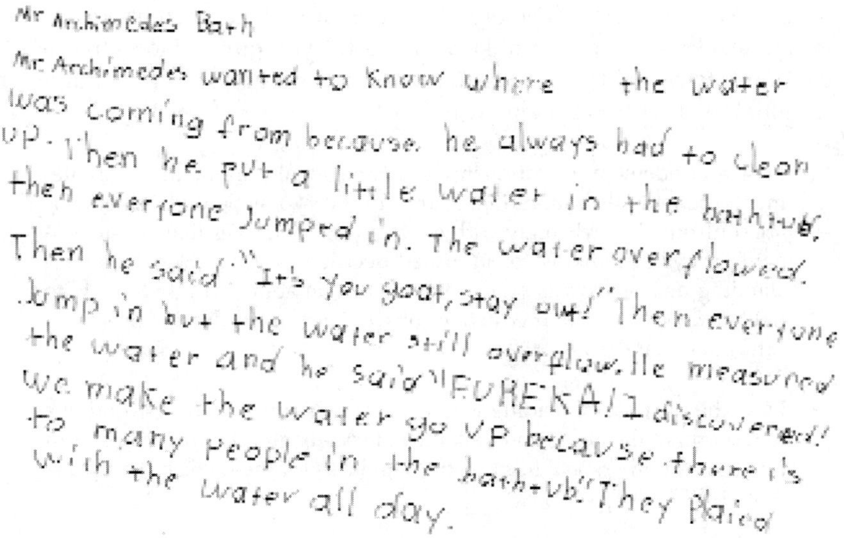

Mr Archimedes Bath

Mr Archimedes wanted to know where the water was coming from because he always had to clean up. Then he put a little water in the bathtub, then everyone jumped in. The water overflowed. Then he said: "It's you goat, stay out!" Then everyone Jump in but the water still overflow. He measured the water and he said "EUREKA! I discovered! we make the water go up because there is to many people in the bathtub." They played with the water all day.

Figure 9.3. Student Retelling.

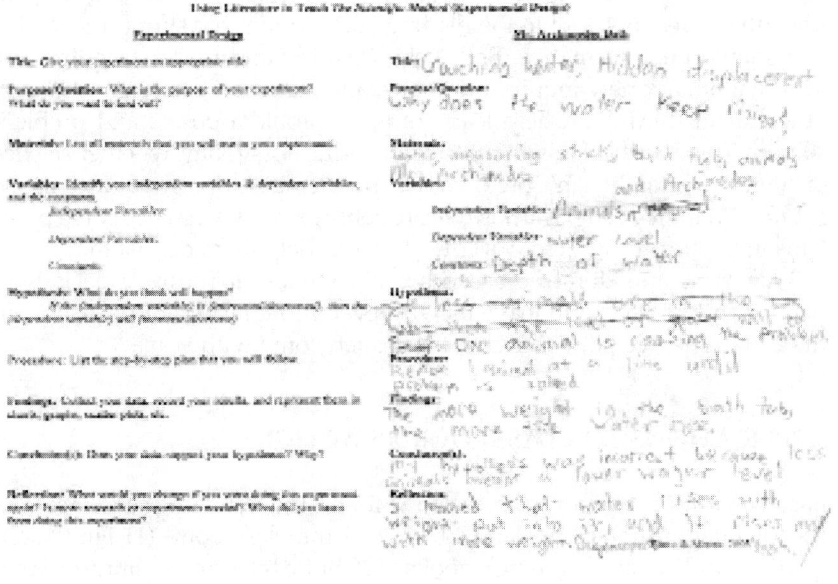

Figure 9.4. Student Experimental Design.

other a science educator (Moore). Based on our educational backgrounds, at one level we seem an unlikely pair. And yet, our collaborative work continues to reveal that we share more common ground than unfamiliar terrain. Consider two statements:

> First, an understanding of science offers personal fulfillment and excitement—benefits that should be shared by everyone. Second, Americans are confronted increasingly with questions in their lives that require scientific ways of thinking for informed decision making...Science understanding and ability also will enhance the capability of all students to hold meaningful and productive jobs in the future (National Science Education Standards, 1996).

> First, the purpose of reading is to acquire new information. Second, it's to respond to the needs and demands of society and the workplace. And finally, it is for personal fulfillment (Standards for the English/Language Arts, NCTE/IRA, 1996).

These are belief statements from two different perspectives, science and literacy. Each is a belief statement about the essence of that discipline. When viewed together, they share some important common ground.

First, the pursuit of science and the process of reading provide "personal fulfillment." Both can be, and should be, exciting. Second, engaging in scientific endeavors, and in the reading and writing that support it can be, and should be, informative. Both help scientists and readers acquire new information, ask new inquiry questions, and start new conversations with others. And third, both help learners to be problem posers and problem solvers. This is critical, given the fact that educators today, whether science or literacy, certainly can't predict what problems students will face in the future. What they can predict is that students today will have to solve problems in the future, and today's education can help them do just that.

We hope using literature-based text clusters in the future, especially in science and literacy, will leave us with even more lasting impressions. In the meantime, we hope this chapter has left some with you.

APPLICATIONS TO CLASSROOM PRACTICE

Based on our own experience, we have found the following sequence useful for integrating science and literacy in the classroom: (1) Find high-quality (and award-winning) books, (2) build classroom libraries that match major themes in science and literacy, (3) organize classroom libraries as a collection of text sets, (4) use curricular engagements with text sets that reflect and support integrated instruction, and (5) invite and encourage students to develop their own text sets.

First, science teachers should familiarize themselves with literature-based science instruction. To do this, we recommend that teachers refer to lists of high-quality and award-winning literature that is on the Web sites of the National Science Teachers Association (NSTA; www.nsta.org), the International Reading Association (www.reading.org) and the National Council of Teachers of English (www.ncte.org). In addition, teachers can refer to NSTA professional publications like *Science and Children* and *Science Scope;* NCTE publications like *Language Arts, Primary Voices,* and *Voices in the Middle;* and IRA publications like *Reading Teacher and Journal of Adolescent and Adult Literacy* for articles on literature-based instruction across the curriculum.

Second, science teachers can build classroom libraries for outstanding trade books in literacy and science. Regie Routman (2004), an internationally renowned literacy educator, suggests that an adequate classroom library will have at least 200 books and an excellent library will have more than 1,000. In building a classroom library, teachers should consider a variety of sources for selecting books. These can include

- Children's and Adolescent's Book Award Winners, for example NSTA, IRA, Caldecott, Newberry, Coretta Scott King Award, The Aesop Prize, and so forth;
- Books by noted authors such as Seymour Simon, Henry Cole, Peter Sis, and so forth;
- Anthologies;
- Book Clubs, such as Arrow, Trumpet, Scholastic, and so forth;
- Professional journals;
- Parent–Teacher Organizations;
- Discount Outlets.

Third, science teachers can familiarize themselves with ways to organize classroom libraries. As noted in this article, we suggest that teachers organize libraries around text sets matched to major themes in the science curriculum. However, many other ways are possible. Here are a few other organizational possibilities (see Routman, 2004, p. 76):

- Paired texts;
- Author sets;
- Illustrator sets;
- Light Reading and Heavy Reading;
- Fiction and Nonfiction;
- Interdisciplinary Sets;

- Hot New Books;
- Award-Winning Books;
- Top Ten List.

In addition, it is important that classroom libraries display books attractively. Once again, Routman (2004, p. 77) is helpful. She suggests the following:

- Use book baskets or bins to sort books;
- Use rain gutters to display books;
- Learn from bookstores ways to display books effectively and attractively;
- Display racks;
- Involve students in classroom library design and organization.

Fourth, science teachers can familiarize themselves with curricular engagements and instructional strategies that are conducive to text clusters and text sets (see Harste, Short & Burke, 1988; Harvey & Goudvis, 2000; Short, Harste & Burke, 1995). Some of these include:

- Scientist study (along the same lines as an Author Study);
- Inquiry projects that integrate science and literacy;
- Paired text with graphic organizers, such as Venn diagrams, H-maps, and so forth.

Lastly, science teachers can help students develop their own texts based on science themes and concepts that are of urgent interest to them.

FOR FURTHER THOUGHT

1. What are major issues and concerns around interdisciplinary curriculum, integrated instruction, and teacher collaboration in literacy and science education? What major obstacles need to be addressed and overcome?
2. How do teachers identify good collaborators? What does it mean to collaborate?
3. How do teachers plan and implement integrated blocks of instructional time?
4. How do teachers recognize high-quality literature to teach science?
5. Where do teachers find funds needed to purchase high-quality literature?
6. What does assessment look like in integrated instruction?
7. How is integrated or multidisciplinary assessment turned into grades?
8. How do teachers talk to administrators and parents about interdisciplinary curriculum and integrated instruction?

9. How do teachers balance literature and hands-on engagements in the science classroom? Where do teachers start?

10. How do teachers encourage students to make connections between disciplines?

REFERENCES

Bintz, W. P. (1995). A-X-Y-N-T means grandma's eyes are getting better. *Language Arts, 72*(1), 50–54.

Bintz, W. P., & Moore, S .D. (2005). What's up with sinking? (teaching through trade books). *Science and Children, 43*(1), 20–22.

Bintz, W. P., Moore, S. D., Hayhurst, E., Jones, R., & Tuttle, S. (2006). Integrating literacy, math, and science to make learning come alive. *Middle School Journal, 37*(3), 30–37.

Camp, D. (2000). It takes two: Teaching with twin texts of fact and fiction. *The Reading Teacher, 53*(5), 400–407.

Casteel, C. P., & Isom, B. A. (1994). Reciprocal processes in science and literacy learning. *The Reading Teacher, 47*(7), 538–545.

Creech, J., & Hale, G. (2006). Literacy in science: A natural fit. *The Science Teacher, 73*(2), 22–27.

Dean, D., & Grierson, S. (2005). Re-envisioning reading and writing through combined-text picture books. *Journal of Adolescent & Adult Literacy, 48*(6), 456–468.

Dunham, W. (1990). *Journey through genius: The great theorems of mathematics.* New York: Wiley.

Dyer, S. (2002). *Five little fiends.* London: Bloomsbury Publishing PLC.

Ebbers, M. (2002). Science text sets: Using various genres to promote literacy and inquiry. *Language Arts, 80*(1), 40–50.

Harste, J. C., Short, K. G., & Burke, C. (1988). *Creating classrooms for authors.* Portsmouth, NH: Heinemann.

Harste, J. C., Short, K. G., & Burke, C. (1995). *Creating classrooms for authors and inquirers .* Portsmouth, NH: Heinemann.

Harvey, S., & Goudvis, A. (2000). *Strategies that work.* Portland, MA: Stenhouse.

Labbo, L. (1999). *Learning more about flying squirrels, cosmic light shows, and other science-related topics from trade books* (A book review column editor's note). Retrieved January 28, 2006, from http://www.readingonline.org/reviews/literature/Andersen

Monhardt, R. (2005). Reading and writing nonfiction with children: Using biographies to learn about science and scientists. *Science Scope, 28*(6), 16–19.

NCTE/IRA. (1996). Standards for English/Language Arts.

National Research Council. (1996). *National Science Education Standards.* Washington, DC: National Academy Press.

Romance, N. R., & Vitale, M. R. (1992). A curriculum strategy that expands time for in-depth elementary science instruction by using science-based reading strategies: Effects of a year-long study in grade four. *Journal of Research in Science Teaching, 29*(6), 545–554.

Routman, R. (2004). *Reading essentials: The specifics you need to teach reading well.* Portsmouth, NH: Heinemann.

Royce, C. A., & Wiley, D. A. (2005). The common ground: A rationale for integrating science and reading. *Science and Children, 28*(6), 40–42.

Saul, E. W. (Ed.). (2004). *Crossing borders in literacy and science instruction:Perspectives on theory and practice.* Newark, DE: International Reading Association.

Saul, E. W., & Dieckman, D. (2005). Choosing and using information trade books. *Reading Research Quarterly, 40*(4), 502–513.

Short, K. G., Harste, J. C., & Burke, C. (1995). *Creating Classrooms for authors and inquirers.* Portsmouth, NH: Heinemann.

Soalt, J. (2005). Bringing together fictional and informational texts to improve comprehension. *The Reading Teacher, 58*(7), 680–683.

LITERATURE

Abrahams, M. (1998) *The Best of Annals of Improbable Research.* New York, NY: Freeman.

Allen, P. (1980). *Mr Archimedes's Bath.* Sydney: Collins Publishers.

Allen, P. (1982). *Who sank the boat?* Ringwood, Victoria, Australia: Puffin Books.

Beveridge, W. (1950) *The art of scientific investigation.* New York: Vintage Books.

Brighton, C. (1987). *Galileo's treasure box.* New York: Walker & Company.

Bunting, E. (1997). *Ducky.* New York: Clarion Books.

Crick, F. (1988) *What mad pursuit.* New York: Basic Books.

Dotlich, R. K. (1999). What is science? In L. B. Hopkins (Ed.), *Spectacular science: A book of poems* (pp. 00). New York: Scholastic.

Eversole, R. (1995). *Flood fish.* New York: Crown.

Feynman, R. (1988) *"What do you care what other people think?" Further adventures of a curious character.* New York: Norton.

Feynman, R. (1998) *The meaning of it all.* Reading, MA: Perseus.

Feynman, R. (1999) *The pleasure of finding things out.* Cambridge, MA: Perseus.

Fisher, L. (1992) *Galileo.* New York: Anthenuem Books for Young Readers.

Gelman, R. G., & Buxbaum, S. K. (1991). *What are scientists?* New York: Scholastic.

Gleick, J. (1992) *Genius: The life and science of Richard Feynman.* New York: Pantheon.

Kanigel, R. (1986) *Apprentice to genius.* New York: Macmillan.

Lasky, K. (1994) *The librarian who measured the earth.* Canada: Little, Brown & Company.

Martin, J. B. (1998). *Snowflake Bentley.* Boston: Houghton Mifflin.

Mullis, K. (1998) *Dancing naked in the mind field.* London: Bloomsbury Publishing.

Sis, P. (1996). *Starry messenger.* New York: Farrar Strauss & Giroux.

Sullivan, O. R. (2002). *Black stars: African American women scientists and inventors.* New York: Wiley.

Wiesner, D. (1992) *June 29, 1999.* New York: Houghton Mifflin.

10

Interdisciplinary Teaching in the Primary Grades: Preservice Teachers' Dilemmas and Achievements Connecting Science, the Arts, and Reading

Janet C. Richards
University of South Florida

Kim T. Shea
University of South Florida

AUTHOR'S NOTE

There are multiplicities of related terms used in the literature to denote interrelationships among subject areas (Gavelek, Raphael, Biondo, & Wang, 2002). In this article, we use the terms interdisciplinary, multidisciplinary, cross-curricula, and integrated curricula interchangeably.

An earlier version of this chapter was published in *The Qualitative Report*, an international on-line journal.

Driven by a search for a new "coherence and integrity in the teacher education curriculum" (Fang & Ashley, 2004, p. 39), scholars now recommend that preservice teachers acquire abilities to organize academic disciplines around broad, interdisciplinary-themed topics of study. An interdisciplinary-themed approach has the potential to introduce preservice teachers to a unified constructivist view of learning as they develop understanding of relationships among subjects (Mendolsohn & Baker, 2005). Interdisciplinary teaching also has the potential to foster democratic school changes needed in a multicultural society when students from diverse cultures engage in collaborative inquiry and decision making (Britzman, 1991; Goodlad, 1984, 2000; National Council of Teachers of English/National Council for the Social Studies/Council for Elementary Science Teachers Association/International Reading Association, 2004; The Boyer Commission on Educating Undergraduates in the Research University, 2001).

Little research has investigated preservice teacher interdisciplinary programs (Akins & Akerson, 2002; Fang & Ashley, 2004). In particular, few studies have examined the subjective realities of preservice teachers who have been encouraged to move from subject-centered to multidisciplinary pedagogy. Yet, Fullan (1982) cautions that ignoring the phenomenology of how human beings experience and make sense of change is "at the heart of the spectacular lack of success of most social reforms" (p. 4). Guided by a phenomenological research perspective, we investigated the experiences of 28 preservice teachers as they learned to offer theme-based creative arts, science, and reading interdisciplinary lessons to kindergarten and first-grade students. We hoped to discover the preservice teachers' subjective realities, including their concerns, achievements, and understandings about interdisciplinary teaching.

WHAT IS INTERDISCIPLINARY TEACHING?

Intermittently popular since the early 1920s, interdisciplinary teaching has once again received favorable attention in the United States as an alternative, or as an extension to a separate subject curriculum (Akins & Akerson, 2002; Goodlad, 2000; Perkins, 1991). Teachers who emphasize a multidisciplinary approach usually keep the content of each subject intact, but they unite disciplines by organizing the curriculum around complex concepts, questions, themes, problems, or projects to capitalize on connections (Akins & Akerson, 2002; Boix Mansilla, Miller, Gardner, 2000; Ross & Frey, 2002). For example, primary teachers might link social studies, visual arts, and reading to help students explore "the first Thanksgiving." Middle school teachers might connect science, language arts, and the creative arts to stimulate students' understanding about "famous scientists" or "rain forest preservation." High school teachers might structure an abstract theme, such as "change" in which students connect the sciences of astronomy and the plant, animal, and physical world with technology, music, and creative and expository writing (Carr, 2003).

Theories Supporting Interdisciplinary Approaches

Several theories of learning support an interdisciplinary approach. New ideas from multiple literacies such as print text, music, the visual arts, and creative and expository writing (Richards & McKenna, 2003) broaden views of learning to encompass all of the diverse ways human beings share information and make sense of their world. Multiple intelligence (MI) theory describes eight intelligences (linguistic, musical, logical-mathematical, spatial, bodily kinesthetic, interpersonal, intrapersonal, and naturalist) that also provide a foundation for subject integration by encouraging students to search for meaning and to problem solve across a wide range of subject areas (Boix Mansilla, Miller, & Gardner, 2000). Moreover, neuroscientists interested in brain-based research suggest that students learn best when they are fully immersed in an educational experience and can consider multiple views and connections across subjects (Caine & Caine, 1991). Similarly, constructivist theorists believe that education is inherently interdisciplinary and that quality learning only occurs when students and teachers together have opportunities to consider, analyze, interpret, and reflect on big ideas and concepts (Kaufman & Brooks, 1996).

An interdisciplinary curriculum is especially relevant in primary classrooms. Research shows that this approach has the potential to meet the needs of all young students—average, gifted, and those who read below grade level (Gaskins & Guthrie, 1994). Equally important, although current accountability mandates in the United States pressure primary teachers to concentrate on reading and writing instruction, many teachers have discovered that a multidisciplinary perspective provides time to include content subjects (Ross & Frey, 2002). For example, primary teachers have begun to infuse science into the literacy curriculum. In both disciplines, students set a purpose, analyze, and draw conclusions, and in some school districts, science is now a tested primary grade subject (Akerson, 2001; Casteel & Isom, 1994).

The Impetus for Implementing our Interdisciplinary Preservice Teacher Preparation Model

Typically, during their training, preservice teachers in our childhood education department take separate-subject course work. Integration among disciplines, such as science, creative arts, and reading, or social studies and language arts has not been attempted. The department of childhood education offers creative arts and reading courses, and the department of secondary education offers science. However, as two supervisors (a professor and a doctoral student) in charge of a creative arts early field experience, we recently made a decision to move from separate-subject to interdisciplinary teaching by connecting the arts with science and reading. The impetus for our decision was fivefold: (1) The elementary school in which our creative arts class operated received a science grant entitled "The Wonderful World of Water," and it made sense for our preservice teachers to link their arts lessons with the new science curriculum. (2) Many of the preservice teachers in our creative arts class had already completed, or were concurrently taking science and reading methods courses. Adding a science and reading component offered opportunities for the preservice teachers to connect three disciplines in an authentic field setting. (3) We wanted to begin to restructure our teacher education program to meet national recommendations that call for preservice teachers to develop abilities to organize academic disciplines around broad topics of study. (4) We saw this as an opportunity for preservice teachers to consider cross-curricula teaching as a way to meet diversity issues in their future classrooms that include race, culture, first language, and ability differences (Bullock, Park, Snow, & Rodriguez, 2002). (5) We hoped to prepare our preservice teachers for what we anticipate will be a multidisciplinary pedagogy of the future. Our belief mirrors that of Kaufman and Brooks (1996) who state," if teachers are to engage in collaborative interdisciplinary endeavors in schools, they must be able to experience and explore such settings in their teacher education programs" (p. 236).

THE CONTEXT FOR OUR INTERDISCIPLINARY PROGRAM, THE PROGRAM STRUCTURE, AND THE PRESERVICE TEACHERS' LESSONS

We offered our interdisciplinary program in a small K–4 charter school located on the campus of a large urban, southeastern university. Charter schools are innovative public schools that offer families opportunities to choose a school most suitable for their children's well being (Center for Educational Reform, 2005). The instructional climate of the charter school where this study took place is student centered, relaxed, and pleasant. Of the approximately 200 students, 80% are African American, 10% are Hispanic, and 10% are Caucasian. The majority of students come from low socioeconomic homes, and students' annual standardized reading and language arts test scores fall at or below the 30th percentile.

The 28 preservice teachers (all female, all in their third year of a four-year undergraduate program of study, and between the ages of 20 and

40), convened at the charter school for 3 hours one morning each week throughout the semester. As course instructors, we met with the preservice teachers for the first 75 min of each class to present multidisciplinary demonstration lessons, to provide lectures, and to lead seminar discussions. Then, with our guidance and mentoring, the preservice teachers were responsible for offering 75-min integrated lessons to small groups of approximately three to five kindergarten or first-grade students (the same groups throughout the semester). The preservice teachers taught their lessons in the students' classrooms or in several adjacent unoccupied school areas, such as the music room, cafeteria, or media center. As supervisors, we continually rotated among the groups to offer suggestions and guidance and to step in and teach mini lessons when necessary.

Through course assignments we encouraged the preservice teachers to link arts, science, and reading with their K–1 students at every opportunity. The preservice teachers began their lessons with dialogue journal activities designed to enhance their students' informal writing abilities and to expand students' understanding of science concepts related to the theme of "the wonderful world of water." Then, the preservice teachers and their students participated in a shared book experience with quality children's literature that portrayed dimensions of the schoolwide "wonderful world of water" science theme (e.g., fiction about such sea animals as whales, turtles, starfish, dolphins, and manatees). The preservice teachers also supported their students' literacy development by offering visual literacy and reading comprehension strategies, such as "What do I see? What do I think? What do I wonder?" (Richards & Anderson, 2003a) "How do you know?" (Richards & Anderson, 2003b), and a science strategy entitled, "What do you think? What do you want to know? What have you learned?"(Akerson, 2001).

In every lesson, the preservice teachers linked fiction with informational sources (e.g., encyclopedias, Internet Web sites, diagrams, charts, maps, and photographs of starfish, dolphins, ocean currents, sea turtles, tides, and river trips). They concluded their teaching sessions by collaborating with their students in creative arts engagements that supported the "wonderful world of water" theme (e.g., group murals, individual creative books, informal dramatic arts enactments, dioramas, rhythm band activities, vocal music, poetry, dance and movement.

THE INQUIRY

Rationale for the Study

As course instructors, we were enthusiastic about our first integrated curriculum restructuring effort, and we assumed that our preservice teachers would also wholeheartedly embrace this teaching approach. However, early in the semester, we recognized that some preservice teachers were unsure about how to connect all three disciplines, and others resisted linking subject matter altogether. It struck us that although scholars note that teacher education restructuring projects are dependent on the individuals who experience the restructuring, we had overlooked our preservice teachers as the most important variable in the change process (see Meister & Nolan, 2001). In our top-down curriculum change mandate, we had neither asked the preservice teachers for their input nor articulated our understanding about the theoretical underpinnings, goals, and benefits of interdisciplinary teaching initiatives. Equally serious, we had not modeled sufficient interdisciplinary demonstration lessons for the preservice teachers before we required them to teach through a similar approach. In short, we had neglected to consider how the preservice teachers might experience the change as they moved from a subject-centered to a multi-disciplinary curriculum.

Mindful of Hargreaves' (1994) cautionary observation that change facilitators must understand the perspectives that teachers bring to the change process in terms of their conceptions of time, power, and the emotional aspects of teaching, we conducted the following inquiry. We wanted to understand our preservice teachers' individual and group experiences and the meanings they attached to their experiences as they learned to offer interdisciplinary lessons. We also hoped to add pragmatic information to the limited research base regarding integrated preservice teacher education programs. Ultimately, we sought to enhance our own practices by fine tuning the content and structure of the program to meet preservice teachers' individual and collective needs in future curricular restructuring initiatives.

After receiving Internal Review Board (IRB) approval from the Office of Grants and Contracts at the University of South Florida, and obtaining signed study participation consent forms from the preservice teachers, we conducted the following inquiry guided by the following four questions:

1. What concerns and achievements did the preservice teachers experience as they learned to offer interdisciplinary lessons to K–1 students?
2. How did the preservice teachers understand and describe their experiences?
3. Did the preservice teachers' subjective realities about interdisciplinary teaching change over the course of the semester?
4. Did the preservice teachers develop an understanding about how to plan and offer an interdisciplinary curriculum?

The Conceptual Frameworks for our Inquiry

A phenomenological interpretive framework grounded our inquiry. The goal of phenomenological studies is to capture commonalities associated with the shared meanings and perceived realities of a group of people in a specific context by systematically examining their "experiences in close detailed ways" (de Marrais & Lapan, 2004, p. 56). Phenomenological methods explore "how human beings make sense of experience—how they perceive it, describe it, feel about it, judge it, remember it, make sense of it, and talk about it with others" (Patton, 2002, p. 104). Through interviews, observation, and language analysis, phenomenologists attempt to enter the conceptual world of study participants in order to "understand it as they do, and to portray that understanding" (Meister & Nolan, 2001, p. 610).

We also viewed our inquiry as a holistic context-specific, intrinsic case study involving a group of individuals who experienced a phenomenon. Case studies analyze critical incidents or stages that can be defined as a specific, unique, bounded system (Stake, 2005; also see Fals Borda, 1998).

Data Sources and Analysis

We employed three types of qualitative data collection strategies to inform the inquiry. The preservice teachers (a) responded to a mid-semester survey (see Appendix); (b) authored an end-of-semester teaching case that portrayed their concerns and problems associated with interdisciplinary lessons, and; (c) participated in a recorded group exit interview that was later transcribed. These three sources along with our observation notes of the preservice teachers' lessons proved helpful in our attempt to understand the meanings the preservice teachers attached to their experiences as they learned to integrate instruction.

In addition, the three multimodal data sets coupled with our field notes allowed us to study the same phenomenon through different lenses, which provided opportunities for triangulation—a method of corroborating evidence from different sources, "a means of reducing ambiguity and the likelihood of misinterpretation, and a process of using multiple perceptions to clarify meaning" (Stake, 2000, p. 443; also see Anfara, Brown, & Mangione, 2002, and Fang & Ashley, 2004, for a discussion of internal validity verification procedures in qualitative research). As an additional check on our assumptions, throughout the semester we presented our summary of the data to the preservice teachers and noted their responses regarding the accuracy of our constructions (Denzin & Lincoln, 2005). All of the preservice teachers confirmed that we represented their views appropriately.

Viewing the three main data sets chronologically seemed most appropriate as a means of providing a systematic review of possible changes over time in the preservice teachers' challenges, achievements, and subjective realities regarding interdisciplinary teaching. Therefore, we ordered the data according to points in time, beginning with the preservice teachers' responses to the mid-semester survey and ending with the transcriptions of the structured group interview.

We began our examination of the data by conducting a careful "line-by-line reading of the text[s]" (Ryan & Bernard, 2000, p. 780). We read and reread the preservice teachers' language and jotted down our assumptions when we believed that certain phrases, sentences, and paragraphs, defined by Hycner (1985) as "units of general meaning" (p. 145), illuminated the preservice teachers' realities. For example, we highlighted individual preservice teachers' responses, such as:

> "So what is my problem? My problem is time."
>
> The first stage involved modeling my own self-created book and discussing the three disciplines of creative arts, reading, and science employed in its creation.
>
> This entire experience has been rough.
>
> Science was mainly left out of my instruction.
>
> It got easier as time went along. Most elementary schools don't even get to science.
>
> I cannot seem to structure my teaching time.
>
> I cannot teach a group of kindergarten students who do not pay attention. I may change majors. I might not be a teacher after all.

Then, we jotted down broad impressions that we believed typified the preservice teachers' perceptions of their experiences, such as, "rough time, especially at the beginning of the semester," "easier as time went along," and, "left out science." Through this process we identified seven topic clusters of meaning. Our next step was to review each of the topic clusters to ensure that they expressed a unified coherency that helped to support our research questions.

Subsequently, following Hycner's (1985) guidelines for in-depth phenomenological analysis, we crystallized and grouped the seven clusters of meaning under two overarching themes, which we labeled "uncertainty, stress, and doubt" (four clusters fell under this first theme), and "positive viewpoints, understanding, and confidence" (three clusters fell under this second theme). This recursive process helped provide us with a sense of the gestalt the preservice teachers attached to the phenomenon of participating in the field-based curriculum restructuring initiative.

Limitations of the Inquiry

Several limitations of the inquiry must be considered before we address the preservice teachers' perceived realities, share our understandings of lessons learned, and discuss next steps for our future interdisciplinary preservice teacher restructuring initiatives. We acknowledge that our assumptions cannot be generalized to other preservice teacher programs. This study investigated 28 preservice teachers' lived experiences in a specific school context, and to a great extent, school contextual influences determine preservice teachers' subjective realities (Richards, Moore, & Gipe, 1996/1997).

We must also note that teachers who author teaching cases consciously identify and write about pedagogical problems rather than about teaching successes (Richards & McKenna, 2003). Therefore, although we placed no restrictions on the preservice teachers' responses to the survey and group interview responses, we directed them to author a teaching case that portrayed a problem or predicament they encountered as they taught interdisciplinary lessons. Their achievements were not included in their case writing. Despite this limitation, we included cases to inform our study because we recognize that they illuminate the context in which teaching occurs (Richards & McKenna, 2003).

Researcher subjectivity is another central consideration in qualitative research. Scholars note the difficulty of separating the researchers from the researched (Alvermann, 2000; Noddings, 1984; Peshkin, 1983). Our previous teaching experiences and our dual roles of researchers and involved supervisors of a newly organized preservice teacher interdisciplinary program influenced how we identified units of general meaning and grouped the units of general meaning into clusters, and how we determined and titled the two overarching themes. Others might draw different conclusions from ours (see Tappan & Brown, 1992, for a discussion of hermeneutics).

A further concern is "the potential limitations of self reported data" (Shavelson, Webb, & Burnstein, 1986, p. 44). From a phenomenological perspective, the preservice teachers' language provided the best view of the meanings they attached to their experiences. However, the inquiry was dependent on their willingness and abilities to describe their realities and reveal their "true" selves. With these limitations in mind, we make the data visible by presenting the preservice teachers' lived experiences in the following section.

THE PRESERVICE TEACHERS' LIVED EXPERIENCES

Theme One: Uncertainty, Stress, and Doubt

For most of the semester, the preservice teachers struggled with two procedural concerns associated with effective teaching practices; time management and group supervision. They also grappled with two pedagogical content knowledge issues[1] directly related to the program; subject matter integration, and preparing and presenting creative arts lessons. We present the preservice teachers' dilemmas in the following section.

Time Management Concerns

The preservice teachers struggled with time management issues in two ways. Early in the semester, some completed their instructional sessions with time to spare because they had not thoroughly planned and prepared their lessons. A preservice teacher explains her underplanning predicament in the following teaching case excerpt:

Under Planning

By the time my students finished their drawings I had more than 20 minutes left in my lesson. Twenty minutes is a long time. I did not know what to do next. I didn't want to seem unorganized but I could not believe that what I had planned only took such a short time. What was I to do? The students were getting bored and they saw other groups making dioramas, painting, and still reading books. I had to think of something quickly. I got out some paper and said, "You can draw anything you like." (I know that is not good teaching).

I learned from this lesson to slow down. Maybe I talk too fast. I tend to rush through things. I also know I should have done more planning. To be honest, I've got to admit that's the real reason my lesson ended abruptly—never mind talking too fast. I could have had more informational material. I did not do a during-reading strategy. I now know it is

---

[1]Pedagogical content knowledge "requires that teachers understand and interpret the subject matter they plan to include, [and] find ways to represent this knowledge for their students"(Gavelek, Raphael, Biondo, & Want, 2002, p. 600).

better to over plan. We could have done some ocean songs, or games to use up the time. That does not sound good either when I say, "Use up the time." It sounds like I am trying to just finish up the lesson and get out of there.

For the most part, however, the preservice teachers believed they did not have enough time to offer a three-subject lesson in 75 min. One preservice teacher confided to us, "I can't seem to pace myself."

Others wrote comparable comments on the mid-semester survey, such as,

"I do not have enough time."

"I can get to creative arts and reading but not science—no time."

"Forget science—there is no time."

"Does anyone notice how stressed I am about time? I have no time."

"I don't like cutting my students off when they are making good connections among subjects, but time runs out."

"I still feel I am cutting them short on their learning because I have to stop them because I run out of time."

"I do not know how long a section of a lesson takes because I have never done this before."

"My only dilemma is the short amount of time. How do I relate the arts, science, and reading when I always run out of time? And I am not sure anyway how to tie it all together."

Supervising Groups of Students

Clearly, a well-defined reality for the preservice teachers was the stress they experienced as they learned to manage groups of students. Excerpts from three of the preservice teachers' teaching cases highlight their management concerns.

Pay Attention, Please!

I shave a suggestion for other preservice teachers. Listen to me. Read my lips. Trust me. Don't take this course with other difficult courses. It is hard to make kids pay attention all the time and it zaps my energy. Every Thursday morning I work with three kindergarten students for an hour and 15 minutes. One student, Jordan, just will not behave at all and the other two students are hardly any better. I have decided I will make this group listen and pay attention if it kills me! Sometimes, Jordan rolls his eyes at me and says, "I am not doing this any more."

Then, the other students act up because they see Jordan getting away with inappropriate behavior. I have tried. I really have. I talk to them. I use positive behavior rewards, such as stickers. I sit next to Jordan. I put kids out of the group for five minutes. I even brought in some clay. I am a failure at group management. How will I make 30 kids behave all day when I have my own class?

How Can They Learn if They Don't Listen?

Last week nothing went right. I'd been prepared since Day One, but I did not expect what happened. From the start the kids wouldn't listen so how can you teach a lesson if they don't listen and hear you? I separated them when one little girl tried to stab another girl with a pencil and then she hit a boy. One boy was disrespectful and another boy must have a physical problem because he has to go to the bathroom all the time (Maybe he just wants to disrupt the group). This is my worst nightmare. I cannot teach because my students will not listen to me.

Marching to the Beat of a Different Drum

My brightest student, Billy, is my biggest behavior problem. When I got to school today, his teacher had already put him out in a separate corner for disrupting the class. Because we were reading about a boy who visits his grandparents on a Caribbean island, I began my lesson by using some literature and pictures about Jamaica that I found on the Internet. I also showed my group a steel drum I bought in Jamaica. In addition, I had a map of the Caribbean area, and I told the students how the steel drum was actually invented in Trinidad. I let each student play the drum. This went well until it was Billy's turn. He beat furiously on the drum, and he refused to pass it to another student. Well, I took the drum away from Billy and with that, he grabbed the drumsticks from another student and began to beat the drum again.

I said, "Class, if you cannot share and be respectful of my drum, then we will not use it."

The students said, "That's not fair. It's all Billy's fault. He's always bad."

Billy responded, "I don't care what you say. I am the best drum player and I am going to play."

We tried again. I helped the students beat the drum and clap their hands to some sea chants. Billy just sat there with a mad face. I used a chart of sea chants next and the students were unable to clap their hands or beat the drum in time to the rhythm of our chants.

Do you think I should have not tried to incorporate music? These kids are hard for me to handle. I know this is more of a behavior case than a teaching case, but I had to write about this dilemma.

Teaching Through an Interdisciplinary Approach

There is no doubt that throughout much of the semester, the preservice teachers had difficulties weaving the subjects of creative arts, science, and reading into a cohesive framework. As one preservice teacher wrote, "Its exhausting. It's too much putting all of this together."

A passage from another preservice teacher's case highlights her dilemma about connecting disciplines.

> Science Was the Last Thing on My Mind
>
> I've been able to integrate creative arts and reading easily. It's when I try to also integrate science that I hit a roadblock. I'm unsure how to tie all three things together and keep it interesting for the students. The bottom line is—I do lots of art. I just can't connect three subjects. It has been very difficult for me to integrate science into all of my lessons. Truthfully, science was the last thing on my mind.

The preservice teachers gave similar responses about connecting subjects on the mid-semester survey. Some wrote:

> "I haven't really connected all three subjects. I just can't get it all together."

> "Science is factual. Art is creative. Literacy is language. There are differences among these three subjects. So, I have problems seeing connections. I am starting to doubt my teaching skills."

> "I have connected science to music. That's about it—not very good is it?"

> "Science = facts. Literature = reading. Creative arts = creativity. Don't ask me how to connect them. The one common thing about all three subjects is they need to be taught."

> "How do classroom teachers do this type of teaching? I assume they can do it because they have the kids all day. Another thing is that I always had to study separate subjects when I was in elementary school so this is all new to me. I have no experience with it."

Preparing and Presenting Creative Arts Lessons

Despite the fact that our restructuring initiative was centered around a required creative arts course, preparing and presenting weekly arts lessons that were linked to science and reading and revolved around the topic of the wonderful world of water remained problematic for all of the preservice teachers. Even though we tried to assuage their doubts, the preservice teachers continued to voice their reservations about their artistic abilities throughout the semester. The following excerpts from the mid-semester survey and the end-of-year exit interview portray their concerns and worries about their self-perceived lack of creativity and their quandaries about offering their students appropriate and worthwhile engagements in the arts.

> Creative arts were hardest—trying to figure out what to do each week.

> It is not easy to be creative all the time.

> I am not an artist, I cannot sing, paint, or dance.

> I am just not a creative person. I do not like to sing at all and I cannot draw.

> Coming up with creative ideas each week made me worry from one week to the next.

> Some people are creative. Some are not. I am not. I am stressed out all the time about my inability to plan creative arts lessons.

> I simply am not artsy. I never will be an artsy type teacher. I don't have the skill—the talent.

> You told us we could not use coloring books and ditto sheets for kids to color in. That left me up a creek so I just tried to ignore the arts.

> The arts are so difficult for me. All I ever did in school was color with crayons. This creative arts emphasis is demanding. Can't you tell us what to do? Must we sing, dance, and do drama?

> I really try to offer arts lessons that are meaningful and valuable. I don't think I am on the right track.

Theme Two: Positive Viewpoints, Understanding, and Confidence

By the end of the semester, the preservice teachers acquired more positive viewpoints about their teaching experiences. They appreciated the benefits of participating in an early field experience. They also recognized the value of subject integration and developed confidence in their abilities to teach through an integrated approach. We present these positive changes in the preservice teachers' perspectives in the following section.

Appreciating the Benefits of Participating in an Early Field Experience. In the end-of-semester exit interview, the preservice teachers mentioned the professional knowledge they acquired by participating in an early field program. They remarked about the value of working with kindergarten and first-grade students, and spoke about the opportunities offered for collaborative interactions with teaching peers and classroom teachers. The preservice teachers explained in the end-of-semester interview:

> I came to like the field experience. It is one thing to get an 'A' in the university classroom, but what about the interactions with K–1 students? Where can you learn that? Only in a field experience could you learn that!

> We could collaborate, learn from each other, and borrow ideas and teaching supplies from each other.

> At first I was nervous and worried because I have never participated in a field-based course. I was actually afraid to teach K–1 and that is crazy because I am studying to be a teacher.

> Whooo—This was a lot of work. All that preparation—getting teaching supplies—being on time to teach kindergarten and first grade students—not being absent. But, it was worth it. I learned a lot. I feel prepared to teach. I am proud of myself.

> This was an eye opener. I would recommend it to anyone who wants to work hard and learn to teach. It wasn't easy. It was hard work. But then, I learned so much teaching K–1 students. Now I know what I am doing.

> I actually feel sorry for my soon-to-be teacher friends who have never participated in an early field experience.

> We could communicate with our classroom teachers and learn from them.

> I can't even say how much I've learned. It was hard—very hard—but well worth it.

> I am now ready to teach after this experience.

Recognizing the Value of Subject Integration.   To our surprise, by the end of the semester, the preservice teachers came to recognize the value of subject integration as a teaching philosophy and method. Their comments in the exit interview indicate they understood theory that supports an interdisciplinary approach, and they connected subject integration to students' learning.

> All three disciplines encourage exploration!! I get it now.

> Teachers can use one subject to teach the other two. It doesn't matter which subject you use. It is easy now.

Students who struggle with learning really get a chance to achieve when teachers connect subjects. I noticed this the more I taught my lessons. One struggling student even authored the best creative book out of all my students in the group. He wrote about grey whales and his illustrations were fantastic.

All good teaching expands students' inquiry and knowledge and that is especially true of interdisciplinary teaching.

I am going to connect subjects as much as possible when I am a teacher. The kids love to learn that way because they can see connections.

I now believe that all primary teachers need to offer this type of approach. There is no other way. As human beings we make connections all the time. That's the way we learn.

Interdisciplinary teaching is not only possible—it is the way to teach.

Literacy events are creative. Use literacy to learn about science. Represent science through the creative arts. There you go—it's like a full circle. One subject can be used to learn about another subject. The creative arts can help students show what they have learned about another subject. In addition, all three subjects—creative arts, reading, and science have similarities, like exploration and discovery—like predictions and conclusions.

Confidence in Abilities to Teach Through an Interdisciplinary Approach.   Despite their initial reservations about planning and presenting interdisciplinary lessons, by the semester's end, all of the preservice teachers gained confidence in their abilities to link subject matter. Their exit interview comments resonated with self-assurance:

It became a confidence booster to recognize I could integrate disciplines and my friends in other courses could not. In fact, they didn't know what I was talking about. Of course that isn't nice of me to gloat.

I wasn't sure at first how to do it but then it was okay. I could actually do it and understand why this type of teaching and learning is so important. Science was the easiest for me because I could look up stuff.

It's easy to integrate now. Many schools don't even get to science. When I'm a teacher I can offer science lessons even if we have to teach reading all day.

It's easy to integrate science and reading. I have new found confidence in me.

I wasn't sure at first how to connect all three disciplines, but as time went on, then it became better.

Yes, now I know it can be done. All subjects are all interconnected.

I have connected it all and I am proud of myself. I never thought I could do that until the end of the semester. The students' journals are now filled with words, pictures, and sentences about science. They read about science concepts. They did creative arts activities that integrated science.

I can use this approach now.

Lessons Learned

Certainly, the results of our inquiry pinpoint some achievements and success. By the end of the semester, the preservice teachers developed considerable insights about the benefits of participating in an early field program. They also recognized how different subjects can support one another in areas commonly shared, and how subject integration has the potential to enhance students' learning.

Yet, just as the literature indicates, our first preservice teacher curricular restructuring effort turned out to be far more demanding and complex than we had anticipated. The language the preservice teachers used to describe a large part of their teaching experiences poignantly illuminates the challenges they faced with procedural teaching concerns of time management and student supervision. They also grappled with pedagogical content knowledge dilemmas directly related to subject integration, and worried about planning and offering meaningful creative arts lessons that supported students' learning in the disciplines of science and reading.

Research indicates that it is common for preservice teachers to overlook time management and planning as important variables in effective teaching (Moore, 2003), and that supervising students is a key concern of beginning teachers (Fuller, 1969; Moore, 2003). A few studies also suggest that most preservice teachers have reservations about their abilities to design appropriate and imaginative student engagements in the creative arts (Gipe, Richards, & Moore, 2001; Halliwell, 1993; Richards, 2005). In addition, a small body of research indicates that preservice teachers who are required to offer an interdisciplinary curriculum initially experience tensions about their abilities to connect subjects, and lack appreciation for subject integration (Young, 1991/1992).

However, research findings that parallel the preservice teachers' experiences in this inquiry do not excuse the significant role we as supervisors played in exacerbating their uncertainties and doubts. Although the field experience offered opportunities for creating new knowledge among our preservice teachers, we now know that we expected them to move too quickly from separate-subject to interdisciplinary teaching. Our desires to

prepare our preservice teachers for what we believe will be a multidisciplinary pedagogy of the future, although well meaning, took precedence
over meticulous planning, coordination of activities, and reflection on the
content base of our program, including our intentions and the goals of our
restructuring initiative. Equally serious, we did not heed Hargreaves'
(1994) cautionary observation that change facilitators must understand
the perspectives that teachers bring to the change process in terms of their
conceptions of time, power, and the emotional aspects of teaching.

APPLICATIONS TO CLASSROOM PRACTICE

Looking back, we can see that over the course of the semester, we learned
a lot about the complexities of educational change. We now have a clearer
understanding about what it takes to engage in a successful preservice
teacher restructuring initiative. Our next agenda needs to begin with a
thorough examination and articulation of our own knowledge, beliefs,
and perspectives about interdisciplinary teaching. We need to clarify our
own uncertainties and dispel any ambiguities we hold about the underlying theoretical foundations of an integrated curriculum before we can
fully inform and support our preservice teachers as they strive to make
connections across disciplines. This support particularly includes helping
our preservice teachers examine and reflect on the theoretical underpinnings of multidisciplinary teaching. It is unacceptable to ask our preservice teachers to adopt interdisciplinary methods if they are not familiar
with the key tenets that support these methods.

It is also essential that we include our preservice teachers in future curricular restructuring planning sessions so that they have opportunities to
develop some ownership of the teaching perspectives we want them to
consider, and understand the approach we encourage them to implement.
For example, we plan to ask our preservice teachers to participate in
designing some of the program's activities. They might also collaborate
with their K–1 students and select individual small groups encompassing
themes of study based on their students' interests rather than respond to
our mandated topic of study.

We also need to ensure that our preservice teachers have the prerequi-
site procedural and pedagogical knowledge base to make a successful
transition from a separate-subject to a multidisciplinary approach.
Offering a multidisciplinary curriculum requires multiple levels of planning and sufficient subject matter knowledge as well as an understanding
about how to represent and adopt that knowledge for students' levels
of development. Relevant course readings, class discussions, and guest

speakers in the visual and performing arts are some of the ways we can provide a clearer direction for our preservice teachers as they strive toward change implementation.

Unquestionably, we need to address course scheduling. Rather than trying to squeeze two or three subjects into a one 3-hour semester course, we need to enlist support from our college administrators and arrange an integrated, contiguous block of field-based courses that might be offered two mornings a week. This schedule configuration would also allow for broader faculty collaboration in which two or three elementary and secondary faculty members work together (e.g., reading and science, or mathematics, language arts, and creative arts courses).

Most importantly, we need to consider the perspectives our preservice teachers bring to the change process as they move from a subject-centered to an interdisciplinary curriculum. As teacher educators, we need to learn to see through our preservice teachers' eyes and recognize that it is unethical and unreasonable for us to teach and expect "great ideas" unless we help our preservice teachers "understand how to [think about and] execute those great ideas" (Stephens, 1998, p. 377).

FOR FURTHER THOUGHT

1. Educators argue that interdisciplinary teaching is more authentic than separate discipline structures because interdisciplinary teaching "parallels real-world tasks and not those developed solely for schooling" (Biondo, Raphael, & Gavelek, 2005, p. 1). Do you think the preservice teachers in this study offered authentic, real-world tasks to their primary students? Why or why not? In the future, how might they better support primary students' learning through real-world interdisciplinary teaching?

2. Do you know any teachers who teach through an interdisciplinary approach? Conduct an informal survey and ask them how they plan their lessons. What aspects of interdisciplinary teaching do they find most difficult and how do they attempt to overcome these content and pedagogical difficulties?

3. Do you think that when the preservice teachers described in this study become classroom teachers they will support their students' learning through interdisciplinary structures? What factors might prohibit them from offering this approach? What theoretical knowledge might help these teachers meet the challenges associated with planning and offering integrated themed units of inquiry in school districts that follow high stakes testing guidelines?

APPENDIX

Preservice Teacher Mid-Semester Survey-Interdisciplinary Project

Dear Preservice Teachers,
    We want to know about your experiences in this interdisciplinary project. We will use the information you provide us to help structure future curricula change initiatives in our College of Education. You have already signed an Internal Review Board (IRB) Consent Form that indicates your willingness to participate in this research project. However, your participation in this survey is voluntary. It will NOT affect your final grade if you choose not to complete the survey. Thank you for your help.
Dr. Richards, Course Instructor and Kim Shea, Doctoral Student
Please use the back of this paper to continue writing your thoughts.

1. What do you think the subjects of creative arts, reading, and science have in common?
2. In what ways have you connected creative arts, reading, and science in your lessons at the charter school? (e.g., dialogue journals? children's literature? arts projects, including music, visual art, drama? creative books? murals?)
3. What were your toughest moments teaching through an interdisciplinary approach?
4. What still puzzles you about an interdisciplinary curriculum?
5. What will you tell others about your experiences planning and teaching interdisciplinary lessons?
6. What positive experiences did you have that centered on teaching through an interdisciplinary approach?

REFERENCES

Akerson, V. (2001). How to teach science when the principal says "Teach language arts" *Science and Children, 38*(7), 42–48.
Akins, A., & Akerson, V. L. (2002). Connecting science, social studies, and language arts: An interdisciplinary approach. *Educational Action Research, 10,* 479–497.
Alvermann, D. (2000). Narrative approaches. In M. Kamil, P. Mosenthall, P. D. Pearson, & R. Barr (Eds.), *Handbook of reading research* (Vol. 3, pp. 123–139). Mahwah, NJ: Lawrence Erlbaum Associates.
Anfara, V., Brown, K., & Mangione, T. (2002). Qualitative analysis on stage: Making the research more public. *Educational Researcher, 31*(7), 28–38.

Biondo, S., Raphael, T., & Gavelek, J. (2005). Mapping the possibilities of integrated literacy instruction. *Reading Online*, (pp 1–12). Retrieved December, 2005, from http ://www.readingonline.org/research/biondo/biondo.html

Britzman, D. (1991). *Practice makes perfect: A critical study of learning to teach.* New York: SUNY.

Bullock, P., Park, V., Snow, J., & Rodriguez, E. (2002). Redefining interdisciplinary curriculum: A journey of collaboration and change in secondary teacher education. *Interchange, 33*(2), 159–182.

Caine, R., & Caine, G. (1991). Reinventing schools through brain-based learning. *Educational Leadership, 52*(7), 43–45.

Carr, K. (2003). A commentary. In J. Richards & M. McKenna (Ed.), *Integrating multiple literacies in K–8 classrooms: Cases, commentaries, and practical applications* (pp. 210–214). Mahwah, NJ: Lawrence Erlbaum Associates.

Casteel, C., & Isom, B. (1994). Reciprocal processes in science and literacy learning. *The Reading Teacher, 47* (7), 538–545.

Center for Educational Reform. (2005). *Making schools work better for all children.* Washington, D C: Author.

de Marrais, K., & Lapan, S. (2004). *Foundations for research: Methods of inquiry in education and the social sciences.* Mahwah, NJ: Lawrence Erlbaum Associates.

Denzin, N., & Lincoln, Y. (Eds.). (2005). *Handbook of qualitative research* (3rd ed.). Thousand Oaks, CA: Sage.

Fals Borda, O. (Ed.). (1998). *People's participation: Challenges ahead.* New York: Apex.

Fang, Z., & Ashley, C. (January/February 2004). Preservice teachers' interpretations of a field-based reading block. *Journal of Teacher Education, 55*(1), 39–54.

Fullan, M. (1982). *The meaning of educational change.* Toronto: OISE Press.

Fuller, F. (1969). Concerns of teachers: A developmental conceptualization. *American Educational Research Journal, 6*(2), 207–226.

Gaskins, I., & Guthrie, J. (1994). Integrating instruction of science, reading, and writing: Goals, teacher development, and assessment. *Journal of Research in Science Teaching, 31*, 1039–1056.

Gavelek, J., Raphael, T., Biondo, S., & Wang, D. (2000). Integrated literacy instruction. In M. Kamil, P. Mosenthall, P. D. Pearson, & R. Barr (Eds.), *Handbook of reading research* (Vol. 3, pp. 587–607). Mahwah, NJ: Lawrence Erlbaum Associates.

Gipe, J., Richards, J., & Moore, R. (2001). Integrating literacy lessons and the visual and communicative arts: Preservice teachers' concerns and challenges. *Reading Online, 4*(8). Retrieved June 22, 2005, from http://www.readingonline.org/articles/art_index.asp?HREF = /articles/gipe/index/html.

Goodlad, J. (1984). *A place called school: Prospects for the future.* New York: McGraw-Hill.

Goodlad, J. (2000). Foreword. In S. Wineburg & P. Grossman (Eds.), *Interdisciplinary curriculum: Challenges to implementation* (pp. vii–xii). New York: Teachers College Press.

Halliwell, S. (1993). Teacher creativity and teacher education. In D. Bridges & K. Trevor (Eds.), *Developing teachers professionally* (pp. 67–78). London: Routledge.

Hargreaves, A. (1994). *Changing teachers, changing times: Teachers' work and culture in post modern age*. New York: Teachers College Press.

Hycner, R. (1985). Some guidelines for the phenomenological analysis of interview data. *Human Studies, 88*, 279–303.

Kaufman, D., & Brooks, J. (1996). Interdisciplinary collaboration in teacher education: A constructivist approach *TESOL Quarterly, 30*, 231–251.

Boix Mansilla, V., Miller, W., & Gardner, H. (2000). On disciplinary lenses and interdisciplinary work. In S. Wineburg & P. Grossman (Eds.), *Interdisciplinary curriculum: Challenges to implementation* (pp. 17–38). New York: Teachers College Press.

Meister, D., & Nolan, J. (2001). Out on a limb on our own: Uncertainty and doubt in moving from subject-centered to interdisciplinary teaching. *Teachers College Record, 103*(4), 608–633.

Mendolsohn, J., & Baker, F. (2005). *The interdisciplinary project model: A workable response to the challenges of multicultural education in out nation's secondary schools*. Retreived June 20, 2005, from http://www.mewhorizons.org/strategies/multicultural/mendolsohn.htm.

Moore, R. (2003). Reexamining the field experiences of preservice teachers. *Journal of Teacher Education, 54* (12), 31–49.

National Council of Teachers of English/National Council for the Social Studies/ Council for Elementary Science Teachers Association/ International Reading Association. (2004). Newark, DE: International Reading Association.

Noddings, N. (1984). *Caring: A feminist approach to ethics and moral education*. Berkeley, CA: University of California Press.

Patton. M. (2002). *Qualitative research & evaluation methods* (3rd ed.). Thousand Oaks, CA: Sage.

Perkins, D. (1991). Enlightening for insight. *Educational Leadership, 49* (2), 4–8.

Peshkin, A. (1983). The goodness of qualitative research. *Educational Leadership, 22*(2), 24–30.

Richards, J. (2005). Integrating sign systems in two field-based literacy methods classes: Preservice teachers' problems and perplexities. *Journal of Reading Education*.

Richards, J., & Anderson, N. (2003a). What do I see? What do I think? What do I wonder? (STW): A visual literacy strategy to help emergent readers focus attention on storybook illustrations. *The Reading Teacher, 65*, 442–444.

Richards, J., & Anderson, N. (2003b). "How do you know?" A strategy to help emergent readers make inferences. *The Reading Teacher, 57*(3), 290–293.

Richards, J., & McKenna, M. (2003). *Integrating multiple literacies in K–8 classrooms: Cases, commentaries, and practical applications*. Mahwah, NJ: Lawrence Erlbaum Associates.

Richards, J., Moore, R., & Gipe, P. (Fall, 1996/Winter1997). Preservice teachers in two different multicultural field programs: The complex influence of school context. *Research in the Schools, 3*(2), 23–34.

Ross, P., & Frey, N. (2002, Winter). In a spring garden: Literacy and science bloom in second grade. *Reading Improvement, 39*(4), 164–174.

Ryan, G., & Bernard, H. (2000). Data management and analysis methods. In N. Denzin & E. Lincoln (Eds.), *Handbook of qualitative research* (2nd ed., pp. 769–802). Thousand Oaks, CA: Sage.

Shavelson, R., Webb, N., & Burnstein, L (1986). The measurement of teaching. In M. Wittrock (Ed.), *Handbook on teaching* (3rd ed., pp. 1–36). New York: Macmillan.

Stake, R. (2000). Case studies. In N. Denzin & E. Lincoln (Eds.), *Handbook of qualitative* research (2nd ed., pp. 435–454). Thousand Oaks, CA: Sage.

Stake, R. (2005) Qualitative case studies. In N. Denzin & E. Lincoln (Eds.), *Handbook of qualitative research* (3rd ed., pp. 443–466). Thousand Oaks, CA: Sage.

Stephens, D. (1998). An agenda for teacher educators. In T. Raphael & K. Au (Eds.), *Literature-based instruction: Reshaping the curriculum* (pp. 371–378). Norwood, MA: Christopher Gordon.

Tappan, M., & Brown, L. (1992). Stories told and lessons learned: Toward a narrative approach to moral development and moral education. In C. Witherell & N. Noddings (Eds.), *Stories lives tell: Narrative and dialogue in education* (pp. 171–192). New York: Teachers College, Columbia University.

The Boyer Commission. (2001). *On educating undergraduates in the research university: Reinventing undergraduate education: A blueprint for America's research universities.* New York: Stony Brook State University of New York.

Young, J. (1991/1992). Curriculum integration: Perceptions of preservice teachers. *Action in Teacher Education, 13*(4), 1–9.

11

Using Science Notebook Writing to Promote Preservice Teachers' Understanding of Formative Assessment

Judith A. Morrison
Washington State University

The research project described in this chapter explored how, through focusing on students' writing in science notebooks, preservice teachers came to see students' writing in science as an important tool to improve teaching and learning. Using science notebooks in science methods courses affected preservice teachers' understanding of and predicted use of formative assessment involving students' writing in science notebooks. The *National Science Education Standards* [National Research Council (NRC), 1996] have called for teachers to continually assess their students' scientific understanding and reasoning and their students' achievement and opportunity to learn. Teachers are encouraged to plan for opportunities where their students can discuss and display their levels of science understanding (NRC, 2001b). In order to implement these recommendations and focus on the learning of each student, teachers may need to employ formative assessments; assessing or helping students assess current levels of understanding and then helping the students with strategies to reach predetermined learning and performance goals (Sadler, 1989).

Having students write about their science experiences in their science notebooks has been claimed to facilitate students' learning of science

(Glynn & Muth, 1994; Ruiz-Primo & Li, 2004). Writing in science notebooks is considered to be a process where students reflect on their experiences and prior knowledge as well as apply new information. Students' science notebook writing has also been shown to be a valid source of information for teachers on students' misconceptions and current understandings (Audet, Hickman, & Dobrynina, 1996; Fellows, 1994). One way for students to increase their understanding of science is to write about their ideas and experiences in science (Glynn & Muth, 1994). Research (Hand, Prain, & Yore, 2001; Rivard, 1994) has shown that writing-to-learn in science has enhanced students' learning when teachers attend to curricular goals, learners' metacognitive knowledge, and the instructional environment. According to Klentschy and Molina-DeLa Torre (2004), students' science notebook writing may be a way for students to strengthen their language skills as they develop an understanding of the world around them.

> The student science notebook serves as an important link between science and literacy when it is utilized in the classroom as a knowledge-transforming form of writing that provides an appropriate opportunity for students to develop voice in the process of constructing meaning from their experiences with the science phenomena. This, coupled with appropriate and timely feedback from the classroom teacher, has strong potential to provide the improvement in student achievement across the curriculum that educators are seeking. (p. 352)

Professional development and preservice teacher training should provide instruction in "how students learn and how learning can be assessed" (NRC, 2001a, p. 309). Teachers need to experience how to implement assessment tools that can provide them with valid inferences about their students' understanding. Teachers must gather knowledge about a variety of methods to use when assessing science learning as well as the advantages and disadvantages of each method (Magnusson, Krajcik, & Borko, 1999). Black (1998) has concluded that assessment in many classrooms is challenging, for instance: (a) Teachers' tests stress memorization and superficial learning even when they say they want to develop students' understanding, (b) assessment methods are not critically reviewed by teachers, (c) in many elementary classrooms, "there is a tendency to emphasize quantity and presentation of work and to neglect its quality in relation to learning" (p. 42), (d) grading and competitiveness seems to be overemphasized whereas providing useful advice is underemphasized, and (e) teachers often use feedback to serve a managerial or social role and students' learning needs are left unaddressed.

It is often the case that preservice training programs present a specific assessment tool without allowing preservice teachers a chance to use the tool or the opportunity to be assessed themselves through that tool. According to Sadler (1998), "teachers need to have professional preservice and inservice training for [the] specific requirements of formative assessment" (p. 83). In this era of high stakes summative tests, it is necessary to balance preservice teacher training with experiences of formative assessment that have "the potential to drive changes in teaching that can improve students' conceptual learning dramatically" (Dougherty, 1997, p. 29). A few of the essential ingredients of teachers' formative assessment strategies are features such as (a) the type of feedback needed to guide students' learning, (b) knowledge of the necessary learning goals for the specified content, and (c) how to guide students to a clear view of the learning goals, their present understanding, and how to move from one to the other (Black, 1998). Ruiz-Primo, Li, Ayala, and Shavelson (1999) found that teachers tended to write "great" as feedback for students' written descriptions of procedures that varied drastically in quality, possibly because no clear criteria for procedure description had been communicated to students. The authors stressed that feedback "should be descriptive, not evaluative or comparative" (p. 25). In another study (Ruiz-Primo, Li, & Shavelson, 2002), the results showed that in 6 out of 10 classrooms, there was no evidence of teacher feedback on students' science notebook entries even though these entries showed poor communication and partial understanding. Certainly, teacher training must include education about the benefits and logistics of providing valuable feedback to students.

There is general agreement that science notebooks are an effective formative assessment tool (Audet, Hichman, & Dobrynina, 1996; Fellows, 1994; Shepardson & Britsch, 1997) allowing teachers to "assess students' understanding and provide the feedback students need for improving their performance" (Ruiz-Primo, Li, & Shavelson, 2002, p. 24). Science notebooks may be defined as individual spiral, hard-bound "composition," or folded paper notebooks where students formulate questions, make predictions, record and display data, analyze results, propose explanations, compose reflections, and communicate hypotheses during inquiry investigations. These notebooks are similar to research scientists' log books and students are encouraged to use them as scientists would, before, during, and after all investigations.

It is important for future teachers to be trained to use science notebooks as an assessment tool; Baxter, Bass, & Glasser (2001) found that the focus of science notebooks in fifth-grade classrooms was dependant on "those aspects of inquiry that teachers attended to" (p. 138). Science notebooks can be a formative assessment tool for both teachers and students to determine a) prior knowledge and existing science ideas, b) how conceptual understanding is being built, c) procedural understanding, d) mastery of curriculum goals, and e) the ability to apply/transfer ideas to new context (Volkmann & Abell, 2003).

Using science notebooks with preservice teachers accomplishes two goals; (1) introducing the preservice teachers to an interdisciplinary strategy involving science and language arts and (2) providing information on the preservice teachers' science conceptual understanding and process skill knowledge. Writing about science in their notebooks is an important step in the development of preservice teachers' science literacy (content knowledge, inquiry skills, and disposition toward using critical thinking/science reasoning in decision making). This project focused on how a formative assessment tool, the science notebook, was introduced in science methods courses and the resultant views held by preservice teachers on the value of this assessment tool for their future practice.

RESEARCH QUESTIONS

In order to explore the understandings held by preservice teachers about formative assessment and using science notebooks as a tool to find out their students' science understanding, the following research questions were devised.

1. How do preservice teachers view using students' writing in science notebooks as a formative assessment tool?
2. How do preservice teachers develop their own use of science notebooks during a science methods course?

Design and Procedure

Participants. The participants in this study were the preservice teachers, both graduate and undergraduate, enrolled in three science methods courses, one each semester for three semesters. The courses were 15 weeks long, meeting 3 hours weekly and covering the pedagogical aspects of teaching science as well as physical, life, and earth science content. All students in the methods classes were given the option to participate in the study or not, none opted to refrain from participating. Out of the 44 preservice teachers studied, no more than two or three participants in each class had a science background. The remainder of the students had typically completed two science courses during their undergraduate course work. These preservice teachers were planning to teach at the K–8 levels. The preservice teachers had completed a course in assessment where they had been introduced to the term formative assessment but they had not had prior experiences with the use of science notebooks. These students had also completed a course focused on teaching writing where they learn how to improve writing skills and how to plan effective writing lessons.

Science Notebook Use.   Throughout the semester-long science methods courses, the preservice teachers were required to maintain a science notebook. The three methods courses remained similar from the first to the third, the use of the science notebook was consistent across all three. Preservice teachers were asked to provide either a hard bound, "composition" book or a spiral bound notebook to be used for the science content parts of the methods course and not to be used for the pedagogy part of the course. During the second class meeting, the preservice teachers were given a short presentation on using science notebooks, examples of scientists' notebooks were reviewed and discussed, and recommendations on what to include in a science notebook were given. Typically, the last half of each class (1.5 hours) was spent in making observations and predictions, collecting data, designing investigations, collecting and analyzing data, testing activities, formulating conclusions, and communicating conclusions and results. Any writing, diagramming, graphing, or drawing about these activities was done in the science notebook. The preservice teachers were also asked to reflect on activities they did in respect to how they could be used in the classroom. The preservice teachers always worked in groups of 3–4 and compared and shared information from their science notebooks throughout their investigations. Often the final communication was a group effort and involved combining the group's results. Collaboration among group members and between groups in the class was always encouraged. At the end of the class session, the preservice teachers were asked to review what they had written in their notebooks, reflecting on how it could have been clearer, how it demonstrated their learning, and how their learning might be assessed by the instruction based on their notebook writings and entries.

The science notebooks were viewed informally during every class session with oral feedback provided and then collected for nongraded, formative assessment at the mid-semester point. At the end of the semester, the preservice teachers submitted their notebooks for both feedback and a final grade. The criteria for this final summative grade was presented to the preservice teachers at the start of the course in the course syllabus; the focus of the assessment was on the level of communication achieved, the degree of completeness and organization of the notebook, and the reflections provided by the preservice teacher on the activities and investigations in which they had been involved.

During the two class sessions on assessment, the role of formative assessment, science notebooks as a formative assessment tool, and using students' writing in their notebooks to assess students' understanding were addressed. As well, the benefits of clear and constructive feedback and the necessity of students communicating their understanding of science concepts in the notebooks were addressed. The preservice teachers were continually asked to reflect on their own notebook use and how they would use science notebooks in their own teaching.

Data Collection

Data were collected from a variety of sources in order to answer the research questions. Preservice teachers used science notebooks as they were involved in inquiry-based investigations in the methods classes. These notebooks were collected and photocopied as a primary data source on how the preservice teachers represented their science understanding and reflected on their use of science notebooks. The preservice teachers received informal feedback from the methods instructor throughout the semester and more formal written feedback on the science notebooks twice during the semester.

The preservice teachers completed a questionnaire (Appendix A) at the end of their methods course where they provided information about their use of science notebooks as an assessment tool, their planned future use of science notebooks, and what they had gained through the assessment of their own notebooks in the methods course.

During the methods course, the preservice teachers wrote one formal paper about the uses of science notebooks as a formative assessment tool, wrote a single page reflection paper at the end of the course on their own use of science notebooks, and also designed a rubric for assessing students' writing in their science notebooks. These were both data sources. Another assignment in the course was writing three lesson plans that each included an in-depth presentation of the planned assessment of the designed lesson. Information presented by the preservice teachers about how they planned to assess future students was a source of data on the views they held about formative assessment and specifically students' writing in the science notebooks. Throughout the three methods courses, the researcher collected data in a researcher's log. Any reference to students' writing, science notebooks, or formative assessment made by the preservice teachers was recorded in the log.

Data Analysis. Data were analyzed by analytic induction (Bogdan & Biklen, 1992). Patterns of similarities and differences in perspectives and approaches and any change in these perspectives were sought. The data were systematically organized and reduced using categories such as the following; a) use of science notebooks as a formative assessment tool, b) formative assessment to inform teaching and learning, c) students' writing in science, d) logistics of using science notebooks, e) evidence of growth in preservice teachers' use of science notebooks, f) beliefs on assessment in general, and g) beliefs on student writing. These categories were used to code and index participants' questionnaires, lesson plans, researcher's log, individuals comments, and all other written work. The preservice teachers' notebooks were collected early in the semester and reviewed for inclusion of questions, predictions, hypotheses, observations, and conclusions. A sample entry from each notebook was photocopied and then compared to a sample entry from the end of the semester. These sample entries were the same for all preservice teachers in each class and selected from an inquiry investigation that had been completed in the classroom.

FINDINGS

The use of science notebooks by the preservice teachers provided a means to strengthen their understanding of formative assessment and to focus on writing in science. The science notebooks were seen by the preservice teachers as a way to continually gather information from students and as an avenue where constructive feedback to students could be provided. The preservice teachers kept their own notebooks and received feedback from the methods instructor on their growth in science understanding and they also reflected on the use of student writing in science notebooks as a formative assessment tool for their future teaching.

Research Question #1

The first research question, How do preservice teachers view using students' writing in science notebooks as a formative assessment tool, was addressed through the preservice teachers' survey responses, assessment plans, rubrics, and a formal paper. When asked to design an assessment plan for the required lessons plans, the preservice teachers consistently included mention of having students write in their science notebooks as a formative assessment tool. The preservice teachers said they would use student writing in science notebooks to assess students' understanding of the content presented in the lesson. The preservice teachers often assigned a specific prompt for assessment of specific content and the majority of the preservice teachers mentioned that they would be able to find out what their students were thinking through the students' writing. A sample of representative quotes follow:

> My assessment plan for this lesson will be based on what they write in their notebooks for homework. The prompt for their notebooks will be "Choose one type of rock out of the three that we studied. If possible, find a rock at home that resembles this type of rock. Based on what you know about this type of rock, write a paragraph saying where you think this rock came from and any questions you have about this rock." When assessing this notebook entry, I will be looking for accurate understanding of the specific rock they picked. Also, I will be looking for creativity when they formulate the questions about the rock. (Melissa)

> There is one clear way of assessing every students' work, their science notebooks. This will be a valuable tool because I am asking to know things that they may be thinking, but the journal gives them space to write it all out. (Candice)

> I will know that everyone has understood the material covered through two different assessment plans. First I will have a conclusion discussion...The second way I will be able to find [student understanding] out is through one of the most valuable assets teachers have, and that is the science notebook. As they will be recording all of their data, then looking back and trying to figure out why some froze and some didn't I will get to see that thought process right before my eyes. (Cary)

These quotes demonstrate the preservice teachers' focus on students' communication of understanding through their writing, the need to use science notebooks as a resource for the students, and the value of the notebook as a venue where the teacher can find out what the student is thinking. Earlier in the semester, all the preservice teachers involved in this study had been required to individually interview a student on a specific science topic. Their feedback was that it is very difficult to know what a student understands or is thinking unless the teacher has time to sit down and do an individual interview. They saw the science notebooks as a tool to use to get an idea of students' comprehension.

Every preservice teacher said that they would have the students record some aspect of science inquiry (recording data, making predictions, designing investigations, proposing explanations, or communicating conclusions) in their notebooks and the teacher would then view the entries and provide feedback in some form or another. When asked on the questionnaires, the preservice teachers all said that they planned on using science notebooks in their teaching Representative quotes included "an assessment tool for students' understanding of concepts," "as a journal, too, to reflect individual style with art and writing," and "to help students with their thought processes, organization." Other representative quotes follow.

> Notebooks is (sic) a perfect form of assessment to see if they have understood the concepts being explored. (Wendy)

> You can certainly check for understanding & assess their experimental procedures. (Lea)

> Great way to note progress, are they completing tasks, are they making conclusions & actually "getting it?" (Jay)

> You can not only assess science understanding, but you can assess the writing (Beth)

This last comment by a preservice teacher demonstrates that they began to see that students' writing in science notebooks would allow them a very complete picture on how the students were doing in both science understanding and in writing abilities. These preservice teachers had also begun to see that the science notebook was a place where both the students' content understanding and process skills could be assessed.

One of the preservice teachers commented "I will use this science notebook in my classroom. This would be great for parent conferences." This demonstrated recognition of science notebooks as a product to show parents student progress. Another commented, "It will make them feel important, I think" recognizing that owning and using their own personal notebook is important to students. The preservice teachers also saw that using science notebooks would be a way to gain feedback from students on their own teaching:

> Great formative assessment on my teaching and students' comprehension levels. (Jana)

> I can be sure students did the labs, gauge their thinking & know what I might need to reteach. (Randy)

> One of the best tools! I can reflect on their progress & comprehension, or lack-there-of, & plan my lessons/units accordingly. (Deb)

The preservice teachers designed rubrics (see Appendix B for examples) for assessing their future students' science notebooks and the analysis of these showed that through assessment of the science notebooks, preservice teachers intend to provide students with information on the quality of the work in the following areas; organization, completeness, content understanding, and process skills. The rubrics were most often designed for assessment of a single investigation rather than the whole notebook. The majority of the rubrics for the science notebooks had a focus on assessment of students' communication of their science understanding through writing. Ruiz-Primo et al. (2002) found that many entries in students' science notebooks are simply mechanical copying of definitions and procedures from textbooks, therefore it was important to note that the preservice teachers planned to assess understanding as well as process skills.

In their formal paper, the preservice teachers wrote about how they planned to assess their students' science notebooks and considered how they might provide feedback other than the rubric scores. Some representative quotes follow:

> Upon completion of the lesson, the science notebooks could be used to determine what students learned. Each student's understanding would be expressed through the questions they asked before, during, and after a unit. The results of their inquiries and other labs would be included, so the teacher could examine students' abilities to create products. (Cherrie)

> I will not grade the notebook on grammar or spelling errors. If I need to communicate to the students through the notebook, I'll write my notes on post-its to maintain the originality. The inclusion of all the required notebook content will [be] a portion of their grade. One of the most important aspects of the notebook that I'll grade will be the students' questions(s) that they'll be required to ask at the end of each inquiry/experiment. (Maria)

> Time will be purposely made for writing in the science notebooks and students will be encouraged to "write as they are thinking" and to add any anecdotal commentary as they reflect on what they have already written. Teacher will read notebooks over-the-shoulder (with permission) and after experimentation to see that scientific inquiry and discovery is taking or has taken place in order to make verbal or "post-it note" commentary and/or to make teaching (inquiry guide) adjustments. Ideally this will be done during and after each inquiry. (Lisa)

Research Question #2

In order to determine how the preservice teachers developed in their own use of science notebooks during the methods course, their science notebooks were analyzed, observations of their use of notebooks were made, their reflections written in a paper on their own use of notebooks, and the comments made on the survey were analyzed. Observations of the teachers revealed that they became more and more dependent on their notebooks as the semester progressed. At the beginning of the semester, many were concerned about the "right" format for their responses in the notebook. Many asked how data were supposed to be recorded or how the conclusions were to look (the teachers were not given any specifications on these points and told to decide for themselves what was necessary). By the end of the semester, all the teachers had become comfortable with the idea that there was not one "right" way to record information in their notebooks and had created individual formats. At the beginning of the semesters, two to three preservice teachers in each class would write all their observations, predictions, data collections, hypotheses, and conclusions on loose notebook paper. When asked why they were doing this, the usual reply was that they wanted to make sure it was right or correct before putting the information in their notebooks.

> At first, I wanted everything in the notebook to be perfect, clean, and complete and I labored over each page, writing carefully and adding drawings. That became too time consuming so I settled for less than perfect, which I'm sure a real scientists would have eventually done as well. (Jan)

> In the beginning I was too concerned about making it too perfect. I was writing the information down on pieces of paper and then transferring it to my journal. A couple weeks of this proved to be too tedious, so I changed my strategy. I also started adding more diagrams and sketches. These strategies illustrated my observations and made them more beneficial to me in the future. (Karin)

These preservice teachers were used to being assessed on the neatness of work they did so they had difficulty doing rough writing and drawing in the notebook even though they had been told that they would not be assessed on neatness, spelling, or punctuation. By the end of the semester, most, but not all, of the preservice teachers were able to let go of their focus on neat work and write with more freedom directly in their science notebooks.

As the semester progressed, the preservice teachers used their notebooks as a reference for the investigations they had already conducted. They seemed to do this in order to assess their own science process skills, content understanding, and communication abilities. The following quotes demonstrate that preservice teachers used the notebooks to communicate their understanding to others as well as a form of self-assessment of their own growth.

By the end of the semester, I was drawing more conclusions because throughout the activities I tended to think of the results and procedures more thoroughly through all the experience I was gaining. I used my science notebook to assess myself by going back and seeing if I could understand what I was trying to communicate and also that I could follow the procedure. (May)

The science notebook started out as a way to present my learning to the instructor. As I began to write my reflections on the classroom inquiries, I realized this notebook could be a tool for me to refer to in the future as a teacher. So, I tried to use the reflections as a way to convey how the inquiries can be applied to a classroom. (Cherie)

[The science notebook] broadened and deepened my learning especially the section used in class when small group discussion was taking place. (Craig)

I was able to regenerate my thoughts and ideas by looking back through my notebook. (Chris)

The preservice teachers came to value their notebooks as a resource to use to reflect on their own science learning and also to use in their own teaching as a model for students' science notebooks. When the preservice teachers were asked to reflect on the activities and investigations they conducted, the science notebook was the source of information they used to remind themselves of what occurred and how their ideas had changed.

CONCLUSIONS

Implications

The use of science notebooks as a formative assessment tool allows teachers to embed assessment into instruction and to retrieve information about students' competence in order to make decisions on adapting instruction to meet students' needs. The preservice teachers in this study came to understand formative assessment as a tool to use in their classrooms and as an avenue to receive information about their own growth in science understanding. The preservice teachers' responses regarding using students' writing to find out if the students understand the science concepts underscores that they accepted science notebook writing as a valid assessment format. Due to their involvement with science notebooks in the methods course (both being assessed on their own notebook entries and predicting their use of notebooks as a teacher), the preservice teachers began to see that this form of assessment is a valuable method to assess students' scientific understanding. The science notebook was presented as a form of assessment that supports individualized instruction, allows for student interaction, contains rich diagnostic data, and provides timely feedback, all criteria for assessment that enhances student learning (NRC, 2001a). Having been assessed through this method themselves, the preservice teachers all predicted they would use science notebooks for formative assessment in their own future classrooms. The preservice teachers involved in this study had been exposed to much discussion on assessing students' understanding. They had conducted an individual interview and read current research on students' misconceptions in science. Their own use of science notebooks and the discussion of formative assessment using science notebooks gave these preservice teachers a valuable tool to use to assess their future students' understanding. As stressed by Ruiz-Primo et al. (2002), teachers need to select notebook entries where students can demonstrate their understanding, improve their performance, and explore scientific inquiry rather than mechanically record data. The preservice teachers in this study explored the use of science notebooks to the extent that they began to see the value of the notebook as a window into students' thinking rather than simply as a place to record data.

The value of science notebooks as a method for improving students' literacy skills was stressed throughout the methods courses. The preservice teachers consistently commented that by requiring students to write about what they are doing and knowing in science, the students' literacy skills and their science understanding can be improved. Because many school districts place instructional and assessment focus on language arts and mathematics, to the detriment of science, in order to comply with standards, educators are recommending linking science and literacy instruction (Hand, Prain, & Yore, 1999; Klentschy & Molina-De La Torre, 2004; Pratt & Pratt, 2004; Saul, 2004).

APPLICATIONS TO CLASSROOM PRACTICE

In order for preservice teachers to be ready to teach when they reach their own classrooms, they must be provided with strategies that make sense to them and that they have had experience using. Providing them with lists of strategies without adequate preparation or experience could result in the preservice teachers putting these strategies on a back burner until they gain assurance and confidence as a teacher. To ensure immediate use of a strategy, such as using science notebooks for formative assessment, it is crucial to provide preservice teachers with experiences using the notebooks themselves as students and to require them to visualize and evaluate the positive aspects of the use of notebooks in their future classrooms.

A science methods course where preservice teachers learn about science pedagogy is an optimum situation for beginning teachers to learn about the interdisciplinary connections between science and other disciplines. If preservice teachers feel comfortable writing in science notebooks for a part of their grade as well as understand the value of using their writing to communicate their science understanding, they will be more likely to employ this method when they are in their own classrooms. Preservice teachers should also be asked to consider how their future students might write in science and how they might assess that writing.

It is essential to provide preservice teachers with experiences and instruction on assessment practices other than the summative assessment methods stressed by federal policies. Formative assessment practices have shown evidence of significant learning gains when teachers are provided with thorough professional development on the effectiveness of formative assessment practice such as appropriate feedback, use of feedback to improve teaching, and the ways assessment can motivate students (Bell and Cowie, 2001). According to Black (1998), "the improvement of formative assessment cannot be a simple matter. There is no quick fix that can be added to existing practice with promise of rapid reward" (p. 46). Black stressed that the substantial rewards of formative assessment will only "happen relatively slowly, and through sustained programs of professional development and support" (p. 46).

FOR FURTHER THOUGHT

Science notebooks can be a useful strategy to incorporate into a science methods course, allowing a focus on formative assessment, alternative assessments, students' writing and identification of students' misconceptions.

Some possible assignments to use in a science methods course are:
1. Reflection Paper Assignments.

   (a) How might you use science notebooks to assess your students? Include the strategies you would use and the things you would have students include in their notebooks.
   (b) What do teachers need to require in science notebooks so that student understanding can be assessed?
   (c) Suggest some prompts students could use in their notebooks in order to communicate their understanding of an investigation.

(d)   How could a teacher ensure that students do more writing than simply recording data in a science notebook?

2. Formal Paper. Discuss the use of your science notebook during this course. How was your science notebook used for you to assess your own learning or present your learning to others? How might you use science notebooks in your own teaching?
3. Rubric Assignment. Design a rubric for assessing science notebooks. Clearly describe the criteria necessary to achieve each level.

APPENDIX A

Notebook Questionnaire

1. What was your reaction to using notebooks in the science methods class? Why?
2. How did using notebooks affect your learning of the science content we have covered?
3. How has using notebooks affected or changed your views of science?
4. How has using notebooks affected or changed your views of yourself as a scientist?
5. How will you use science notebooks in your classroom?
6. How will the students you work with react to using science notebooks?
7. Describe how you might use science notebooks as an assessment tool in your classroom.
8. How might you use the notebook you generated in this class in the future?

Appendix B
Preservice Teachers' Science Notebook Rubrics

	1	3	5
Table of Contents Page Nos.	More than two entries not filled out completely. Sloppy work done and little effort put into it. Page numbers not listed.	All but one or two entries completely filled out and labeled correctly. Some missing information but most done correctly.	Clearly written and labeled table of contents, including subject, date, and page numbers for each entry Page numbers are listed correctly.
Illustrations	More than two illustrations left out with inaccurate labels. Drawings done very sloppy, little effort put into the drawings.	All but one or two illustrations are done completely and accurately, with correct labeling.	Clear and accurate drawings are included and labeled correctly for every entry. They are neat and accurate.
Steps	Little effort put into the steps. Not clear what steps were taken and unable to understand what took place during the entry.	Steps are written out, but some are difficult to understand. Not written clearly, but still pretty good effort.	Steps are written out completely and accurately. Reader is able to. clearly understand what steps were taken.
Predictions	Predictions are not included, or little effort was given with no scientific reasoning present.	Predictions are included but not supported through scientific explanations.	Predictions are included with scientific reasoning for their predictions.
Results	Results either not recorded for more than two entries. No effort put into recording the results.	Results were missing for one or two entries, and/or entries are somewhat vague.	Results were clearly labeled for each entry. Reader can easily understand what happened for each step.

Appendix B (Continued)

	1	*3*	*5*
Conclusions	Conclusions are brief and missing the essential parts of the conclusion. Or conclusions are missing altogether.	Conclusions are missing from one or two entries. Some are missing student thought and reasoning, but pretty good effort.	Students clearly write a conclusion to each entry. Included are their thoughts and reasoning for each experiment.

Science Notebook Rubric

Science Notebook Criteria	NA 0	Not Present 1	Lacking 2	Meets 3	Exceeds 4
Inquiry question or purpose • Stated					
Prediction • Stated • Clear, reasonable • Relates to purpose					
Planning • Relates to purpose • Clear, sequential					
Observations • Notes • Diagrams • Data • Materials used					
Conclusions • Based on purpose and evidence • Clear statement of what was learned • Reflection					
Communication • Focused on purpose • Complete • Organized					

Science Notebook Rubric

	5	3	1
Notebook has a clear purpose and states what the student hopes to learn from the inquiry	• Complete • Accurate • Topic that relates to science	• One part missing • Mostly accurate • Topic relates to science	• Not complete • Many inaccuracies • Topic not related to science
Notebook has a prediction of what the student expects his findings to be	• Reasonable • Relates to purpose	• Fairly reasonable • Relates somewhat to purpose	• Not reasonable • Does not relate to purpose
Notebook is organized with a table of contents, numbered pages and title page	• Table of contents • Pages numbered • Title page	• Incomplete table of contents or • Pages not numbered completely	• One or more parts missing • Sloppy
Entries relate to question and includes student generated drawings, charts, graphs, and narratives	• At least 5 drawings • At least 1 chart and graph • Daily narratives	• At least 3 drawings • At least 1 chart or graph • Some narratives	• 2 or less drawings • No chart or graph • Few narratives
Notebook contains conclusion - a clear statement summarizing what was learned - that is reflective and creative	• Conclusion relates to purpose and prediction • Clear summary • Reflective and creative	• Conclusion relates somewhat to purpose • Fairly clear summary • Somewhat reflective	• Conclusion vague or unrelated to purpose • Unclear summary • Little thought demonstrated

REFERENCES

Audet, R. H., Hickman, P., & Dobrynina, G. (1996). Learning logs: A classroom practice for enhancing scientific sense making. *Journal of Research in Science Teaching, 33,* 205–222.

Baxter, G. P., Bass, K. M., & Glasser, R. (2001). Notebook writing in three fifth-grade science classrooms. *The Elementary Science Journal, 102*(2), 123–140.

Bell, B., & Cowie, B. (2001). The characteristics of formative assessment in science education. *Science Education, 85*(5), 536–553.

Black, P. (1998). Formative assessment: Raising standards inside the classroom. *School Science Review, 80*(291), 39–46.

Bogdan, R., & Biklen, S. (1992). *Qualitative research for education: An introduction to theory and methods.* Boston, MA: Allyn & Bacon.

Dougherty, M. J. (1997). Formative assessment: Using an instructional model to improve conceptual learning. *The Science Teacher,* 29–33.

Fellows, N. (1994). A window into thinking: Using student writing to understand conceptual change in science learning. *Journal of Research in Science Teaching, 31,* 985–1001.

Glynn, S. M., & Muth, K. D. (1994). Reading and writing to learn science: Achieving scientific literacy. *Journal of Research in Science Teaching, 31* (9), 1057–1073.

Hand, B., Prain, V., & Yore, L. (2001). Sequential writing tasks' influence on science learning. In G. Rijlaarsdam (Series Ed.) & P. Tynjala, L Mason, & K. Lonka (Vol. Eds.), *Studies in writing: Vol. 7. Writing as a learning tool: Integrating theory into practice* (pp. 105–129). Netherlands: Kluwer.

Klentschy, M. P., & Molina-De La Torre, E. (2004). Students' science notebooks and the inquiry process. In E. W. Saul (Ed.), *Crossing borders in literacy and science instruction* (pp. 340–354). Newark, DE: International Reading Association.

Magnusson, S., Krajcik, J., & Borko,H. (1999). Nature, sources, and development of pedagogical content knowledge for science teaching. In J. Gess-Newsome & N. Lederman (Eds.), *Pedagogical content knowledge and science education* (pp. 95–132). Netherlands: Kluwer.

National Research Council. (1996). *National science education standards.* Washington, DC: National Academy Press.

National Research Council. (2001a). *Knowing what students know: The science and design of educational assessment.* Washington, DC: National Academy Press.

National Research Council. (2001b). *Classroom assessment and the national science education standards.* Washington, DC: National Academy Press.

Pratt, H. & Pratt, N. (2004). Integrating science and literacy instruction with a common goal of learning science content. In E. W. Saul (Ed.), *Crossing borders in literacy and science instruction* (pp. 395–405). Newark, DE: International Reading Association.

Rivard, L. P. (1994). A review of writing to learn in science: Implications for practice and research. *Journal of Research in Science Teaching, 31*(9), 969–983.

Ruiz-Primo, M. A., Li, M., Ayala, C., & Shavelson, R. J. (March, 1999). *Student science journals and the evidence they provide: Classroom learning and opportunity to learn.* Paper presented at the annual NARST meeting, Boston, MA.

Ruiz-Primo, M. A., Li, M., Shavelson, R. J. (2002). Looking into students' science notebooks: What do teachers do with them? (CSE Tech Rep 562). Los Angeles, CA: University of California, Center for the Study of Evaluation.

Ruiz-Primo, M. A., & Li, M. (2004). On the use of students' science notebooks as an assessment tool. *Studies in Educational Evaluation, 30,* 61–85.

Sadler, R. (1989). Formative assessment and the design of instructional systems. *Instructional Science, 18,* 119–144.

Sadler, R. (1998). Formative assessment: Revisiting the territory. *Assessment in Education, 5*(1), 77–84.

Saul, E. W. (2004) Introduction. In E. W. Saul (Ed.), *Crossing borders in literacy and science instruction* (pp. 1–9). Newark, DE: International Reading Association.

Shepardson, D. P., & Britsch, S. J. (1997). Children's science journals: What can students' science journals tell us about what they are learning? *Science and Children, 37*(6), 39–33.

Volkmann, M. J., & Abell, S. K. (2003). Seamless assessment. *Science & Children, 40*(8), 41–45.

12

Using Critical Literacy in the Science Classroom

Ingrid Graves
Indiana University

Teddie Phillipson-Mower
University of Lovisville

The human being is a profoundly complex organism. Childhood begins with the innate ability to question, beginning with the proverbial "no" in questioning an adult's authority to the more complex "why?" The need to know and understand is replicated with essential comments from children such as, "Mommie, why is the sky blue?" and "Daddy, where do babies come from?" These scientifically situated questions meet with mixed responses depending on those to whom the questions have been posed but are very real contextually based inquiry.

Although there are differences between children's science and the western science practiced by scientists, it is well accepted that children engage in inquiry as they explore and test their environment to make sense of their world. In science education, as well as in elementary education in general, there has been a return to a more organic inquiry-based acquisition of knowledge that builds on the student's interests, experiences, strengths, and needs (Harste, Short, & Burke, 1988; National Research Council, 1996; Raphael et al., 1992; Wells, 1986). This attention to the student's prior knowledge and experience as a necessary starting place for teaching and learning is based on constructivist learning theory.

Theorists such as Gutierrez, Rymes, and Larson (1995) challenge teachers to form more inclusive forms of instruction by understanding the interplay of communities and schools by employing critical literacy into the reading and writing classroom. From a more anthropological framework, there is recognition that children are always in the process of learning whether or not a teacher or adult is in the active process of explicit instruction. Other theorists (Erickson, 1982; Freebody & Herschell, 2000) who examine identity through discursive practice explain that students are routinely engaged in moral decisions about what constitutes acting as a student. These procedures usually involve completing a clearly delineated series of tasks that end with the ability to comprehend and know clearly identifiable things. Understanding is placed in clearly identifiable cultural and moral reference groups.

Candela, Rockwell, and Coll (2004) point out the notion of incidental learning which possibly can strengthen misconceptions of scientific principles in that these conceptions were never explicitly attended to. When students build knowledge on scientifically inaccurate preconceptions (weak foundations), they tend to try to make sense of the new information within their old inaccurate frameworks. For this reason, students may tenaciously hold on to their misconceptions, not because they did not learn the content but that new knowledge may not gel well with the old.

Additionally there is an increase in pressure in the United States and in Europe to assess teaching and learning through standardized measures. These standardized tests require students to give scientifically acceptable answers. According to Keeley, Eberle, and Farrin (2005), "a major challenge for science teachers is to build conceptual bridges from student's own ideas to scientifically accepted views" (p. 4). This challenge to build bridges to new information has the potential to leave elementary teachers with multiple view points and forms of information that are never challenged or questioned and blindly accepting that any sort of scientific view in the end is acceptable. This could have the effect of leaving students in states described by Perry (1970) of dualism, where science (Authority) always provides the right answers or multiplicity, the wherein all opinions are equally valid. Routinely teachers in these Perry Positions are left wondering at what point students will learn the "right" answers for the test. The philosophical framework from which Keely et al. come from should be addressed. Constructivism, or interactive teaching methods, is often advocated without attention to the epistemic and ontological commitments. Matthews (1994) points out that this is one of the difficulties with constructivism in teaching, "it frequently overreaches itself. It uses claims about learning processes and developmental psychology (the heart of constructivism) to establish educational and social positions." Western science establishes a public standard through the open communication of ideas and critical peer review of the evidence. While the resulting product of this public standard is both tentative and durable, it is the accepted measure of "reality" in science. Philosophical frameworks that deny reality reduce "knowledge" to a "belief."

According to Denzin and Lincoln (2003), "critical theorists tend to locate the foundations of truth in specific historical, economic, racial, and social infrastructures of oppression, injustice and marginalization." The basis for critical theorists is grounded in duality, raised consciousness and the possibility of social change. The basic premises of truth and power, the essence and mode of the transformation of power relations, and provided the discourse that allows researchers to talk to each other about specific classroom practices that involve speaking one's power, knowledge, and identity.

We contend that critical literacy and a critical stance become an imperative and effective cognitive function of the classroom that has the potential to allow students the opportunity to reach their own conclusions, build their own knowledge base consistent with a variety of cultural models, and take personal ownership of the knowledge they take from a given context Early research in the field of assessment (Graves, 2001; Hickey, DeCuir, Hand, & Kyser, 2002; Lemke, 1990; NRC, 2003) backs up this claim by showing that using argumentation and effective discursive practices in the elementary classroom has a positive effect on high stakes tests. Additionally, the Benchmarks for Science Literacy (AAAS, 1993) state that evidence and logical reasoning are at the core of scientific inquiry and students should "understand what constitutes good reasoning, and practice judging reasons in others' arguments and in their own."

ARGUMENTATION IN LANGUAGE ARTS AND SCIENCE

What we know about learning and the teaching of language arts and science instruction has shifted dramatically over that last 50 years. Initial understanding of the reading process in any genre focused primarily at the word level with instruction centered on the use of phonetic rules and formulas.[1] Using transactional theory (Halliday, 1980; Rosenblatt, 1978; Wells, 1986) to guide instruction, meaning occurs through interaction with the reader and text. Readers construct meaning in the internal cognitive space

---

[1] Which always seem to change their meaning and are very difficult to understand out of context.

of the mind and the knowledge one gains from the text is dependent on the reader. This type of knowledge transmission is dependent on the reader having contextual knowledge and understanding of the subject matter. The teacher is expected to supplement instruction or use the text as official representation of knowledge.

From a modernist perspective (Street, 1984), reading and the linguistic process are used to transmit knowledge and cultural norms. Readers are expected to learn through formal instruction, which often privileges some ways of knowing above other ways. For example, science may be taught as the sole source of objective knowledge and truth. In perhaps a response to monolithic forms of inquiry, postmodernist perspectives seek to decenter the subject and instead claim that language is central to the production of knowledge, including scientific knowledge, which can be most readily found in discourse. In general, the postmodernist position is critical of truth claims and monological texts or readings, recognizing that teaching is a political endeavor. There is a fundamental acknowledgement that truth claims, and transmission of its forms, involve a certain degree of power and that *sponsors of literacy*[2] are those who are in direct control of socially reproduced norms. As part of the postmodern movement, critical theorists (Luke, Freebody, & Land, 1997; Young, 1992) contend that reading and information cannot be separated from the cultural, historical, and political context in which they were written. In western science education, constructivism holds that science is a human endeavor that is socially and culturally embedded and tentative yet durable. However, where postmodernism and extensions of constructivist learning theory move from here to claims that all knowledge is relative, western science requires on the one hand that knowledge is held against a public standard with claims that are based in evidence while depending on the notion that the advancement of scientific knowledge relies on challenging ideas of truth against a public standard. Our theoretical problem arises at the intersection where science, postmodernism, and social constructivism come together. We are left wondering if they can indeed be fused despite the fact that postmodernism is not subject to skeptical argument in light of the notion that truth in an absolute sense does not exist.

Definition of Critical Literacy in the Context of Building Argumentation Strategies

As we struggle to fuse the ability to engage in critical discourse with science principals, we are reminded of the interdisciplinary nature of elementary

---

[2]Deborah Brandt (2001).

classrooms. National Science Education Standards (NRC, 1999) currently expect teachers to engage in inquiry and constructivism as organizing frameworks. Teachers in the elementary setting focus on student understanding and use scientific knowledge, ideas, and inquiry processes to guide students in active and extended scientific inquiry. Gee (2004) points out that, "a child in a science classroom engaged in real inquiry and not passive learning, must be willing to take on an identity as a certain type of scientific thinker, problem solver..." (p. 53). This active identity as a scientific thinker does not emerge simply by providing inquiry-based lessons. Teachers may also need to directly instruct students in the socially acceptable method through which argumentation in a classroom setting might be used to legitimize both ones identity as well as ones knowledge.

Lewison, Flint, and Van Sluys (2002) described the journey of elementary school teachers as they learned to negotiate the use of critical literacy in their own classrooms through the support of workshops. Teachers were surprised to find the increased engagement of students in literature discussions. They also grew in their awareness of "how sociopolitical systems and power relationships impact [their] teaching" (p. 389). Additionally, the researchers found that the multiple perspectives method of instruction stood in direct opposition to the heritage of the testing model found in most schools. For the purposes of this chapter, the term critical literacy is used as that described by Lewison, et al. (2002) that focused on four primary categories; (a) disrupting the common place, (b) interrogating multiple viewpoints, (c) examining sociopolitical aspects of the text, and (d) taking action and/or promoting social justice.

Expounding on the notion of critical literacy is not a new idea in language arts and social studies (Lewison, Flint, & Van Sluys, 2002) and has been used effectively to engage students in active class discussions, to build comprehension as well as to become actively involved in problem solving through service learning, peace initiatives, and so forth, however little has been written about critical literacy as it might be effectively incorporated into content areas such as math and science. This lack of incorporation in these areas may have more to do with the philosophical associations and assumptions associated with critical theory than with the possible outcomes. In addition, most preservice and practicing teachers of both elementary and secondary levels have experienced science as "a rhetoric of conclusions" (Schwab, 1962) involving disconnected right answers. The uncertainty, social and cultural implications, use of a theoretical lens, and rules of evidence that define science as one way of knowing are seldom addressed and reflected on. Because teachers teach as they were taught (or were not taught but modeled), the challenge here is to use critical literacy to enhance scientific exploration.

Critical Literacy From the Perspective of a Scientist

As expected, many science curriculums are examining methods through which a curriculum can provide opportunities for scientific discussion and debate among students while at the same time continually assessing student understanding. This demonstrates support for the building of a classroom community through cooperation, shared responsibility, and respect. The National Science Education Standards Board continues with this theme when they state that,

> Science teaching must involve students in inquiry-oriented investigations in which they interact with their teachers and peers. Students establish connections between their current knowledge of science and the scientific knowledge found in many sources; they apply science content to new questions; they engage in problem solving, planning, decision making, and group discussions; and they experience assessments that are consistent with an active approach to learning. (National Science Education Standards, 1996, p. 20)

Additionally, as expected, there are also active discussions surrounding reform issues in the scientific community. Windschitl (2006) points out that "students have ideas about science that everyday classroom activity never reveals." He also points out that, "people's core values and beliefs are not that easily changed" (p. 355). Using a critical stance, students learn to examine scientific knowledge from multiple perspectives with students bringing in the evidence for and against a particular stance. For instance, deeper comprehension of the solar system can be derived from early writings done from theories of earth as the center of the solar system to early writings of astronomers who were attempting to prove that the earth revolved around the sun. Students learn the history, the societal aspects of why scientific theories come to pass and, in some cases, the contradictions that lead to the evolution of scientific theories. Most important is the notion that science by its very nature is transformed by changing empirical data,[3] informed by more clearly identifiable information. Employing a critical stance is not always that comfortable within scientific endeavors. The facts and knowledge that drive our understanding of the world are long held and significantly impact the manner in which research in

---

[3]According to NOS, scientific knowledge is subject to change with new observations and with reinterpretations of existing observations.

science is both perceived and taught. The scientific method[4] is used in order to substantiate claims.

Zeidler, Sadler, Berson, and Fogelman (2003) point out several cases where cultural bias has been at the heart of "scientific" claims. Noting instances where social norms were reflective of the greater community and using "data-driven" information to justify the oppression of individuals, they point out the need for teachers to "combat the blind acceptance of any authority without critical evaluation" (p. 144) Whether consciously done or not, marginalized students may find themselves internalizing the notion of exclusion as a reflection of their own lived experience.[5]

THEORY INTO PRACTICE

Originally one of the authors incorporated critical literacy into her elementary reading methods class in order to allow preservice teachers the opportunity to understand the manner in which some students in their classes might be marginalized by the type of literacy activities found in a typical mainstream classroom. Each semester, as a class activity, they were asked to critically evaluate K–12 textbooks to find perspectives and voices that seemed to be missing from the text. In one of the textbooks, a student found a paragraph describing the Southwest with a picture of the Alamo next to it. This example proved to be an effective way to benignly incorporate multiple viewpoints. Using examples of social studies textbooks that showed Native Americans in traditional "tribal" costumes,[6] preservice elementary teachers

---

[4]Center for Science, Mathematics, and Engineering Education (1996) embedded in the notion of the scientific method is the need to (1) form a testable hypothesis and "demonstrate appropriate procedures, a knowledge base, and conceptual understanding of scientific investigations," (2) learn the major concepts in the area under investigation, (3) collect evidence to prove hypothesis, (4) formulate an explanation, (5) recognize alternative explanations and models, and (6) learn to effectively communicate findings both written and oral.

[5]Most problematic are those students who are living with categorical labeling such as at-risk minority, bilingual, low socioeconomic status (SES) and other factors from purely biological standpoints such as the hyphenated American (i.e., African-American, Asian-American, and Native-American).

[6]Many indigenous populations would prefer the garment to be regarded as religiously significant and not "tribal costumes." I would like to also add that textbooks are becoming more and more sensitive to many aspects of the American experience and we are not attempting to criticize the textbooks in any way. We are simply attempting to move students into a new method of "seeing the world."

were asked to consider the type of stereotypes that had the potential to be perpetuated. During this process of exploring the nature of bias found in textbooks, we broadened our perspectives by engaging preservice elementary teachers in the examination of math and science textbooks. In an effort to make science accessible to students with physical challenges, a class period each semester was devoted to the discussion of how to design science lessons that would take into consideration diverse needs. We then carried this notion of diversity into discussions of what children from diverse backgrounds might think of the big bang theory if they had been brought up with differing perspectives on the origins of the universe. What differing perspectives would come to bear when competing metaphorical cultural representations of the universe came into direct conflict with that found in the science community? What were the potentials in the classroom to replicate marginalization through the monolithic style of presenting theories? What internal and external conflict might arise in the classroom when specific subject matter was presented? Did this conflict really matter? Most importantly, could one use this conflict as space for marginalized perspectives and identities the opportunity to practice the language of the science community?

In the science methods classroom, attention was paid to developing critical thinkers who asked for evidence for stated claims, who could detect false reasoning in arguments and assertions, who understood the difference between knowledge and opinion, who sought to identify sources of biases among advocates and detractors of ideas, and who could describe possible social and cultural consequences of science. In doing this, a couple of methods were employed. The first involved learning how to structure a debate using Johnson and Johnson's Structured Controversy Model as guidance. Individually, students write about their ideas on the topic statement. This provides clarity for their original positions. Next, they are asked to give reasons for their ideas, arguments that could be made against their ideas, how they would counter these arguments, and what evidence they would use doing this. Following this, students were randomly assigned to two teams, for and against the topic statement, and required to repeat the steps as a team. They are encouraged to draw from each individual's statements and required to investigate literature, provided and individually attained, to help support their position and anticipate possible rebuttals. Once this stage is completed, the students are asked to count off by 2s and placed into new teams. Initially this meets with resistance because each team has developed an identity in realtionship to the issue. The work done up to this point has only been shared within each group, which has the tendency to reinforce the "rightness" of the group's argument. However, after the formation of new groups, the arguments developed previously have a better chance of being scrutinized and leads to separation of 'fact' from opinion. Furthermore, this attention to forming better arguments and rebuttals provides justification for the regrouping. Through peer interaction and teacher guidance, students learn about credibility of sources, the importance and types of evidence to back up claims, "poking holes" in claims, and social and cultural components and consequences of decision making.

The second strategy used in the science classroom involved a modified electricity lesson plan created by former graduate student, Debi Hanuscin, a simulation, and a science materials and textbook analysis. Two students were given ear plugs, two students were blindfolded, two students were asked to use wheelchairs, and two students were given written directions and materials that were nonsensical. The class was told that no special provisions would be made for these individuals because we needed to "get through the material." The "engage" stage of the five E lesson plan uses a magic ball that lights up and makes noise when it is involved in a closed circuit. The teacher, without speaking, shows the class various ways to create a circuit to turn on the magic ball. Throughout the explore stage, the students are asked to use their senses and abilities to explore various concepts of electricity. The students are brought together in the explain stage to discuss the science concepts being presented with explanations being sought from those with "special needs." These students are generally frustrated and more than willing to turn the discussion to the importance of special provisions to ensure access to classroom participation. These ideas are implemented in the extend stage with a follow-up discussion on possible revisions. Science textbook and materials analysis followed with the first author guiding discussion on the marginalization of groups of individuals and the second author facilitating discussion on the misrepresentation of how science is done—the scientific method, and the image of what science is.

Our interest lies with the effects that taking a critical stance in a scientific context might have on both misconceptions students retain after they have been instructed otherwise and the conditions in which a deep understanding of a scientific theory might be generalizable to other domain-specific dimensions of knowledge production.

Methods and Participants

We examined the notions that preservice teachers at the university brought to both an elementary language arts and science curriculum by asking the question, "Is intelligent design science?" What is the difference between creativity in language arts and science? What does it mean to be creative in expository text as opposed to scientific inquiry? We argue that linguistic practices in these two settings are similar but are based on significantly different representations of knowledge.

Reform documents indicate that students starting in K–2 should receive instruction in the evolution of life (AAAS, 1993; NRC, 1996). However, few teachers, especially at the elementary level, have had coursework in evolution or have even a basic understanding of what evolution is. Coupled with the controversy of the idea of intelligent design fronted by the Discovery Institute and the general public's misunderstanding of what science can and cannot address, we can understand why the topic of evolution is bypassed. Furthermore, research has not clearly addressed best practices in this important area at the elementary level. Nelson (NSTA, 2000) advocates six strategies that include active learning; teaching critical thinking processes instead of a set of conclusions; encouraging students to develop criteria to judge the strength of scientific theories; positioning evolution in terms of scientific strength among other scientific theories (evolution is much stronger); helping students understand that those with differing views disagree about consequences; and taking into account the students' intellectual and ethical developmental levels when structuring approaches. More recently, Verhey (2005) contrasted the teaching of evolution in a traditional sense and discussions comparing intelligent design with evolution along with a focus on the nature of science. Undergraduates in the traditional course produced almost no change in their views of evolution whereas those involved in the comparison group were found to have developed much more scientifically viable views.

PRACTICAL USE OF CRITICAL THEORY TO ENGAGE STUDENTS

The Evolution Debate

Recent controversy surrounding the teaching of intelligent design seems to place many educators in uncomfortable positions. Striving to design classroom inquiry that would explore the use of critical literacy in the science classroom while at the same time challenge university students, we chose to focus on the recent debate over the inclusion of intelligent design in classrooms around the country. Cognitively, much of what students process and internalize is not necessarily empirical in nature. Most learn the norms of their community through the socialization process, not from teachers or the text. Both intelligent design and evolution compromise similar dogmatic stances; the difference is held only in the "proofs" that are allowed to enter the dialogue.

Advocates of teaching intelligent design or creationism along with evolution make assumptions that if taught, they will be taught as equally valid or with evolution being critiqued and others not (Wallis, 2005). This is both morally and factually wrong. If intelligent design is taught in the science classroom it must be held to the same scientific rigor and critique as evolution (Nelson, 2005).

Scientific minds evolve and scientific model must be learned through practice. As scientists, we should be willing to mentor students into the nature of collecting evidence by collecting it. In the process, students become more capable of sorting empirical data into that which can either be measured or considered endurable.

A learning unit, which seems to produce deep thought for a broad range of students K–16, is one that is designed to provoke active involvement of most students. We chose to begin a unit on evolution by reading a creation story from around the world, mindful that one should discuss creation stories as versions of people's culture not as an opportunity to discredit sources outside of scientific debate. We discuss the fact that these histories have been passed on, in many cases for over 10,000 years, and embedded in cultural perspectives.

Next, the class was asked to read the following "warning label" recently placed in science textbooks.

Disrupting the Commonplace

> "This textbook contains material on evolution. Evolution is a theory, not a fact, regarding the origin of living things. This material should be approached with an open mind, studied carefully and critically considered." Sticker was placed in science textbooks in Dover, PA and Cobb county, GA. (NSBA, 2006)

We continued with the lesson by critically examining the warning label for problematic knowledge or understanding. What do the writers want you to know or understand after reading this text? Do I agree or disagree? What motivates me to disagree? After this discussion, students are asked to learn of how school has changed since its inception in the United States by examining artifacts. We then moved on to using the critical literacy guide (Table 12.1) to examine the evolution debate within cultural and historical context. Students follow the historical timeline of evolution in the public schools by critically examining the history of Darwin and evolution debate through examination of excerpts from original artifacts from the following resources.

- 1859—Darwin published *On the Origin of Species by Means of Natural Selection, or the Preservation of Favoured Races in the Struggle for Life.* Natural selection added to the field of philosophy.

- 1925—Scopes "Monkey Trial"—transcripts from trial, political cartoons from the era.
- 1982—*McLean v. Arkansas Board of Education*, 529 F. Supp. 1255 [ED Ark. 1982]; the judge ruled that "creation science" did not qualify as a scientific theory.
- 1987—United States Supreme Court outlawed the teaching of creationism in public schools.
- 2003—NSTA Board of Directors publish position statement on the teaching of evolution stating the board "strongly supports the position that evolution is a major unifying concept in science and should be included in the K–12 science education frameworks and curricula." NSTA www.nsta.org
- 2004—Ninth-grade biology teachers in Dover, Pa., must include "intelligent design" in their instruction. http://www.csmonitor.com/2004/1123/p11s02-legn.html
- 2004—Wisconsin, the Grantsburg school board voted to allow teachers to discuss various theories of creation in their classrooms, opening the door to intelligent design.
- 2005–2006—Litigation continues for and against intelligent design vs. creationism as currently taught in schools. (Pew, 2006)

As students learn to critically read text the students should ask the following questions:

1. Who is supposed to read the text?
2. How is the text attempting to convince me to accept a position?
3. What if I don't agree with the position taken in the text?
4. What are we supposed to learn from the text? Why?
5. Whose voice is missing? Pay attention to and learn to seek out voices of marginalized people or perspectives.
6. How does the use of multiple perspectives change how I read the text?
7. How can we us the knowledge created in the classroom to improve the greater community?
8. How are the scientific principles/thought process used within the text?
9. What empirical evidence is presented?

TABLE 12.1
Critical Literacy Guide

Name of Artifact/Article	How is This Text Trying to Position Me?	Whose Voice is Missing?	So What? Why Does This Matter?
1859-Excerpts from *The Origin of the Species* (Darwin, 1995)			
1925-Excerpts from Scopes Monkey Trial (Liner, 2006)			
1982- Findings of *McLean v. Arkansas Board of Education*			
1987- United States Supreme Court ruling on outlawing creationism in public schools			
2003- NSTA Board of Directors Position Statement on the teaching of Evolution			
2004-Newspaper article ninth-grade biology teachers in Dover, PA must teach "intelligent design" (NSBA, 2006)			
2004- National School Boards Association news article			

Taking Action and/or Promoting Social Justice.   Perhaps the imperative of critical literacy is this last challenge to the classroom, that of taking action or promoting social justice. In our setting, the social justice to be found is the recognition that as elementary school teachers, we position students in certain ways. The challenge toward social justice here should be to seek multiple methods through which students are able to learn the same content. Students have the opportunity to write evolution lesson plans for their future classrooms that will include content from the standards, science for all (inclusion and valuing all belief systems), and attention to the nature of science with an emphasis on how they would teach NOS.

Most importantly is the need to comprehend that some students will never accept evolution (or scientific theories for that matter) as a lived reality or meld the need to use their moral base to make sense of new scientific knowledge. As teachers, we need to be very careful not to reject out-of-hand this information as it becomes part of the discourse but learn to use all student voices to engage in Western scientific inquiry.

RESULTS AND DISCUSSION

Interesting for us was the fact that despite the intense involvement with the scientific context of intelligent design and evolution theories, students left the lesson with unchanged philosophies about evolution. The vast majority of students felt that intelligent design could be considered a science because one could apply scientific methods (as taught in their university science course). Few students felt intelligent design could not be considered a science because scientific "claims" could not be empirically measured. We were particularly interested in the fact that students felt empowered to answer the questions in response to their personal religious convictions and their enculturation into the elementary mindset of the university, which is to respect all viewpoints. As such, we concluded that students have a tendency to pick out and pay attention to only those facts that support their own belief system or that which is perceived to be true of the educational system. Students in lower developmental stages would not have the ability to use or understand the rules of evidence involved in justifying ones position. For some students, evidence has no meaning in a world where knowledge is always certain and given to them through authority. Second, unlike students that sign up for an evolution or other science course, we have found that elementary preservice teachers feel less capable of doing science than do their secondary peers. For some, science content background is at an elementary level and their experience with higher order thinking skills such as judging, analyzing, synthesizing, and drawing conclusions based on deep scientific understanding is limited. Third, western school systems value individualism, equal time, and a democratic tradition. This misleads the public into a false idea that all ideas are equally valid. However, science is not democratic. One can interpret reality through multiple lenses but in science, this information does not constitute scientific validity. We found the use of this exercise most useful when explaining to preservice teachers the misconceptions of scientific thought, using the exercise to further classroom discussions around the difference between multiplicity in language arts and that found in the science curriculum. Additionally, we found that after thoughtful discussions, students were more able to synthesize new scientific information in a manner that was meaningful to a particular setting.

CONCLUSION

As students learn how to ask questions in a way that stimulates thought instead of simply soliciting answers, the potential for deep scientific understanding occurs. Using a critical lens, students can begin to use scientific methods toward a more thoughtful understanding of scientific theories and contextually based application of facts. For some educators, the prospect of moving away from traditional models of instruction can seem daunting, however, many preservice teachers, who have engaged in critically examining basal readers and science textbooks, have come to realize the importance of seeing knowledge from the perspective of the learner. Additionally, the intersection of context and legitimacy cannot be ignored when it comes to effectively engaging learners whose comprehension of the world is not necessarily shared by those found in the science classroom. Through active discussions, multiple perspectives, and the right to know, children become active participants in their own enlightenment.

From an educator's perspective, we should remember that there are certain truths that will never be changed. As such, perhaps the answer to the question of is intelligent design a science, lies not with the answer but with the question. The question should be changed to how well did my students learn to use scientific inquiry?

APPLICATIONS TO CLASSROOM PRACTICE

Currently there are no less than 100 articles (Pew, 2006) discussing aspects of intelligent design. The National Center for Science Education as well as science and science education organizations (for example, AAAS and NSTA) are fighting to keep Intelligent Design out of the science classroom, some communities and School Boards with help from the Discovery Institute are fighting to include multiple perspectives of the origins of the universe (Hopkins, 2006; Wilgoren, 2006). The debate has the potential to cause a significant gulf between schools and communities but on a more positive note, holds an abundance of rich materials through which scientific hypothesizing can be directed. With careful thought, I believe the metacognitive skills needed while learning to use scientific reasoning can be realized.

FOR FURTHER THOUGHT

Before critical stances to content can effectively be implemented in your classroom, it is imperative that students feel safe. Safe to bring knowledge to the classroom that might not be shared by others. Therefore, teachers K–16 should answer important questions about the incorporation of critical literacy activities before engaging in such.

1. Does your classroom community support diverse perspectives?
2. In this light, students should be mentored into acceptable classroom discursive practices and have ample opportunity to practice less offensive or controversial subjects before endeavoring to engage in controversial issues.
3. In K–12 settings, one should actively engage parents as well as community members in discourse in order to afford them the opportunity to become active participants in the knowledge base you bring to the learning environment. Additionally, in some cultural contexts, alternative discursive practices hold the potential to bring contentious subjects into what might seem to be very clear notions of traditional teaching strategies.

Questions you might want to contemplate before implementing critical literacy in your classroom:

1. How can you adapt critical literacy activities into your particular classroom/context?
2. What difficulties might arise as you learn to implement critical literacy in your particular context? What will you do if students use disparaging words such as "that is stupid" or "where did you get that?"
3. What constitutes critical literacy? Is it action or simply the activity of learning to see the world through a new lens?
4. What difficulties might arise in your particular setting when you begin to turn over the responsibility of learning to your students?

5. What is it that you really want students to learn? Would it be more advantageous to delve deeply into this topic? What are the distinctive characteristics between surface and deep understanding of this topic? How do you propose to assess what has been learned?[7]

REFERENCES

American Association for the Advancement of Science. (1993). *Benchmarks for science literacy: A project 2061 report*. New York: Oxford University Press.

Brandt, D. (2001). *Literacy in American lives*. New York: Cambridge University Press.

Candela, A., Rockwell, E., & Coll, C. (2004). What in the world happens in classrooms?: Qualitative classroom research. *European Educational Research Journal*, *3*(3), 692–713.

Center for Science, Mathematics, and Engineering Education. (1996). *National Science Education Standards* [National Committee on Science Education Standards and Assessment]. Washington, DC: National Academies Press

Darwin, C. (1995). *The origin of the species*. New York: Gramercy.

Denzin, N., & Lincoln, Y. (Eds.). (2003). *The landscape of qualitative research: Theories and issues* (2nd ed.) Thousand Oaks, CA: Sage.

Erickson, F. (1982). Classroom discourse as improvisation: Relationship between academic task structures and social participation structures in lessons. In L. C. Wilkinson (Ed.) *Communicating in the classroom* (pp. 153–181). New York: Academic Press.

Freebody, P., & Herschell, P. (2000) The interactive assembly of social identity: The case of latitude in classroom talk. *International Journal of Inclusive Education*, *4*(1), 43–61.

Gee, J. (2004). *What video games have to teach us about learning and literacy*. New York: Plagraves Macmillian.

Graves, I. (2001). *Teaching in a high stakes testing environment: One teacher's practices and perspectives*. Unpublished master's thesis, Texas Tech University, Lubbock, Texas.

Gutierrez, K., Rymes, B., & Larson, J. (1995). Scripts, counter scripts, and underlife in the classroom: James Brown versus Brown v. Board of Education. *Harvard Educational Review*, *65*, 445–471.

Halliday, M. (1980). Three aspects of children's language development: Learning language, learning through language, learning about language. In Y. Goodman, M. H. Haussler, & D. Strickland (Eds.), *Oral and written language development research* (pp. 7–19). Urbana, IL: National Council of Teachers of English.

Harste, J., Short, K., & Burke, C. (1988). *Creating classrooms for authors: The reading-writing connection*. Portsmouth, NH: Heinemann.

Hickey, D. T., DeCuir, J, Hand, B., & Kyser, B. (2002, April). *Technology-supported formative and summative assessment of collaborative scientific inquiry*. Paper

presented at the Annual Meeting of the American Educational Research
Association, New Orleans.

Hopkins, M. (2006). The talkorigins archive: Exploring the creation/evolution
controversy. Retrieved January 20, 2006 from http://www.talkorigins.org/
fagu/organizations

Keeley, P., Eberle, F., & Farrin, L. (2005). *Uncovering student ideas: 25 formative
assessment probes*. Arlington, VA: NSTA Press.

Lemke, J. (1990). Talking *science: Language, learning, and values*. Norwood, NJ:
Ablex.

Lewison, M., Flint, A., & Van Sluys, K. (2002). Taking on Critical Literacy: The
Journey of Newcomers and Novices. *Language Arts*, 79(5), 382–392.

Liner, D. (2006). Tennessee vs. John Scopes: The Monkey Trial. In *Famous Trials in
American History*. Retrieved January 20, 2006 http://www.law.umkc.edu/
faculty/projects/ftrials/scopes/scopes.htm

Luke, A., Freebody, P., & Land, R. (1997). Shaping the social practices of reading.
In S. Muspratt, A. Luke, & P. Freebody (Eds.), *Constructing critical literacies*
(pp. 185–225). Cresskill, NJ: Hampton Press.

Matthews, M. R. (1994). *Science teaching: The role of history and philosophy of science*.
New York: Rutledge.

National Center for Science Education. (2006). *Defending the teaching of evolution in
the public schools*. Retrieved January 17, 2006 from http://www.ncseweb.org/

National Research Council. (2003). Bridging the gap between large-scale and
classroom assessment: Workshop report. In J. M. Atkin (Chair) *Committee on
assessment in support of instruction and learning*. Retrieved January 27, 2006
fromhttp://www7.nationalacademies.org/bota/Bridging_the_Gap.html

National School Boards Association. (2006). Alexandria, VA. Retrieved January 20,
2006 from https://secure.nsba.org/site/doc_cosa.asp?TRACKID=&DID=
34983&CID=164

NSTA. (2003). *Position statement on the teaching of evolution*. Retrieved January 21,
2006 from www.ncst.org.

Nelson, C.E. (2000) Effective strategies for teaching controversial topics. In James
W. Skehan and Craig E. Nelson (Eds.) *The Creation Controversy and the Science
Classroom* (pp. 19–47). Arlington: NSTA Press.

Perry, W. G., Jr. (1970). *Forms of intellectual and ethical development in the college years:
A scheme*. New York: Holt, Rinehardt, & Winston.

Pew Forum on Religion and Public Life. Retrieved January 17, 2006 http://pewfo-
rum.org Washington, DC.

Rosenblatt, L. (1978). *The reader, the text and the poem*. Carbondale, IL: Southern
Illinois University Press.

Schwab, J. (1962). The teaching of science as inquiry. In J. Schwab & P. Brandwein
(Eds.), *The teaching of science* (pp. 1–103). Cambridge, MA: Harvard University
Press.

Street,B. (1984). *Literacy in theory and practice*. Cambridge: CUP.

Verhey, S. (2005). The effect of enaging prior learning on student attitudes toward creationism and evolution. *Bioscience, 55*(11), 996–1003.

Wallis, C. (Aug 15, 2005) The evolution wars. *Time*, p. 0.

Wells, G. (1986). *The meaning makers: Children learning language and using language to learn*. Portsmouth, NH: Heinemann.

Wilgoren, J. (2006). In evolution debate, a counter attack. *New York Times*. January 1, 2006, page 3.

Windschitl, M. (2006). Why we can't talk to each one another about science education reform. *Phi Delta Kappan, 87*(5) 348–355.

Young, R. (1992). *Critical theory and classroom talk*. Philadelphia: Multilingual Matters, Ltd.

Zeidler, D., Sadler, D., Berson, M., & Fogelman, A. (2002). Bad science and its social implications. *Education Reform, 66*, 134–146.

13

CLASP: An Approach to Helping Teachers Interpret Children's Science Journaling

Susan J. Britsch
Purdue University

Daniel Philip Shepardson
Purdue University

For several years we have been working with teachers on the integration of science and literacy through children's journaling as a teaching, learning, and assessment tool. Recently our work was supported by the Toyota USA Foundation, which funded our *Children's Literacy and Science Project* (CLASP). The aim of CLASP was to collaborate with teachers on the integration of science with literacy in the elementary school curriculum through children's self-produced journals. A key component to this professional development was the enhancement of teachers' abilities to take a more multimodal stance toward the use of science journaling; that is, the incorporation of representational resources beyond the written word. For many teachers, this requires not only a new way of thinking about scientific literacy but also sustained practice in ways of incorporating both linguistic and extralinguistic resources into science journaling. In this chapter, we detail what we have learned about ways of engaging teachers as intellectual and reflective practitioners in learning to look at children's science journaling beyond the written word as the sole means of constructing and conveying both knowledge and science experience. First, however, we provide a brief review of the literature in order to locate our work within a more multimodal approach to scientific literacy. We next provide a general description of CLASP as a context for understanding our collaboration with teachers. Finally, we detail two experiences, the first addressing ways of analyzing children's journal work and the second presenting a case study that illustrates just such an analysis by a teacher.

PERSPECTIVE

To begin, our view of scientific literacy involves more than acquainting children with the use of technical terminology or specific written genres (Martin, 1993). In fact, Maienschein (1998) differentiates scientific literacy from science literacy; whereas science literacy involves knowledge of science facts and information, scientific literacy consists of the acquisition of scientific thinking processes, the ability to conceptualize and view phenomena as scientists do. Although children's journaling in science (through drawing and writing) can be linked with this view of scientific literacy, journals can assist children in making observations, in remembering events, and in communicating understandings instead of simply retaining science facts. By creating their own journal entries, children are able to depict their ways of seeing and understanding science phenomena, constructing or reconstructing these phenomena through their own lens of experience (Britsch, 2001; Shepardson, 1997). In addition, through the use of visual and written modes, children's journal entries express their differing perceptions of salient versus tangential elements of the science experience, and their "emerging sense of 'scientificness'" (Kress, Jewitt, Ogborn, & Tsatsarelis, 2001, p. 140) through their uses of visual and verbal language for different purposes.

Children's science journals can also serve as assessment tools for the teacher, as guides to the development and nature of children's science understanding (Elstgeest, Harlen, & Symington, 1985) as well as diagnostic tools that inform teacher practice (Shepardson & Britsch, 2001). Because students convey their science understandings through writing and drawing, journals provide a window for viewing these ideas (Britsch, 2001; Doris, 1991). The purpose of CLASP is to help teachers examine what children's science journals can reveal about what children are learning, and how these journals can best be used in the elementary classroom for interdisciplinary science-literacy teaching, learning, and assessment.

In the current society, however, all students are disserved if classroom instruction treats "...literacy (or language) as the sole, the main, let alone the major means for representation and communication" (Kress, 2003,

p. 35). Students need the ability to create and carry out meanings via channels other than language alone. CLASP views science journaling as a process that encompasses the visual image as well as the use of oral and written language (Kress, 2003; Manguel, 2000; Shaw-Miller, 2002). Science journals do not simply contain a set of genre templates to be superimposed on a given science activity. Instead, the journaling experience incorporates visual as well as verbal language through which students synthesize science and literacy instead of taking each as a separate domain that is independently taught. This means that, in the context of science-literacy inquiry, child-composed science journals function as more than artifacts or products. The science journal, as part of scientific literacy, enhances children's familiarity with scientific ways of thinking and knowing, thus contributing to their participation in the culture of science on a personal and social level. Thus, children's science journals work as an integral part of the investigation—not simply as a duplication of the investigation.

The teacher, too, conveys a particular notion about science by means of the instructional approach taken, requiring the children to use their journals in different ways. The instructional approach can be made richer or poorer according to the teacher's own scientific understanding. In addition, the teacher's view of scientific literacy can either enhance the child's engagement with science or portray science as a mechanical set of steps to be followed. All of these factors influence the ways in which children make use of their science journal to make meaning as well as the ways in which teachers look at children's work.

OVERVIEW OF CLASP

The Children's Literacy and Science Project (CLASP) prepared practicing elementary school teachers to use and analyze children's self-produced science journals in the curricular integration of science and literacy. Teachers participated in the project in collaborative teams of two from each school site, representing kindergarten through fifth grade. CLASP provided elementary teachers the opportunity to:

- enhance their science and literacy content knowledge, including a focus on the use of visual representations in children's science journaling,
- develop teaching strategies that incorporated children's self-produced journals as a way to integrate science and visual/verbal literacy, and
- develop tools to assess children's learning from this integrative perspective.

CLASP began with a 2-week summer institute, followed by a teacher-researcher phase in which teachers investigated and documented children's science and literacy learning in their own classrooms, constructed case studies, and documented their own instructional design. These academic year workshops also explored various pedagogical aspects of science-literacy integration. During a week-long summer institute at project end, teachers revised and finalized their instructional designs and case studies. An overview of the initial 2-week summer institute is shown in Table 13.1. For more information on CLASP and a detailed description of project activities and video clips, please visit http://clasp.education.purdue.edu/.

The first summer institute began with a focus on the background knowledge undergirding appropriate science and literacy instruction for children. Teachers first examined the nature of inquiry, exploring the types of questions that are appropriate, the differences between explanation and interpretation, and the kind of planning that is involved. Teachers also examined the concept of genre as a response to context (Britsch, 2002; Kress, 1999) in lieu of a set of forms to be filled in, but they also gained exposure to several conventional science genres and the text features of science genres as correlated with science functions (e.g., classification, explanation, procedural experiments, experiment recounts; Martin, 1993).

Next, teachers analyzed sample student science journals that reflected children's visual as well as verbal representation of meaning. This approach to analysis stressed the "joint significance of visual and written elements of texts" (Kress et al., 2001, p. 141) and ways in which science journal entries composed by children made use of talk, drawing, and/or written language. The children's use of oral language as part of the entire science experience was integral to this assessment of children's science learning and representation of understanding. Finally, the summer institute also guided teachers in ways of observing children's talk in the context of science experiences, in constructing their own definitions of productive versus unproductive talk, and in defining the relationship of this talk to journal entries.

To model the use of journals in inquiry, teachers participated as learners in several activities (e.g., stream tables, dissolving substances) that demonstrated different types of science inquiry as well as different genres. Teachers then reflected on their journal work and on the demonstrated instructional techniques to deepen their understanding of the role of journals in science-literacy learning. After reading Maienschein (1998, p. 917) and discussing the concept of "scientific literacy" (and understanding of scientific thinking processes) as opposed to "science literacy" (knowledge of science facts), teachers used four types of science journals as part of their participation in different science contexts, each of which required a different type of journal response. Experiences of each type as

TABLE 13.1
Overview of the CLASP Summer Institute

Day	Topic
Day 1 Monday	Background knowledge in science and literacy instruction for children: • the structure of different types of science texts and the language used in them; • the influence of children's prior ideas on their observations and science understandings, the ways that this knowledge is shown in science journal entries; • an emergent literacy approach and children's journal productions; • the nature of inquiry and the dimensions of scientific literacy.
Days 2–4 Tuesday–Thursday	Project staff modeled the integration of literacy into a unit using different inquiry approaches and journal types. Teachers: • experienced literacy-science instruction at the primary and intermediate grade levels based on different approaches to inquiry and journal genres; • reflected on their own journal work and discussed pedagogical techniques for the effective use of journals; and • interpreted children's journal work from the perspectives of emergent literacy and the development of science understandings.
Day 5 Friday	Goals: 1. To engage participants in thinking about science and non-science genres 2. To facilitate reflection on the week's activities by requiring participants to critique existing science programs that incorporate children's self-produced journals 3. To introduce participants to the CLASP model for designing instruction
Days 6–9 Monday–Thursday	Participants designed integrated science and literacy units for use in their own classrooms.
Day 10 Friday	Teachers shared their instructional designs.

appropriate for K–2 and Grade 3–6 levels were provided. Taking the learner's role in these science-literacy experiences provided teachers with perspective and information to guide their instructional design as well as their further assessment of samples of children's science journals.

Teachers carried out (a) an exploration, (b) a controlled experiment, (c) a field observation, and (d) a narrative observation, and engaged in the following functions within these contexts.

Exploratory journals involved:

- design of a focus question or problem (not a controlled experiment);
- manipulation and measurement of materials to see what happened.

Experimental journals involved:

- design of a focused question that generates a hypothesis;
- specification of variables (independent, dependent, controlled) and measurement

Field journals involved:

- documentation of observations gathered in the field, as in a nature study;
- development of questions based on those observations.

Narrative journals involved:

- observation and detailed description in indoor or outdoor contexts;
- generation of a narrative that contextualized or interpreted the observations.

Other summer institute sessions focused on the use of trade books in elementary science experiences and on prescriptive versus descriptive views of science genres. At the end of each day, teachers responded in reflection journals to a single question posed by CLASP staff. The aim was to enable teachers to take stock of their own views and ways in which these views had changed or had been further reinforced (e.g., "How has your view of scientific literacy been reinforced or changed during the past week?"). The reflection journals also provided space for teachers to think about ways of applying ideas to their own classrooms (e.g., "What's one exploration I could do with my students? How could I turn this into an experiment?").

Teachers then engaged in the design of instructional materials integrating science and literacy in interdisciplinary curricular units that they could use in their own classrooms the following fall semester. Teachers also reviewed state and national standards in science and literacy and questioned the ways in which standards can be used to inform classroom practice. This instructional design involved peer sharing and critique of developed materials.

LEARNING TO LOOK AT CHILDREN'S JOURNAL WORK

We next describe our approach to helping teachers learn to look at children's journal work. We begin by detailing an analysis of children's journals as presented via a real-world classroom vignette. We then provide an overview of a case study as a means of learning to look at children's journal work.

Analyzing Vignettes

Through journal assessment, teachers engage in a kind of research that is based on their own learning about children's science ideas, but journal pages can provide access to misconceptualizations as well (Dana, Lorsbach, Hook, & Briscoe, 1991). Nonetheless, teachers who are aware of children's existing conceptualizations based on a combination of visual, verbal, and actional evidence are better equipped to plan and implement instruction (Driver, Squires, Rushworth, & Wood-Robinson, 1994), a view that is reflected in the NRC standards:

> Effective teaching requires that teachers know what students of certain ages are likely to know, understand, and be able to do; what they will learn quickly; and what will be a struggle. Teachers of science need to anticipate typical misunderstandings and to judge the appropriateness of concepts for the developmental level of their students (NRC, 1996, p. 62).

One aim of CLASP was to help teachers learn how to assess the visual and verbal representations on children's journal pages as well as the talk that takes place around the journals. The vignette recounted in the text below comes from a fourth grade classroom. We present the analysis as we do when working with teachers—by first presenting a set of questions to focus reading and thinking about the vignette. We follow this with our own reflections about the vignette.

CLASSROOM VIGNETTE

Set-Up. During the first week of a unit about sound (Shepardson & Britsch, 2001), the children investigated the phenomenon of pitch. They

---

WHAT DO YOU THINK?

• Based on her journal entry, what might be some of Kim's prior ideas about sound?
• Which of the children seem to contextualize their ideas about sound with reference to the real world? Do the children contextualize their ideas with reference to the science experience itself?
• What do Tom's journal entries tell you about his ability to design and conduct an investigation? Do they evidence an ability to record data and draw conclusions?
• How does Laurie use visual representation as opposed to, or in combination with, the verbal representation of her ideas?
• What kinds of visual representations does Laurie include? Does this differ from Tom's use of visual resources on the page?
• How does the group's talk influence Tom's journal entries? Would you consider this talk to be productive or unproductive?

---

used their science journals to explore their prior knowledge about sound and to document their small-group investigations of rubberband pitch.

The teacher first invited the class to identify several sounds that she produced by tapping on water-filled bottles. She then asked, "What is sound?" and "How is sound made?" The children were to respond to this prompt by using written language, visual images, or both on their journal pages. Kim's journal entry, shown in Figure 13.1 (Shepardson & Britsch, 2001), thus included visual images as well as verbal descriptions in response to these questions.

The teacher followed up by initiating small-group investigations of the variables affecting the relative pitch of rubber bands. She focused this phase by posing another guiding question, "What makes the pitch different?" Each group of four children was then supplied with a single set of materials consisting of seven rubber bands of various colors, lengths, and thickness, and a ruler. Each group designed, conducted, interpreted, and documented their investigations in individual journals.

Tom's entry began with a categorization of the rubber bands by color and length followed by a hierarchical representation of his testing procedure. At this point, the others in the group decided to trace all of the rubber bands in order to record visual distinctions in their sizes. Michael suggested this idea as follows:

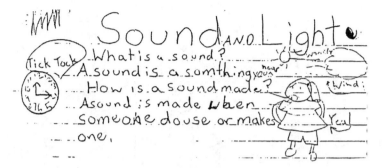

Figure 13.1 Kim's journal entry (from Shepardson & Britsch, 2001).

Michael: I know what we could do. We could like trace their—trace 'em.

Teacher: Tom has a chart going here and the rest of you have pictures. Okay after you get these pictures drawn, then what are you going to do?

Michael: Label 'em. We're gonna draw these pictures and label them so then we can write like Brandi (labels rubber bands ABCDEFG).

Tom: I'm not doing ABCDEFG.

While Tom returned to measuring and recording the lengths of the rubber bands, Michael continued his trace-and-label procedure while also fishing for group support by means of an oral narration of his own activity:

Michael: Here's what I'm doing. You guys, here's what I'm doing. This way's easier because you make how big the rubber band is and then label it, and all you have to do is ABCDEFG, down the table.

Tom: I am going to put that on the bottom part.

Michael: Too bad.

Nonetheless, Tom did include seven labeled ellipses in his journal entry but relegated them to the lower half of the lefthand page shown in Figure 13.2 (Shepardson & Britsch, 2001). He also separated these shapes from measuring with a horizontal line, graphically disconnecting the two approaches—one independent and the other social in origin.

In fact, Tom never actually used any of the information from the tracing activity. He measured the smallest rubber bands in centimeters because he was unable to interpret the smaller units in inches (e.g., 1/8 or 1/16 of an inch) and documented his measuring procedure by drawing a ruler captioned with, "How I measured it."

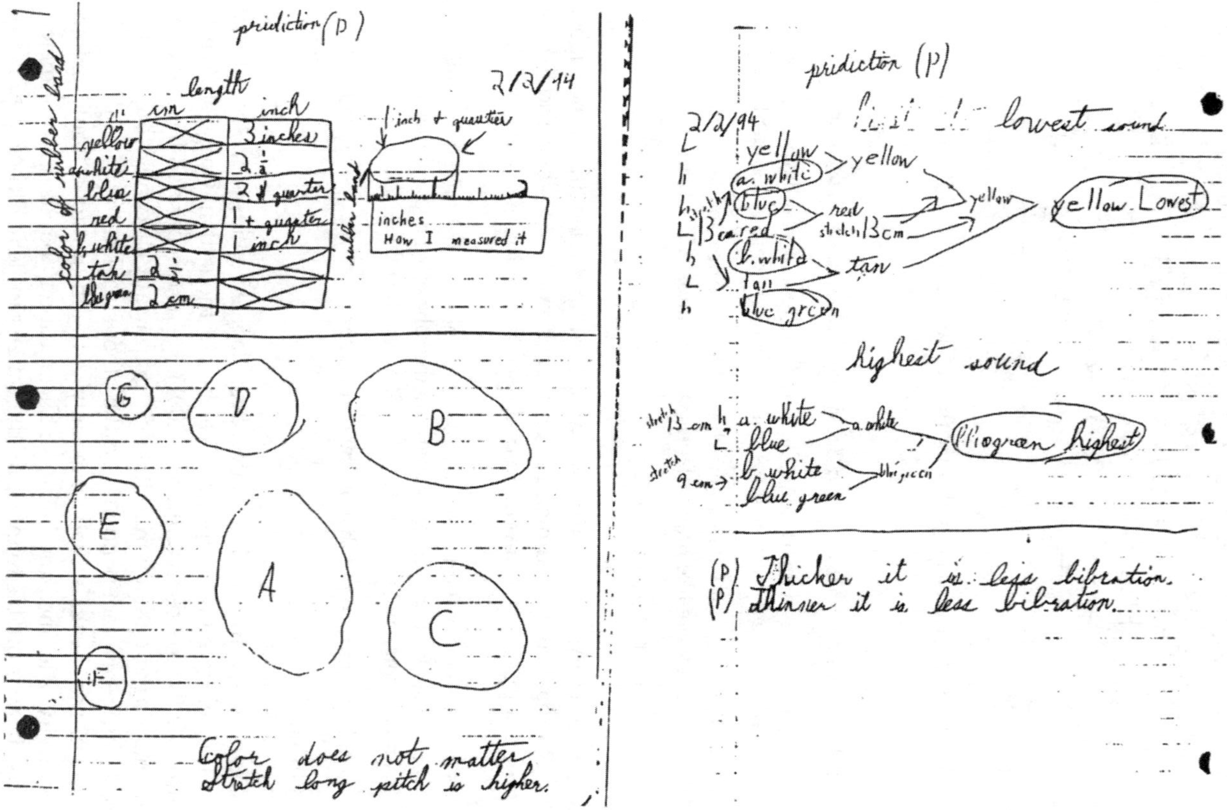

Figure 13.2 Tom's journal entry (from Shepardson & Britsch, 2001).

Next, he paired the rubber bands by length to test for differences in pitch by stretching the rubber band either 13 or 9 centimeters. He recorded this testing procedure and results directly across from these measurements by drawing the tree diagram shown on the righthand page of his journal entry (i.e., Fig. 13.2). He also recorded his predictions for two possible outcomes: "(P) Thicker it is less bibration [sic]" and "(P) Thinner it is less bibration [sic]."

Laurie characterized her understanding of pitch differences by developing a data tablelike chart for her journal entry, shown in Figure 13.3 (Shepardson & Britsch, 2001). Laurie's data entry distinguished the rubber bands by size and color as well as by real world events or objects in her own experience; for example, the 1 millimeter white rubber band sounded like a "guitar string." Laurie encoded these ideas using written language alone; however, she did use a curved line to separate her measurement and color data from her descriptive real-world data, framing all inside a rectangular box. She made two notes in the margin outside this box: "thin fast" and "thick slow."

Our Reflections. As part of the CLASP approach to professional development, we engaged teachers in discussion and reflection about these kinds of vignettes to work toward as a set of shared views. Focusing the discussion about the "sound" investigation on the previous questions, our view was that Kim's visual responses merely occupied the space around the edges of her verbal ones. Both her clock and her girl-with-open-mouth (at left and right in Fig. 13.1) were always accompanied by verbal descriptions of sounds. Kim verbally specified "wind" next to the visual index provided by her sketch of a cloud. Her prior ideas about sound as well as the visual signs she uses were based on her experiences. For her, objects or people make different sounds and people hear sounds. Despite the highly experiential nature of these understandings, she conveyed them by literally placing language at the center of her journal entry.

In contrast, Tom's entry graphically organized written language that reflected his talk with the small group as well as his individual activity. The teacher's comments implied that she valued Tom's chart more highly than the "pictures" of the rubber bands and probed for the other participants to articulate some logical consequence to their trace-and-label procedure (i.e., "Tom has a chart going here and the rest of you have pictures. Okay after you get these pictures drawn, then what are you going to do?"). Although Tom eventually gave in, his placement of the traced rubber bands at the bottom of his page reflected their adjunct nature to his chart. He also separated these shapes from his measurement data with

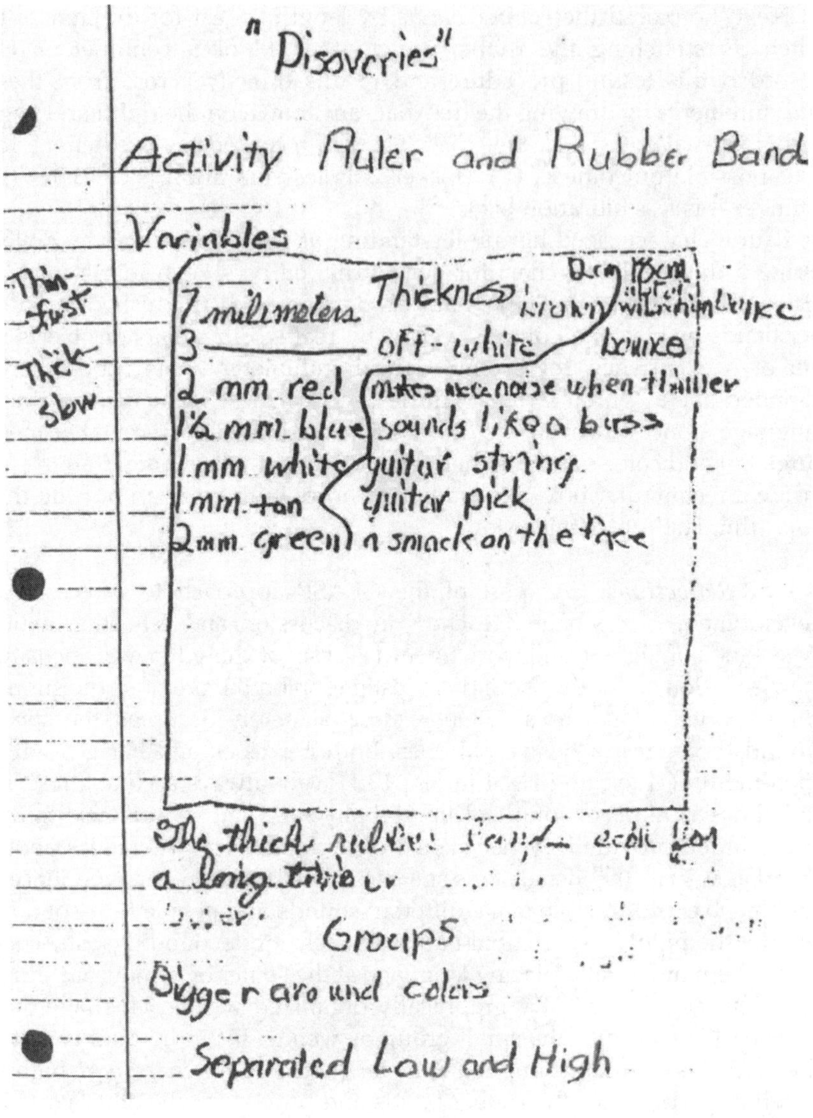

Figure 13.3   Laurie's journal entry (from Shepardson & Britsch, 2001).

a horizontal line, graphically disconnecting the two approaches—one independent and the other social in origin.

Tom's conceptual and procedural process of elimination was reflected in the tree diagram he composed on the next page of his journal, first eliminating rubber bands with a high sound, "h" (as shown on right side in Fig. 13.2). He also recorded his "pridiction (P)," representing his view of the two possible outcomes, under the diagram of his testing procedure. Thus, although Tom seemed to understand the notion of testing rubber bands by comparing the pitches of two at a time, he did not appear to understand how to control for variables during the test. He recorded his procedures, the rubber band sizes, and the identity of the rubber bands he tested, but not in a data table. Tom's conclusions (a) that color does not matter and (b) that the longer a rubber band is stretched, the higher the pitch, are accurate and reflect his interpretation of his data.

Finally, in Laurie's entry, color and measurement appeared to serve no purpose as variables and were not based on an interpretation of her data. Even her ideas about sound opposed "thin fast" to "thick slow" were relegated to the left margin of her journal page—outside the box framing her data table. Tom's data entry, however, documented his testing procedure within the context of the investigation itself, identifying color as an insignificant variable. In these cases, the representation of visual and experiential data was left unconnected to the procedural context of the science investigation and they became virtually extraneous.

Based on these kinds of analyses of classroom science experiences, accomplished in collaboration with teachers, we derived a set of principles for supporting teachers in their own efforts to interpret children's science journals as a foundation for designing instruction. We next discuss some of the central features that can support teachers in their independent analysis of and reflection on children's journal entries.

Conceptualizing the Science

One factor that would contribute to the ability of elementary teachers to assess children's journal work is the further development of the teachers' own scientific conceptualizations of the science content (NRC, 1996; NRC, 2001). This provides a scientific lens for looking at and appreciating children's journal work. This begins most productively by collaboratively conceptualizing the science to be taught together with teachers; for example, if teachers understand that pitch means how high or low a sound is (not its volume) and that a higher pitch has a greater frequency of vibration, they can more perceptively analyze children's work for ideas about the cause of high- versus low-pitched sounds. It is also essential to make resources available to teachers so that they can conceptualize the science as a part of instructional design prior to assessing children's work.

Identifying Children's Prior Conception

We have also found that it is useful for teachers to review the research literature to identify possible conceptions and misconceptions that children might bring to the science experience or derive from it. This informs teachers about what to look for in children's journal work by facilitating their thinking about possible differences between children's ideas and the conventional scientific perspective (Driver et al., 1994). For example, the research on children's ideas about sound indicates that children may think that:

- sound is produced as a result of the physical attributes of the object (i.e., the object makes the sound);
- a force is needed to produce a sound;
- sound production involves vibration (context-specific); younger children do not relate sound to vibration (Driver et al., 1994).

Teachers might examine children's journals based on these identified understandings. In Figure 13.1, for example, the child indicated that the clock makes a "tick tock" sound or that people can "Yeal" [sic] to make a sound. These written statements reflect understandings based on objects or events as perceived by the children but not on the vibration of the materials of which the objects are made. Further instruction can then be planned on this basis.

Deciding What to Look at and For

Linking science content knowledge with this knowledge about children's ideas then allows teachers to more perceptively distinguish what to look at and for in children's journal entries as these are integrated into the context of particular investigations. For example, in the pitch investigation, teachers might look for the following concepts:

- A rubber band produces sound when it is plucked. (A force is used to move the rubber band).
- The number of vibrations determines rubber band pitch; the higher the pitch the more vibration.
- The thickness (diameter), length, and tightness (tension) of the rubber band influences its pitch. A thick rubber band vibrates more slowly and thus has a lower pitch. A short rubber band vibrates faster and thus has a higher pitch.

The teacher might then examine the children's drawings for evidence of the idea that thickness and length influence pitch. A child might, for example, draw a guitar and visually indicate that thick strings vibrate more slowly and have a lower pitch. The teacher might next look for the understanding that a higher pitch means more vibration. This kind of specificity then determines what counts as evidence for children's science ideas and abilities. For instance, the journal entry shown in Figure 13.1 reflects the child's ideas prior to instruction (i.e., for her, objects or people make sounds, different objects make different sounds, and people hear sounds). From a scientific perspective, the child's journal entry reflects the following:

- sound travels outward from the source, but not necessarily as a wave;
- sound can move through air, but there is no indication that sound can move through liquids or solids.

We can also see, however, that the child does not show an understanding that:

- the vibration of the object produces the sound (i.e., objects cannot produce sound unless they are vibrating);
- pitch is caused by the frequency of vibration; the higher the pitch, the greater the frequency of vibration;
- an object's thickness, length, and tightness influences its pitch by affecting its vibration.

Based on this interpretation of the child's work, a teacher can make decisions about the child's learning and about further instructional responses. The teacher might use a tuning fork to demonstrate that sound is produced when the fork vibrates. The vibrating fork could then be placed in water or next to a suspended ping-pong ball (Friedl, 1997) to show how sound is produced by vibration (i.e., water splashes, ping-pong ball moves).

Yet, another way to collaborate with teachers in looking at the role of children's journal work in designing science experiences is through the compilation of case studies. We illustrate this process with a CLASP example in the next section.

LEARNING FROM CASE STUDIES

CLASP teachers also designed and conducted case studies of children's science-literacy journaling as teacher researchers who were investigating their own classroom practice so as to better understand it (Cochran-Smith & Lytle, 1993). The case studies were adapted from InTime case studies (University of Northern Iowa, 1999–2001, http://www.intime.uni.edu). These required teachers to identify and refine a framing question that would help them to reexamine or refresh their own perspectives about the learning of a particular child. Next, teachers identified data sources for building the case study, analyzed and interpreted their data, and shared the case study with the CLASP community. To illustrate this process, we share excerpts from the case study developed by one teacher participant; pseudonyms are used throughout to ensure confidentiality. The framing question for this case study focused on the impact of the journal structure on the student's journal work. As Ms. F (the teacher) stated it: "How does the amount of structure provided by the teacher within the journal impact the amount of thought displayed in the student's work?"

Data sources used to build the case study included the child's journals from two science investigations; the first focused on environmental factors that affect plant growth and the second focused on animal responses to environmental factors. Other data sources included teacher–child discussion, the CLASP checklist of observable scientific literacy behaviors (Table 13.2), and peer conversation from the science investigation contexts. Both investigations were similar in inquiry level, but varied by the degree of journal structure as Ms. F. noted in her case study:

> The first journal used during a plant experiment did not have a teacher-created format. The second journal used during an experiment with mealworms did have a teacher-created format, including the guiding question, headings for the different sections of the journal, and diagrams to use when recording results.

As Ms. F. analyzed her checklists for the focal child, she noted that the child conveyed more of her own thinking in the less structured plant journal, reproduced in Figure 13.4, than in the mealworm journal shown in Figure 13.5.

Figure 13.4 includes both visual and verbal data to document plant growth as of Day 9 of the investigation as well as detailed quantitative information for Day 12. As stated by Ms. F:

> Cynthia was able to include evidence of prior knowledge (Plants, p. 1, Hypothesis), identify variables and constants (Plants, p. 1 and 3), record patterns to show classification and composition through illustrations (Plants, p. 4 and 5), record quantitative data in her observations (Plants, p. 3–7), recount a sequence as a set of steps or stages (Plants, Days 5, 8,

Table 13.2

CLASP Checklist of Observable Scientific Literacy Behaviors

Use this checklist to record what you observe about the child's literacy behaviors in the science/literacy experience. You'll need to use several of these checklists in order to record the child's response throughout the unit so that you can see change from the beginning of the unit to the end.

Date: _____   Lesson: _____

Observable Behaviors	Check Behaviors You Observe	How is the Student Demonstrating the Observable Behavior? What Exactly is Happening? Which Journal Pages Show This? (Attach Xeroxes of Journal Pages)
Includes evidence of prior knowledge		
States question or problem		
Indicates a focus		
Shows procedure/method		
Details apparatus		
Identifies variables & constants		
Includes prediction related to problem & basis		
Details attributes of persons, objects or environment		
Records patterns to show classification or composition		
Includes data table or graph		
Records quantitative data		

TABLE 13.2 *(Continued)*

Observable Behaviors	Check Behaviors You Observe	How is the Student Demonstrating the Observable Behavior? What Exactly is Happening? Which Journal Pages Show This? (Attach Xeroxes of Journal Pages)
Recounts a sequence as a set of steps or stages		
Recounts process as a narrative (what happened)		
Shows change/contrast (over time, across perspectives)		
Shows similarities		
Interprets observations		
Explains observations and interpretation		
Identifies possible sources of error		
Notes application to new context/situation		
Raises further question(s)		

and 9), and show similarities in her illustrations (Plants, p. 4, 5). Many of these behaviors demonstrated thought that went beyond minimal reports of her findings.

Ms. F. also noted that the teacher-structured mealworm journal inhibited the extent, amount, and detail of her focal child's journal entries in comparison with the child's plant journal entries. In the less teacher-structured journal, Cynthia used a range of visual elements to encode a sort of classification of variables:

> …in her plant journal there was no limit to the number of pages that could be used to record her observations. As a result, Cynthia incorporated detailed pictures (Plants, p. 3–6) which recorded variations in plant

Day 9 We are going to take the Plant ⑤ plastic wrap. Our sand grew 13 blades of grass. Our mixture grew 2 blades of grass. Our soil grew 6 blades of grass.

Day 12 Our tallest grass in the soil is 5cm. Our tallest grass in the mixture is 4cm. Our tallest grass in the sand is 4cm and a half. We have 13 blades of grass in sand. We have 7 blades of grass in mixture. We have 11 blades of grass in soil. The grass in the sand is dying because the grass is bending.

Day 9

Figure 13.4   Cynthia's plant journal entry.

height and number of blades of grass. These same pictures also used color, shading, and/or labels to distinguish which material was used for planting the seed (soil, sand or a mixture) demonstrating Cynthia's ability to show classification and composition and distinguish similarities

Observations:

At the start

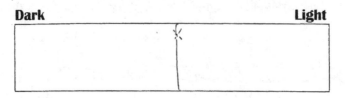

After 30 sec. ,

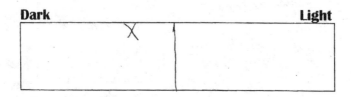

After 60 sec.

Figure 13.5 Cynthia's mealworm journal entry.

and differences. Her comments in her observation section of the plant journal suggested her understanding for the need to hold certain variables constant. For example, on page 3 of her journal, Cynthia writes, "We put 20 drops [of water] in sand, soil, and mixture."

Ms. F. also noted that Cynthia used written language to record her logical thinking as she carried out her observation:

She later writes (Plants, p. 5) "that the sand is dying because it is bent, and the roots of the grass in the sand were visible" (Plants, p. 6). This demonstrates a beginning understanding of why the sand is not the best medium in which to plant rye grass seed.

In contrast, in the teacher-structured mealworm journal shown in Figure 13.5, Cynthia's observations were limited to recording the position of the mealworm on a teacher-drawn diagram with an "x." A further point is that this circumscribed the child's responses during an investigation that took place approximately one month after the plant experiment—in other words, after Cynthia had accumulated additional experience with science journals. Ms. F. noted other limiting features of the page format in terms of Cynthia's written expression:

> When creating the format for the journal, I did not provide additional space in the observation section for written comments. Cynthia, thus, did not provide any (Mealworms, p. 3–6). There were behaviors of the mealworm that went unnoted or were only mentioned in the more open-ended conclusions section of the journal (Mealworms, p. 7). For example, many of the mealworms burrowed in the sand and others moved between the layers of foil on the sides of the runway. Cynthia did not note this. In her conclusions (p. 7), she did note that during one trial the mealworm was slower than in the next trial. The greatest evidence of Cynthia's thoughts during the mealworm activity occurs in the more open-ended hypothesis and conclusions sections (p. 1, 7). It is here that she added illustrations of the setup and offered some interpretations of what would and did happen.

Through her comparison of the child's plant and mealworm journals, Ms. F. did observe that the more structured mealworm journal helped to ensure consistency in the data collection procedures used by all of the children. In contrast, Cynthia's entries in the open-ended plant journal switched from documentation of both (a) plant height and number of blades of grass to (b) numbering only the blades of grass to (c) numbering neither feature. (This, however, may also have been an artifact of the relatively long 2-week duration of the investigation.)

Ms. F. reflected, in her words, "…on the fine dance between giving too much structure and not enough":

> I have decided that the structure need not lie directly on the page with a teacher-created format. Rather I think it should be found in teacher modeling…I think establishing blocks of time for reflection and discussion of thoughts and concepts should further provide the structure.

In fact, one recurring conclusion, across CLASP teachers, was that the level of structure applied to the journal page in fact limited students' journal use. This resulted in low-level learning—in labeling rather than synthesis, for example, on the journal page. This means that the teacher must not over-dictate the structure of the journal page. Even teachers who divided the journal page into writing and drawing sections noted that this specification actually limited children's writing and drawing to the space provided. For example, one teacher found that more structured journal pages also minimized the responses of a developmentally delayed student (aged 8 years).

> When [the] journal was structured to following instructions and re-writing (copying) of teacher's words in [the] journal the child wrote less and did not use drawing. Instruction was a "road block." When journal use was less structured the child responded with more writing and drawing, displaying a greater understanding of the science.

Another teacher investigated the impact on an English Language Learning child's (aged 7 years) use of both writing and drawing, concluding that teacher-imposed structuring tended to circumscribe the child's use of drawing to represent detailed science content.

> Journal structure greatly impacted the ELL child's writing and drawing. A journal designed with blank space and lines resulted in the child only drawing in the blank space and only writing on the lines. Although a journal designed with only blank space resulted in the child using writing and drawing together to communicate their science understanding, less writing occurred, but the drawings were more complete and detailed and communicated their science understanding better than their writing.

The knowledge that emerged from the case study process helped teachers to make their own connections between principles and practice. We might simply have presented some of these points of knowledge—and probably several others as well—through lecture or even through example, but the points that teachers questioned and proved to themselves became much more valued and firmly instantiated than the most well-crafted presentation could have done.

APPLICATIONS TO CLASSROOM PRACTICE

Although a number of classroom applications resulted from the CLASP research and teacher case studies, we emphasize what we believe to be three key points as related to classroom practice; journal structure, purposes for journal work, and teachers' conceptual understanding and knowledge of the research on children's ideas.

First, our findings from CLASP suggest that teachers did view scientific literacy as inclusive of the children's use of verbal (oral and/or written language) and visual (drawn) modes to represent meaning. Perhaps as expected, 71% of the K–2 curricular units prominently featured both visual and verbal expression; however, only 14% of the units for Grades 3–6 explicitly featured this verbal/visual choice. Although the opportunity to make a choice between modes or to use different modes for different purposes (Kress et al., 2001) was frequently not noted in the activity plans, the upper grade units most often offered visual expression only for unit closure activities such as poster making. Although teachers did view both verbal and visual representations as part of scientific literacy, they also gained an increased awareness of conventional science genres. This, in fact, helped them to appreciate the unconventional contributions of the children (Britsch, 2002). This knowledge did not seem to tie their analyses of sample children's science journals to a prescriptive point of view; instead, it freed teachers to see the original contributions of the children's work.

A second key finding from CLASP was that journaling as a multimodal process involves a broader context than that of the page alone; in other words, journaling must be regarded as much more than a paper-and-pencil task. For example, children who were aware they were going to use their journal entries in future activities (e.g., to talk with other children in large or small group settings) attended more closely to the content of their journal entries. Sharing with other students during the investigation also prompted listener-viewers to think further about their journal entries and to enter additional observations in their journals. It is also pedagogically important to require that children look back at their previous journal entries to answer questions and to share information. In other words, the journal cannot be viewed as the final product in the learning process; instead, it works as a mediational resource on which children can continually draw (Shepardson, 1997; Shepardson & Britsch, 1997).

As shown in the vignette from the rubber band investigation, encouraging children's talk fosters observation and production of graphics during the science lesson. The teacher, however, must realize that the children's talk does not always lead to a productive strategy or to a scientific way of knowing. This means that the teacher must attend closely to the children's talk and to the moment-to-moment production of journal entries. In the rubber band vignette, the teacher's close observation of these journal entries signaled that the children needed assistance. In this way, children's journals can act as guideposts for teacher intervention and assistance with the group's inquiry process.

This suggests a third key finding from the CLASP project: A central limiting factor for elementary teachers in looking at children's journal work is the level of scientific understanding possessed by the teachers themselves. Although teachers clearly saw the need to include the use of science processes in the curriculum, such a process-oriented stance is not enough. Teacher knowledge of science content needs to solidly undergird the implementation of science experiences in the classroom. If not, the development of new practice often begins with familiar unit topics that do not necessarily reflect either science literacy or scientific literacy. Research into science content information may be a new part of the curricular development process for many teachers, but it provides a crucial foundation for appreciating children's journal work. Closely related to this is the teachers' knowledge of the research literature about children's conceptions of science phenomena. We have found that this not only informs teachers about what to look for in children's journal work but also facilitates their thinking about possible differences between children's understandings and the conventional scientific perspective.

FOR FURTHER THOUGHT

Teacher evaluations of the implementation of their CLASP units showed that they saw benefits in terms of enhancing children's ability to observe, to note and record detail, and to carry out scientific procedures and processes. The reflections of some K–2 teachers and their conversation with project staff, however, suggested some worry that the emphasis on scientific literacy (as science process) might unseat children's own ideas in the face of adult convention. Thus, professional development for K–2 science instruction in particular might include explicit ways of introducing scientific literacy as a positive link with children's own connection-making cognition. In the upper grades, this might extend to ways of including more extensive incorporation of multimodal discourse for science learning and for the representation of understanding. For all grades, teacher analysis and assessment of children's work should more centrally acquaint teachers with ways of observing and understanding the use of different modes for different purposes by individual children (Kress et al., 2001).

Professional development also needs to give attention to the use of conceptually based models of science instruction instead of, or at least as an accompaniment to, long-instantiated activity-based approaches to teaching. We had thought that a unit template based on inquiry and a conceptually based model of science instruction would lead teachers away from an activity-based model of teaching. For some teachers in both upper and lower grades, this change did occur. In other cases, however, teachers continued to redesign and redevelop units focused on familiar unit topics instead of units that developed the ability to design and conduct an investigation. Perhaps change is less likely to take place if the activity, and not the science content, continues to be the teacher's focus. This is doubly true if the use of standards reinforces the retention of unit topics such as "animals" despite the fact that the activities therein do not lend themselves to the use of a scientific literacy stance. It is too often possible to link almost any activity to one standard or another instead of thinking scientifically.

To stimulate discussion, reflection, and analysis of classroom practice in light of these findings, we present the following questions:

- How is science journaling used in the meaning making process? Does the classroom process emphasize written language alone? Is drawing suggested only as a replication of written meanings—or vice versa?
- In what ways do you, as a teacher, structure the science journal page and how might this influence the ways children use the journal (i.e., their science learning)?
- Is the inquiry level of the science activity helping or hindering the children's science journal use?
- Does every science lesson have to include children's journal work?
- Should children's science journals be used even if they are not assessed by the teacher?
- How does the children's talk productively shape their science journal use? How does it unproductively influence their observation and journal use?
- How does encouraging children to talk about their science experience before using their journals influence their entries and their science learning?
- How might you investigate children's science journal use in your classroom to learn more about your students and the ways in which they use science journals?

In closing, we recommend that the incorporation of science processes into concrete science experiences as ways of thinking be a central focus of professional development programs for science instruction. Scientific literacy means more than simply providing science journals for children to fill out; instead, journals need to function as part of the child learner's construction process, reflecting and perpetuating that process. This, in turn, helps the teacher to offer new possibilities and new tools tailored to the child's process, ever broadening the context that incorporates the child, the teacher, and literacy as a part of science.

REFERENCES

Britsch, S. J. (2001). Emergent environmental literacy in the non-narrative compositions of kindergarten children. *Early Childhood Education Journal, 28*(3), 153–159.

Britsch, S. J. (2002). *Beyond stories: Young children's nonfiction composition.* Larchmont, NY: Eye on Education.

Cochran-Smith, M., & Lytle, S. (1993). *Inside outside: Teacher research and knowledge.* New York: Teachers College Press.

Dana, T. M., Lorsbach, A. W., Hook, K., & Briscoe, C. (1991). Students showing what they know: A look at alternative assessments. In G. Kulm & S.M. Malcom (Eds.), *Science assessment in the service of reform* (pp. 331–337). Washington, DC: Association for the Advancement of Science.

Doris, E. (1991). *Doing what scientists do: Children learn to investigate their world.* Portsmouth, NH: Heinemann.

Driver, R., Squires, A., Rushworth, P., & Wood-Robinson, V. (1994). *Making sense of secondary science: Research into children's ideas* (pp. 133–137). New York, NY: Routledge.

Elstgeest, J., Harlen, W., & Symington, D. (1985). Children communicate. In W. Harlen (Ed.), *Primary science: Taking the plunge* (pp. 92–111). Portsmouth, NH: Heinemann.

Friedl, A. E. (1997). *Teaching science to children: An inquiry approach.* New York: McGraw-Hill.

Kress, G. (1999). Genre and the changing contexts for English language arts. *Language Arts, 76*(6), 461–469.

Kress, G., Jewitt, C., Ogborn, J., & Tsatsarelis, C. (2001). *Multimodal teaching and learning: The rhetorics of the science classroom.* London: Continuum.

Kress, G. (2003). *Literacy in the new media age.* New York: Routledge.

Maienschein, J. (1998). Scientific literacy. *Science, 281,* 917.

Manguel, A. (2000). *Reading pictures: What we think about when we look at art.* New York: Random House.

Martin, J. R. (1993). Literacy in science: Learning to handle text as technology. In M. A. K. Halliday & J. R. Martin (Eds.), *Writing science: Literacy and discursive power* (pp. 166–202). London: Falmer Press.

National Research Council. (1996). *National science education standards.* Washington, DC: National Academy Press.

National Research Council. (2001). *Classroom assessment and the National Science Education Standards.* Washington, DC: National Academy Press.

Shaw-Miller, S. (2002). *Visible deeds of music: Art and music from Wagner to Cage.* New Haven: Yale University Press.

Shepardson, D. P. (1997). Of butterflies and beetles: First graders' ways of seeing and talking about insect life cycles. *Journal of Research in Science Teaching, 34*(9), 873–889.

Shepardson, D. P., & Britsch, S. J. (1997). Children's science journals: Tools for teaching, learning, and assessing. *Science and Children, 34,* 13–17, 46–47.

Shepardson, D. P., & Britsch, S. J. (2001). The role of children's journals in elementary school science activities. *Journal of Research in Science Teaching, 38*(1), 43–69.

University of Northern Iowa, College of Education. (1999–2001). InTime: Integrating new technologies into the methods of education. Retrieved July 19, 2002 from http://www.intime.uni.edu.

14

Semiotics for Integrating Geosciences Into Literacy in Teacher Education

Lucia Y. Lu
Longwood University

This research is based on the teacher candidates' practicum in Atlanta Public School (APS) system in Georgia. Elementary school teachers are trained as generalists of all disciplines, and many teacher candidates are intimidated by mathematics and science. When the teacher candidates in my Reading and Literacy classes went to the field elementary schools for clinical and practical experience, I invited them to conceptualize hyper-textuality into their practicum by integrating mathematics and geosciences into their planning, tutoring, instructing, and assessing. I am excited by the results—teacher candidates felt more comfortable in this integration, the coordinating teachers at the field elementary schools became interested in implementing this integration approach into their classrooms, and their students are motivated to learn science.

SEMIOTICS FOR INTEGRATING GEOSCIENCES INTO LITERACY IN TEACHER EDUCATION

Two Incidents: "Don't Cut the Tree!"

Four years ago, Ms. Shauna Fair, one of my students in the Teacher Education Program, came to me to borrow an easy book for her 10 students in the afterschool program in the Atlanta Public School system, where 75% of the student population is African American. Later, she picked up *The Giving Tree* (Silverstein, 1964).

Two days later, Ms. Fair came to me and showed me her students' responses to this book. One response was "We are not supposed to cut the tree!" I encouraged Ms. Fair to go back to the students and ask them why. Two days later, Ms. Fair came back to me with her students' answers. With the help of Ms. Fair, her students, most of whom were second graders, listed several functions of the tree; growing fruits for us, providing nests for the birds, supplying building materials for humans, giving children shade when they were playing under the tree, and so forth.

Ms. Chastie Gamble, the other student in my class, showed me her students' response to *The Lorax* (Dr. Seuss, 1971). Five of her second graders created a puppet show—"Don't Cut the Tree!" Her students used the construction paper to make five puppets; Lorax, Truffula Treeman, Bar-ba-loot, Swomee-Swan, and Humming-Fish. Her students dictated their suggestion of spraying the Truffula seeds in the woods to grow more Truffula trees in the future.

These two incidents inspired me to integrate geosciences into the classes of reading and literacy. Whenever my students, the teacher candidates went to the field schools for practicum, one of the assignments was to integrate geosciences into their planning, tutoring, instructing, and assessing.

I used this idea to write a grant proposal for Service Learning and was funded. Some of the grant was used to support one elementary school students' field trip to the zoo, to Callaway Garden in Georgia, to the city aquarium. The purpose is to activate students' interest in learning science.

STATEMENT OF PROBLEM

The Gap in Science Education in Teacher Education Program

We all know that elementary school teachers are educated to be generalists of all disciplines (El-Hindi, 2003; Lundstrom, 2005). For the elementary school teachers, teaching science is frequently a challenging task, and sometimes it can even be intimidating (King, & Sudol, 1998; Koch, 2005). The students in the Teacher Education Program, especially those with early childhood education majors, always feel unprepared and lack confidence to deal with the depth of inquiry-based questions in science.

Students' Performance in Science

According to the recent state of Georgia's annual report on K–12 student achievement, most students' performance on science in APS does not meet Georgia standard on Criterion-Referenced Competency Tests (CRCTs) and Iowa Test on Basic Skills (ITBS). If early intervention of science were not provided immediately in the elementary school setting, the problem would soon go beyond the scores of science.

OBJECTIVE

The No Child Left Behind Shift led by Education Secretary Spellings (U.S. Department of Education, 2006) declares that global competition has changed the rules of the game; school students must be offered more rigorous coursework with a strong emphasis in math and science. The No Child Left Behind Act (2001) mandates that during the 2007 school year, students must be assessed in science for the first time. Science is again at the hotline of U.S. classrooms. The integration of geosciences into literacy is to make the exploration of science more interesting through semiotic inquiry—which is artistic (Eisner, 1990) and scientific, and more productive through the authoring cycle. The goal is to get the children on the right track of school success in science, and to become competitive in business and industry that require a workforce with improved critical thinking skills and substantial knowledge in science (Ellis, 2003).

SEMIOTICS AS THE THEORETICAL FRAMEWORK

Hypertextuality

Because technology has shifted the paradigm of learning and instruction (Smolin & Lawless, 2003), the author conceptualizes hypertextuality (Genette, 1997) into her design of research. Hypertextuality is the semiotic notion of the computer-based texts that take the readers directly to other texts for information, exploration, evaluation, and communication of their interpretation of the text. Lundstrom (2005) is pragmatic about the integration in her advocacy,"… with all the techniques and contents you need to teach and your students need to master, you have to integrate everything as much as you can" (p. 1–4).

In this research, teacher candidates were invited to go over the Internet for free and interesting lesson plans from www.lessonplanspage.com, and for other information for scientific investigation.

Semiotics

Semiotics is the science of signs (Cunningham, 1992; Sebeok, 2002). Vygotsky proclaimed that semiotic emphasis on the use of signs brings with its focus on meaning as central to human activity (Moll, 1997). The four components of semiotics are (a) signs—anything bears meaning; (b) semiosis—the construction of signs; (c) inference—reasoning of signs; and (d) reflexivity—the reflection of the process of learning signs.

Based on semiotic theory, languages, arts, music, dance, drama, puppet shows, mathematics, cultural modes, and so forth are all signs or sign systems that humans created to mediate the world (Cunningham, 1992; Deeley, 1994). According to semiotics, a good language arts curriculum must be able to expand learner's potential for understanding and communicating through a variety of signs, not only languages (Hubbard, 1989; Leland & Harste, 1994; Short, Kauffman, & Kahn 2000; Suhor, 1992). When learners are striving to communicate and construct different sign systems to interpret their comprehension of the text, and because the connection between different sign systems does not exist a priori, it would be an "anomaly" to learners (Siegel, 1995). To Pierce, the great American philosopher, anomalies that learners encounter in their daily lives drive the process of inquiry into the endless cycle of inference (Neilson, 1989; see Fig. 14.1); abduction (generating hypotheses), deduction (testing hypotheses), and induction (accepting, rejecting, or modifying the previous hypotheses). Learners should be provided with opportunities to become actively involved in the construction of knowledge through these reasoning processes. In education, the shift from knowledge transmission model to an inquiry-oriented model of teaching and learning can be achieved through the process of inference, or reasoning, in a social context (Siegel, 1995).

In this integration, readers' response (Beach, 1993), transactional theory (Rosenblatt, 2002), semiotic theory (Cunningham, 1992; Sebeok, 2002), and constructivist theory (Zahorik, 1995) are all involved to create an inquiry-based integration of geosciences into literacy.

The Authoring Cycle

The author believed that social interaction provided the opportunities for children to learn more about the world (Goodman & Goodman, 1997; Halliday & Hasan, 1985), and there is growing evidence that collaborative learning between peers, regardless of ability, activates the zone of proximal development (Tudge, 1997). The author implemented "the authoring cycle" (Short, Harste, & Burke, 1996) as a framework for her semiotic inquiry into geosciences. Usually, there are two to six students in the

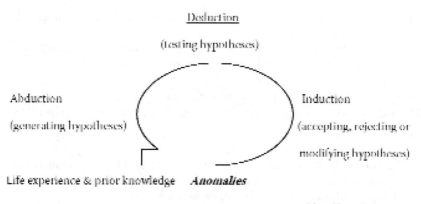

Figure 14.1   An endless cycle of reasoning–inference.

authors' circle for peers' interaction. When learners come from socioeco-nomically diverse backgrounds, they can see with different eyes (Oster, 1989), listen to different drums (Watson, Burke, & Harste, 1989), speak with different voices, think from different perspectives, and ideas will flourish when they resonate with others (Short & Burke, 1991).

DESIGN OF RESEARCH

Lesson Plans

The teacher candidates in my Literacy and Reading classes were invited to create their own lesson plans or browse the Web site of www. lessonplanspage.com for free and interesting lesson plans created by edu-cators. The teacher candidates looked for the grade level, the interesting discipline subjects, and modified it by adding the student information, objectives, state standards like GA QCC and VA SOL, constructivist teach-ing (Zahorick, 1995) activities step by step, and their assessment tools for checking students' performance in terms of comprehension, essay writing, observation reports, hand-on artifacts, and so forth.

Samples of Teacher Candidates' Lesson Plans

Sample 1: Why Do Leaves Change Color in the Autumn

Teacher candidate: Ms. Harris   Supervisor: Dr. Lucia Y. Lu

Students: K–1 at one Atlanta Public School

Objective: 1. Students will be able to investigate the leaves change color in the autumn;
2. Students will be able to trace the leaves they picked up in the playground and to color the leaves.

Georgia QCC Standards: Language Arts, Science, and Arts
Materials: *Sky Tree: Seeing Science Through Art* (Locker & Christiansen, 1995).
Activities:

1. Teacher will take students to the playground and pick up some leaves.
2. Students will be invited to tell the colors of the leaves they have and the color of the leaves in the other seasons.
3. Students will be invited to trace the leaves on the construction paper and color their leaves.
4. Teacher will read the science trade book *Seeing Science Through Art* to the class and explain the reason why leaves change color in the autumn.

Assessment: Students will be able to answer the questions the teacher posts.

Sample 2: Making the Water Cycle

Teacher candidate: Ms. Ross   Supervisor: Dr. Lucia Y. Lu

Students: fourth graders at one Atlanta Public School

Topic: Making the water cycle

Objectives:

1. Students will synthesize the water cycle through a model and through a drawing.
2. Students will draw an illustration of the water cycle.
3. Students will label the parts of the water cycle effectively.
4. Students will describe what effects water pollution has on other parts of the environment.

Materials: A lesson from www.lessonplanspage.com The Water Cycle.
Georgia QCC Standards: Demonstrate and describe the water cycle and the role of evaporation, precipitation, and condensation, examine the process of change as it relates to water in the atmosphere.

Activities:

1. The teacher will have a drawing of the water cycle on the board. The students will label the land, body of water, clouds, evaporation, condensation, precipitation, and run off. The teacher will review the answers with the students.
2. The teacher will group the children into four groups of three and give each group one bowl, some green paper or Easter grass, cotton balls, and one small cup of water. Then they will construct an environment model. They will make grass on one side of the bowl from the paper or Easter grass. They will pour the water in the other side of the bowl to represent the body of water. They will soak some of the water up with the cotton ball to represent evaporation. They will use the cotton balls in the "sky" above their model as clouds/condensation. They will squeeze the cotton balls to make rain/precipitation over the land or water. If it "rains" on the land, they should observe the run off.
3. The teacher will ask about what happens when the water is polluted. To synthesize this, the teacher will put some food coloring in the "lake." The students will complete the water cycle as described above with the "pollutant" from the lake. They will notice that the "pollutant" evaporates, condensates, and precipitates onto the land. Thus, polluting one factor pollutes all. The students will clean up and return to their seats in their groups.
4. The students will each receive a sheet of white paper and will be asked to draw the water cycle and label the parts (precipitation, evaporation, condensation, clouds, land, run off, body of water). They will color it and use all of their creativity.

Evaluation & Assessment:

During the model activity: Did the students build the model correctly? Were the students able to connect the fact that polluting the water will pollute the cloud and the land?

The Drawing: Did the students stay on task? Were the drawings labeled correctly (precipitation, evaporation, condensation, clouds, land, run off, body of water)?

Sample 3: Does the Moon Really Change?

Teacher candidate: Ms. Cooke   Supervisor: Dr. Lucia Y. Lu

Students: second grade, seven male, six female, and two ESL

Lesson: Teach one scientific unit based on my favorite topic of the lunar system

Materials: *The Moon Seems to Change* (Branley, Emberley, & Emberley, 1987) and teacher-made assessment tool.

Objective: The students will know how to identify the different phases of the moon in a given time period by making the lunar flip book.

Georgia QCC Standard: Science/Space/Astronomy 19, 20, 2:19 Observes and discusses apparent notion of sun and moon. Understands that the sun, moon, and stars appear in the east and set in the west. Plots the apparent movement of the sun and moon in the sky using shadows or other devices; 2:20 Describes motion of earth, moon, and planets in our solar system. Describes how the earth rotates once a day and revolves around the sun each year, how the moon revolves around the earth each month and how the planets revolve around the sun in a periodic manner. Constructivist Teaching Activities:

1. Activate students' prior knowledge: asking students about the different phase of the moon.
2. Help students acquire new knowledge: reading the book and get familiar with the eight lunar phases.
3. Help students acquire the new knowledge: students will be able to identify the eight different phases of the moon by creating a lunar flip book.
4. Help students use the new knowledge: the students will use the book as a guide to draw and label phases of the moon for the lunar flip.
5. Reflect: students will explore the Internet, Google.com to find out the phase of the moon for that given day.

Assessment tool: The students will be given a handout where they have to label the moon phases with the correct diagram.

Sample 4: The Erosion in the Environment

Teacher: Ms. Diggs   Professor: Dr. Lucia Y. Lu

Students: first grade at one elementary school in Virginia

Objective: Students will learn the concept of "erosion" and the causes of erosion in the beach

Materials:

1. two 9" x 12" aluminum trays
2. white sand
3. pebbles
4. video with the image of beach, river, soil, and the process of erosion on beach, river, and soil

Activities: The Concept of Erosion

1. Students watch the video, and see the process of erosion on beach, river, and soil by water, wind, and digging.
2. Teacher explained the concept of erosion.
3. Teacher put the sand on the tray, and let one side of the tray stand on two books.

Erosion out of Water

1. Teacher poured some water from the top side of the tray, and the sand moved because of the wash of the water.
2. Teacher explained the erosion of the beach.

How to Prevent Erosion

1. Teacher put some pebbles on the top side of the tray.
2. Teacher poured some water from the top side of the tray, but the sand moved very slowly because of the pebbles.
3. Teacher explained that the pebbles can be constructed near the beach to prevent the erosion of the beach because of the wash of the water.

Erosion out of Wind

1. Teacher told students to close their eyes because she would blow the sand on the tray.
2. Teacher blew the sand, students saw the move of the sand.

Students' Oral Report on Erosion Investigation

1. Teacher asked students the meaning of "erosion."
2. Teacher asked students the causes of erosion in the beach.
3. Teacher asked students how to prevent erosion in the beach.

(The author observed that all students raised their hands to answer the questions, and all the answers were right.)

DISCUSSION

Student-Centered Science Curriculum

Before the teacher candidates conducted any science investigation with the students in the field school, I gave them the interest inventory to know their students' favorite topics in science. This is the student-centered science curriculum. The inventory is the base on which the teacher candidates selected their students' favorite topics. Because the topics were from the students, they might have ownership in the science investigation. They were very passionate in doing science, talking about science, reading about science, and writing about science (El-Hindi, 2003).

Topics in Science in the Early Childhood Education

Teacher candidates' lesson plans covered the popular topics in science curricula developed within the past 10 years:

- Astronomy—Solar System—Does the moon really change (by Ms. Cooke)
- Atmosphere & Weather—Cloud & the water cycle (by Ms. Ross)
- Biology—Insects—The life of ants (by Ms. Stewart)
- Biology—Plants—Why do leaves change color in the Autumn? (by Ms. Harris)
- Biology—Plants—The plant's life cycle (by Ms. St-llme)
- Ecology—Creating a simulated landfill to prevent erosion (by Ms. Diggs)
- Geology & Earth Science—Exploration of volcanoes (by Ms. Dean)
- Geology & Earth Science—The formation of the fossil (by Ms. Dean)

Holistic Approach Across Language Arts and the Curriculum

The teacher candidates used the holistic approach integrating language arts of thinking, listening, speaking, reading, and writing in their classroom activities (Pearson, 2002). The students read about science, talked about science, wrote about science, thought about science (El-Hindi, 2003). The interesting contents motivated students to use various comprehension strategies to understand science.

This is also the holistic approach integrating science across the curriculum with arts (the K–1 students traced the leaves and colored the leaves), social studies (the students talked about the hurricane in Florida, and expressed their sympathy for the victims), mathematics (the students calculated the damage from the hurricane), and they talked about the erosion in the beach, and how to prevent the erosion in Ms. Diggs' classroom. The students talked about air pollution, water pollution in Ms. Ross's instruction of the water cycle.

Inquiry-Based Science Curriculum

In the inquiry-based classroom activities integrating geosciences into literacy, students were invited to exercise their reasoning ability throughout the class activities: They observed, they made predictions, they generated hypotheses, they tested hypotheses, and finally they accepted, rejected, or modified the previous hypothesis (Neilson, 1989).

The Value of Teaching Science

Koch (2005) assures that a good science program teaches science ideas, processes, and attitudes that prepare students for further, more complex studies in science. Science in the early grades has the potential to help students become critical thinkers, to reason carefully, to solve problems, and to make informed decisions. Elementary school students who engage in scientific activities in their classroom build confidence in themselves as thinkers, and by cultivating scientific attitudes, we can help students improve their abilities to explore a problem from many perspectives, confer with their classmates and their teacher, and become knowledge builders and meaning makers.

The goals of constructivist teaching are application, discovery, extension, and invention through understanding, thinking, and creation. These goals are more than the goal of direction instruction, which leads to reproduction only (Zahorik, 1995).

Promoting scientific literacy is a strategy to enhance the nation's understanding of scientific research and its contribution to economic development and community quality of life. As knowledge becomes a driving force in the new global economy, research institutes, universities, government, and corporations must work together to make sure that knowledge is generated, transmitted, and used for social and economic good (Hubbs-Seaworld Research Institute, 2005).

Science Motivated Students to Read

Based on the research conducted by The University of Maryland's Literacy Research Center, literacy and science belong together, and growing evidence shows that test scores go up when science and literacy are matched. In just 4 months, third-grade children who were taught a science-literacy curriculum advanced one and a half grade levels in reading comprehension because science immerses children in content that is so interesting and important to them that they want to learn about it, which motivates them to read.

APPLICATIONS TO CLASSROOM PRACTICE

Science Trade Books

Most science trade books focus on a single topic with great detail and provide for depth of exploration (King & Sudol, 1998). The science trade books published within the turn of this century are with a lot of visual strategies for active learning by beautiful, full-color illustrations, maps, diagrams, photographs, charts, and graphs that organize the information and capture young students' attention (Bromley, Irwin-DeVitis, & Modlo, 1995). In addition to the science trade books, the teacher candidates in my Reading and Literacy classes adopted and modified the free lesson plans from the web site of www.lessonplanspage.com by adding their own objectives, Georgia State Standard QCC, or Virginia State Standard SOL, and their own assessment tools. King and Sudol (1998) designed a checklist for evaluating nonfiction trade books. The most important criteria are the accuracy of the contents and illustration, organization and layout, cohesion of ideas. The teacher candidates used this checklist to evaluate the science trade books and the lessons from the Web site.

Integrating Technology to Enrich Scientific Resources

Because technology has shifted the paradigm of instruction and learning (Smolin & Lawless, 2003), technology became the tool for scientific inquiry (Koch, 2005). Web-based resources enrich the contents and activities of science investigation. For example, Ms. Ross's students explored the Internet for the information of temperature. Ms. Dean's students explored the Internet for the damage of hurricane in Florida. Ms. Harris' students explored the Internet for the trees and leaves in different season. Teacher candidates and their students used hypertext links for more related information.

Constructivist Teaching

Constructivist teaching theory (Zahorik, 1995) is aimed for application, discovery, extension, and invention. The instructing and learning activities cover five steps; (1) Activating learners' prior knowledge; (2) Helping learners acquire new knowledge; (3) Fostering learners understand new knowledge; (4) Providing learners with opportunities to use new knowledge; (5) Reflecting the process of acquiring new knowledge.

Visual Strategies for Active Learning

For effective instruction and comprehension, visual strategies like semantic maps, overview webs, tables, illustration, diagram, and graphic organizers will be used to make texts more explicit (Bromley, Irwin-DeVitis, & Modlo, 1995).

Integrating the Language Arts

Using the holistic approach integrates science investigation with language arts through thinking, listening, speaking, reading, and writing (Pearson, 2002). Using the holistic approach to integrate science across the curriculum in arts, language arts, mathematics, social studies, and so forth (Pearson, 2002) will broaden readers' view of science investigation.

Formal and Alternative Assessment Tools

Assessment is always an ongoing process. Alternative assessment tools like hands-on experiments, observation reports, science portfolio, readers theatre, storytelling, drawing, and so forth will be counted as well as the standardized tests in science education.

FOR FURTHER THOUGHT

The following issues serve as the further thoughts for this integrated approach and allow you to see whether you are successfully integrating science and literacy.

1. Did I give students time and opportunity to ask questions?
2. Did I give students time and opportunity to explore the topics of their interest?
3. Did I give students time and opportunity to share their exploration?
4. Did I shut students' voices when their exploration goes beyond my expectation?
5. Did I encourage students' different voices after their exploration?
6. Did I encourage students to initiate further exploration?
7. Did I encourage students to go beyond the textbooks?

REFERENCES

Beach, R. (1993). *Reader-Response theories*. Urbana, IL: National Council of Teachers of English.

Branley, F. M., Emberley, B., & Emberley, E. (1987) *The moon seems to change*. New York: Harper-Collins.

Bromley, K., Irwin-DeVitis, L., & Modlo, M. (1995). *Graphic Organizers*. New York: Scholastic Professional Books.

Cunningham, D. J. (1992). Beyond educational psychology: Steps toward an educational semiotic. *Educational Psychology Review, 4*, 165–194.

Deeley, J. (1994). *The human use of signs*. London: Rowman & Littlefield Publishers.

Dr. Seuss (1971). *The Lorax*. New York: Random House.

Eisner, E.W. (1988). *The Role of Discipline-Based Art Education in America's Schools*. Los Angeles: Getty Center for Education in the Arts, 1988.

El-Hindi, A. E. (2003). Integrating literacy and science in the classroom: From ecomysteries to readers theatre. *The Reading Teacher, 56*(6), 536–538.

Ellis, J. D. (2003). *Fostering change in science education*. Washington, D C: National Science Foundation.

Genette, G. (1997). *Palimpsests* (trans. Channa Newman & Claude Doubinsky). Lincoln, NB: University of Nebraska Press.

Goodman, Y. M., & Goodman, K. S. (1997). Vygotsky in a whole-language perspective. In L. C. Moll (Ed.), *Vygotsky and education* (pp. 223–250). New York: Cambridge University Press.

Halliday, M. A. K., & Hasan, R. (1985). *Language, context, and text: Aspects of language in a social-semiotic perspective*. Victoria, Australia: Deakin University Press.

Harste, J. C., Short, K. G., & Burke, C. (1988). *Creating classrooms for authors*. Portsmouth, NH: Heinemann.

Hubbard, R. (1989). *Authors of pictures, draughtsmen of words*. Portsmouth, NH: Heinmann.

Hubbs-Seaworld Research Institute. Orlando, FL.

King, C. M., & Sudol, P. (1998). *Fusing science with literature*. Ontario, Canada: Pippin Publishing Corp.

Koch, J. (2005). *Science stories: Science methods for elementary and middle school teachers* (3rd ed.). New York: Houghton Mifflin.

Leland, C. H., & Harste, J. C. (1994). Multiple ways of knowing: curriculum in a new key. *Language Arts, 71*, 337–345.

Locker, T., & Christiansen, C. (1995). *Sky tree: Seeing science through art*. New York: Harper-Collins.

Lundstrom, M. (2005). Link science & literacy. *Scholastic Instructor*. March, 2005 pp. 25–28.

Moll, L. C. (1997). Introduction. In L. C. Moll (Ed.) *Vygotsky and education* (pp. 1–27). New York: Cambridge University Press.

No Child Left Behind Act, 107 U.S.C. (2001).

Oster, J. (1989). Seeing with different eyes: Another view of literature in the ESL class. *TESOL Quarterly, 23*(1), 85–103.

Pearson, P. D. (2002). American reading instruction since 1967. In N. B. Smith (Ed.), *American reading instruction (special ed.,* pp. 419–486). Newark, DE: International Reading Association.

Pierce in Neilson, A. R. (1989) *Critical thinking and reading: Empowering learners to think and act.* Urbana, IL: National Council of Teachers of English.

Rosenblatt, L. M. (1989). The transactional theory of the literary work: Implications for research. In C. R. Cooper (Ed*.), Researching response to literature and the teaching of literature: Points of departure* (pp. 33–53). Norwood, NJ: Ablex.

Sebeok, T. (2002). *A global sign.* Bloomington, IN: Indiana University Press.

Short, K. G., & Burke, C. (1991). *Creating curriculum.* Portsmouth, NH: Heinemann.

Short, K. G., Harste, J. C., & Burke, C. (1996). *Creating classrooms for authors and inquirers* (2nd ed.). Portsmouth, NH: Heinemann.

Short, K. G., Kauffman, G., & Kahn, L. H. (2000). "I just need to draw": Responding to literature across multiple sign systems. *The Reading Teacher, 54*(2), 160–171.

Siegel, M. (1995). More than words: The generative power of transmediation for learning. *Canadian Journal of Education, 20,* 455–475.

Silverstein, S. (1964). *The giving tree.* New York: Harper Collins.

Smolin, L. I., & Lawless, K. A. (2003). Becoming literate in the technological age: New responsibilities and tools for teachers. *The Reading Teacher, 56*(6), 570–577.

Suhor, C. (1992). Semiotics and the English language arts. *Language Arts, 69,* 228–230.

Tudge, J. (1997). Vygotsky, the zone of proximal development, and peer collaboration: Implications for classroom practice. In L. C. Moll (Ed.), *Vygotsky and education* (pp. 155–172). New York: Cambridge University Press.

U.S. Department of Education (2006). Margaret Spellings, U.S. Secretary of Education—Biography. Retrieved April 4, 2007 from http://www.ed.gov/news/staff/bios/spellings.html

Watson, D., Burke, C., & Harste, C. (1989). *Whole language: Inquiring voices.* New York: Scholastic, Inc.

Zahorik, J. A. (1995). *Constructivist teaching.* Bloomington, IN.: The Phi Delta Kappa Educational Foundation.

15

Using Action Research Projects to Help Preservice Elementary Teachers Effectively Use Interdisciplinary Language Arts and Science Instruction

Valarie L. Akerson
Indiana University

Elementary teachers are often generalists, having no special training in either science content or pedagogy (Cox & Carpenter, 1989; Perkes, 1975; Tilgner, 1990). Elementary teachers are most often specialists in language arts education, with an interest and expertise in helping children learn to read and write. They are more often likely to avoid teaching science, or feel uncomfortable teaching science because they have not been adequately trained to do so. There have been recommendations that training in interdisciplinary science and literacy instruction can help elementary teachers improve their science teaching because they can use their strengths in language arts instruction in their science teaching (Flick, 1995). However, it should be noted that teachers could interpret interdisciplinary instruction as simply reading a book about science—after all, it is a book about science and it is reading, right? Without appropriate preparation, there is a risk that the science instruction is actually left out in an interdisciplinary science and language arts approach. So the real question remains—how do we help elementary teachers effectively use interdisciplinary instruction to enable their own students to meet language arts and science objectives?

Action research has been shown to help elementary teachers develop science teaching strategies (Van Zee, 1998). Because action research provides evidence-based strategies for science teaching, it can also be used to find evidence for effective strategies that can enable appropriate language arts and science interdisciplinary instruction. Not all strategies are effective for teachers, and it is necessary to find ways of preparing teachers to use the best interdisciplinary strategies.

In this chapter, I describe a strategy for preparing elementary teachers to use action research to explore the best ways to use interdisciplinary science and language arts instruction. Also included are specific research-based strategies found by elementary teachers for effective language arts and science instruction.

ACTION RESEARCH

Action research, simply put, is a classroom-based focused study in which teachers investigate their own teaching situations. Feldman and Minstrell (2000) describe teacher research as teachers inquiring into their own teaching in their own classrooms. The teacher systematically designs a study, collects data, analyzes the data, and interprets and reports the results, a process that parallels scientific inquiry. Teacher research is also an iterative process—containing cycles of action followed by data collection, data assessment, reflection, and further action (Hopkins, 1993). In fact, it can be defined as inquiry into one's own teaching. The study can be used to inform teaching practice, and develops a reflective practitioner (Hubbard & Power, 1993). The questions investigated in classroom-focused research generally spring from what teachers see as problems that arise in the classrooms, or strategies that they would like to try.

Interdisciplinary Instruction

Reading, writing, prediction, creative and critical thinking are integral processes to scientific inquiry. Language arts skills of verbal and written communication are critical to help scientists share their research findings. Scientific inquiries and investigations can be used to provide a purpose for reading and writing instruction. It seems sensible to capitalize on the reciprocal processes of language arts and scientific inquiry, as noted by Casteel and Isom (1994). The similar processes for language arts and scientific inquiry, such as raising a scientific question, or setting a purpose for reading, and making predictions about investigations and for what will happen in the book, make these disciplines particularly good for interdisciplinary instruction. Indeed, given that elementary teachers generally have expertise in language arts instruction, through using interdisciplinary language arts and science instruction to tap the parallels in both disciplines, it is possible to improve science instruction at those grade levels.

For the purposes of this chapter, the definition of interdisciplinary instruction will follow that recommended by Lederman and Niess (1997) wherein "interdisciplinary instruction maintains the integrity between the disciplines, the distinctions between the disciplines remain clear, and connections between the subject matters are emphasized" (p. 57). In other words, interdisciplinary language arts and science instruction means that language arts processes, such as reading and writing, will be used for science instruction and scientific investigations in the class may be used to support language arts instruction. The disciplines remain distinct, and students are made aware of when they are using strategies from each discipline to support learning in the other discipline.

PREPARING ELEMENTARY TEACHERS TO USE ACTION RESEARCH TO EXPLORE INTERDISCIPLINARY LANGUAGE ARTS AND SCIENCE INSTRUCTION

Instruction in using action research to explore classroom-focused teaching issues can be used as part of a graduate course or in an inservice teacher institute. Action research can aid teachers to better understand how their instruction influences student learning. Indeed, because elementary teachers tend to enjoy and emphasize language arts, it is not unexpected that many of these teachers select language arts strategies for which they want to test effectiveness. Some teachers have wished to explore the effectiveness of the use of literature circles, for example, on student self-selection of reading materials. To encourage them to investigate science instruction, which may be a perceived weaker area, the course or workshop facilitator needs to require that teachers connect the selected language arts strategy to a science content area or inquiry area. For instance, if the teacher wanted to explore the influence of literature circles on students, the teacher could use science trade books and explore how the use of these trade books in literature circles influences student understanding of the science content.

Teachers should be asked to design a proposal for their project, through which they develop a problem statement that will help them describe the need for exploring a particular strategy. They should then review related literature that will immerse them in the related problem— showing them other research that can help support their ideas, as well as showing them research strategies and instruments. I ask teachers to design an alignment table in which they list their research question(s), the data they will collect to help answer the questions, and then the time-frame for acquisition of that data. Teachers should develop a design through which they use the most practical and feasible classroom-based methods for gathering data to answer their question. I have had a group of inservice teachers at a summer institute brainstorm a common design for a research question, and then implement similar designs in their own classroom settings for their smaller subquestions. They need instruction in rigorous methodology, such as appropriate construction and use of survey instruments, as well as interview techniques if they decide to interview some of their students. They need instruction in data collection procedures, and in the importance of maintaining dated records, as well as in embedding the data collection in day to day classroom practice. If their research question leads them to explore how well they implement specific teaching strategies, they should be instructed to collect data that will track their instruction, such as videotapes of their instruction, obser-vations by a principal or other outside person, or to record reflective notes in a researcher log directly after instruction. If their research ques-tion leads them to explore the influence of their instruction on student outcomes, they should be instructed to use data collection methods such as collection of student work, collection of pre and postinstruction data, possibly interviews of subsets of students, and recording reflective notes in a researcher log of the instruction as well as perceptions of student reactions to the instruction. The importance of collecting multiple data sources should be stressed.

Along with considering methods for data collection, teachers should also describe data analysis procedures. Many action research studies fol-low a qualitative paradigm, and teachers need to understand that the data must be thoroughly analyzed to give them the best determination of the outcome of the teachings strategies. Instruction in tracking patterns in data, and in considering primary and secondary sources is important. Teachers can compare pre- and postdata, and note patterns in their instructional practice through viewing videotapes or reviewing notes in their researcher logs. Through rigorous data analysis, teachers can gain an understanding of their instruction and the influence of that instruction on student outcomes.

They may also consider expected outcomes, or what they hope to find based on using the particular strategies. By considering their expectations, they can seek to guard against "finding what they hope to find" and ensure that they are focusing their attention on data-based outcomes.

This approach to teacher research may seem daunting and similar to scholarly research, but to get the best information from their work, and to ensure they fully learn the action research process, it is necessary to have a rigorous design. Without a rigorous design, teachers and readers of the research may get the idea that teacher research is not "worth it" and is of lesser quality (Lederman & Niess, 1997).

Examples of Interdisciplinary Language Arts and Science Action Research Studies

In this section, I describe interdisciplinary language arts and science action research studies carried out by preservice and inservice elementary teachers. The results of these studies are also included and will enable me to later draw conclusions for what strategies seem most appropriate for using interdisciplinary language arts and science instruction at the elementary grade levels. The four research studies shared in this section have either been published in peer-reviewed journals, or presented nationally at science education conferences.

Determining How to Use Graphic Organizers in a Sixth-Grade Science Classroom. In this study (Stine & Akerson, 2001), the sixth-grade teacher endeavored to find out how to most effectively use a science textbook to enable his students to gain the most information from the text. The teacher had students use graphic organizers to encourage metacognitive awareness of the text in the content areas of states of matter, kingdoms of living things, cell organelles and functions. The teacher used three graphic organizers in the study—vocabulary development strategy (VOC strategy), Venn diagrams, and concept map patterns. The VOC strategy is a worksheet that provides students with the opportunity to examine textbook vocabulary and to make personal connections with the vocabulary terms—hopefully ensuring a deeper understanding of the words. Venn diagrams represent the similarities and differences between two concepts that are addressed in the text. Concept pattern maps present information in the form of a web, in which the circles in the web contain definitions, categories, properties, and examples of a specific concept that are connected by appropriate lines. Students used the Venn diagram three times to explore differences and similarities between states of matter. Students used the VOC strategy once when they explored a reading about a fourth state of matter, plasma. The students' work was collected as data to help the teacher explore any changes in their understandings over the course of instruction. The teacher also videotaped six lessons to ensure he was properly teaching about the use of graphic organizers, and kept a researcher log in which he recorded notes regarding his teaching and perceptions of how his students were responding to instruction.

The teacher used the concept pattern map the most because he believed it was the most useful because it allowed students to describe connections among concepts. He had students construct concept maps in small groups, and individually, to describe relationships among science concepts they were reading about while researching plant kingdoms.

To track the effectiveness of the strategy, he conducted interviews of students to track the influences of the organizers on the information they were gleaning from the texts. He videotaped classroom sessions to watch his own instruction on the use of these organizers, and kept a researcher log for reflections on the students' use of these organizers. Following his data collection, the teacher reviewed the videotapes, making notes of his instruction, and then reviewed his researcher log, making notes in the margins regarding when students seemed to be using the strategies, or when he may have been emphasizing the strategies more effectively. The interviews of the students were combined with a review of their work using the graphic organizers to see whether there was any change in how well students were able to use the organizers to gain information from text.

The teacher found that his students required an extensive amount of guidance and direct instruction for how to use an organizer each time he taught a new form. He noted that students were very concerned with "correctly using the organizers," and less so with how to use the organizers to glean the most information from the text. He suggests a slow introduction to each organizer, with ample time for practice and reflection on its use.

Although students needed direct instruction for how to use the organizers, it was also apparent that they needed to construct these organizers on their own—that the teacher should have no role in directly telling students where to find information to put on the organizer, or where to place the connections. Making the students self-sufficient in using the organizers for their own ideas is more effective at helping them gain information from the text than having them organize predetermined information.

Another finding that the teacher emphasized was the importance of follow-up activities and closure. These follow-up activities and concluding discussions allowed students to further practice the strategies, and to recognize how these organizers helped them to gain understandings from the text they were reading. The follow-up closure activities often took the form of an extended response question that allowed students to describe what they had gained from the reading as it was organized on their graphic organizer. Additionally, they were able to make connections to the hands-on portions of their science investigations.

Science and Language Links: A Fourth-Grade Intern's Attempts to Use Language Arts to Improve Scientific Inquiry Skills. In this action research study, the teacher (Liu & Akerson, 2002) explored ways in which he could use language arts skills to improve scientific inquiry skills for his fourth-grade students. He noted that "using language arts is a natural connection for exploring scientific ideas." He felt particularly strong in language arts instruction, but not so strong in his science instruction, and wanted to see how his strengths in language arts could be used to improve his perceived weakness in science. To explore how he could use language arts skills to improve science inquiry skills, the teacher collected data in the form of investigative worksheets that were filled out by the students during scientific inquiries, conducted audiotaped interviews of the students, and used observations a field specialist made of his instruction while he was teaching and making explicit connections between language arts and science. He analyzed the data collected by noting patterns in the investigative worksheets over time, compared pre and postinterview data of the students. He compared this data for low, average, and high ability students. He tracked patterns in the observation notes made by the field specialist.

The science content taught during this time was animal habitats and land and water. As part of the land and water unit, students were required to reflect on controversial issues such as the Snake River dam issue and whether to breach the dam to save salmon.

To make the connections between language arts and science, the teacher used the "gradual release of responsibility" model (Reutzel & Cooter, 1999) to enable students and the teacher to gain experience in allowing the students to take more responsibility and leadership in their science investigations. The teacher required students to reflect orally and in written form on the issues explored in class. He used open questions, such as "The town experiences occasional flash floods. The town council has asked your company to find a solution to this problem. Think also of the environmental impacts of this solution. What will your company do to solve this problem?" He then had students use an investigative sheet to design an inquiry to solve the problem. By having them discuss the problem and devise a written plan for addressing the problem through a scientific inquiry, the teacher was hoping to use writing to improve inquiry skills. He noted that the language arts skills used in these investigations included recording observations, making predictions, communicating findings, listing materials needed in an investigation, and making conclusions.

The teacher found that, overall, there were no noticeable changes in students' abilities to use language arts to support scientific inquiry. However, this lack of change was masked by the ability level of the students. For high ability students, there was no change in writing ability or scientific inquiry skills. The teacher noted that these students were already receiving high marks for these subjects in their class. They were able to verbalize their ideas orally and in written form. However, for the average and low ability students, there was room for improvement. These students showed some growth in their ability to use language arts skills for their scientific inquiry. Thus, for lower ability students, it seemed that the relevance of science encouraged them to use their written skills.

Connecting Science, Social Studies, and Language Arts: An Interdisciplinary Approach. This action research study was also conducted in a fourth-grade classroom and focused on the connections the students made between science, language arts, and social studies (Akins & Akerson, 2003). The teacher wanted to know how she could enable her students to see the differences and connections between science, social studies, and language arts. She believed an interdisciplinary approach would help her improve her students' understandings of the connections and distinguish between the disciplines because she noted that students had sometimes confused the subjects of social studies and science. By using an interdisciplinary approach, she hoped to keep the disciplines separate, yet help students recognize when they were using different disciplines to support learning in other areas. She also wanted to ensure that students were able to meet objectives of all disciplines using this approach.

She designed an interdisciplinary unit that centered on exploring electricity for science, and exploring the American Revolution, as well as biographies of scientists connected to electricity (Benjamin Franklin, Samuel Morse, Thomas Edison, and Michael Faraday) as the social studies piece. During the unit, the students researched the scientists and wrote biographies about their contributions as part of the language arts component. Students also kept reflective connection journals recording what they were learning in electricity, and journals recording notes about people of the revolution as the rest of the language arts component.

To track the effectiveness of her approach, she conducted interviews with the students pre and postinstruction to discern their views of social studies, science, and language arts. She made daily notes of her perceptions of instruction in her researcher log. She used copies of the students' connection journals to note where students were seeing connections and distinctions among the disciplines. She collected copies of student work and used her record and plan book to note student progress. She analyzed the data by comparing student perceptions of the disciplines pre and postinstruction through their interview responses. She compared student entries in the connection journals over time, to see whether there would be change in the kinds of connections between disciplines that students noted. She reviewed her researcher log and record and plan book to note patterns in the kinds of disciplinary and interdisciplinary instruction she implemented.

She found that her students seemed to easily find connections between language arts and science, and language arts and social studies, but did not note many connections between social studies and science. However, as their participation in the unit progressed over time, so did their ability to note connections k and distinctions among all the disciplines. She found that at the conclusion of the project, her students had a considerably easier time defining language arts, social studies, and science, than they did at the beginning of the project. They also were able to note more connections between the subjects, and when they were using different disciplines to support learning in other disciplines.

She recognized that implementing an interdisciplinary program is difficult, but important. She found that explicit instruction in the nature of the disciplines is necessary, as well as explicit discussion regarding the connections between the disciplines to help students see the interdisciplinary as well as disciplinary natures of the subject matter.

Building Bridges: Using Science as a Tool to Teach Reading and Writing. The "building bridges" study focused on exploring the ways that science could be used to teach reading and writing skills (Nixon & Akerson, 2004). The fifth-grade teacher wanted to track the influence of science on developing reading and writing skills for her students. She also wanted to note whether using science as a purpose for reading and writing influenced students' nonfiction reading choices.

Her science curriculum consisted of an ecosystems unit. She used the PAR lesson framework strategy to help her students use writing for science. This framework for content-reading instruction included; (a) Preparation, which considers textual features and student background knowledge, (b) Assistance, where the instructional context for the lesson is provided, and (c) Reflection, which provides critical thinking opportunities and openings for extension activities and enhancement. In each case, the students were required to include writing that focused on the science topic being investigated.

During the preparation phase, students wrote their ideas about what they already knew about ecosystems, and what more they wanted to know, and what they learned from reading. During the assistance phase, the teacher used guided-reading procedures as well as required such graphic organizes as Venn diagrams and concept mapping to track ideas. During the reflection phase, the students were given the opportunity to ask themselves what they learned and to demonstrate their knowledge by writing a formal paper on the topic.

To track students' development of reading and writing through science, the teacher collected data that included student written work throughout the study, daily recordings of science and language arts instruction in a researcher log, 16 hours of videotaped instruction that recorded student science investigations prior to writing their papers, and science and language arts instruction, collection of student science journals, and a weekly checklist that recorded book choices made by students during the time of the study. The videotaped instruction and researcher log were analyzed for patterns of instruction in using science for language arts development. Patterns were sought in student writings and science journals to see whether and when the science instruction influenced writing skills. The book choice checklist was used to note whether there were any changes in the kinds of books students selected to read on their own over the course of the study.

From a review of the videotaped instruction, the teacher found that for reading skills, there was substantial success from science instruction. Students used their texts often as resources to answer content questions, and student responses on the "what I learned from reading" sheets indicated good growth in understanding from reading. This use of the text as a resource grew stronger over time. Initially the teacher needed to prompt the students to look to the text for information, but as the study progressed, students began to do so on their own. However, students did not tend to select more nonfiction science books as a result of reading and science instruction.

As far as interdisciplinary science instruction with writing skills, from a review of student writings over time, the teacher noted several disadvantages. For instance, although the teacher gave note-taking guidelines, these guidelines reduced the insightful science thinking while they promoted appropriate writing conventions. Thus the students were constrained to one writing style that did not always help them share their scientific thinking. The writing structures to be taught did not always match up to the science content being taught. Students began to respond to prompts solely through the structures and lost the reflective piece that had been in their earlier writings about science. Additionally, the teacher noted that there was no change in the kinds of books students self-selected for reading.

The teacher concluded her study by recommending that when inter-disciplinary language arts and science instruction makes sense and the objectives are compatible, then it is appropriate to do so. However, it is not appropriate to "force" the disciplines together when there is not a match as far as one discipline supporting the learning in the other. At times it is necessary to have separate disciplinary instruction in each area. Appropriate times to use science as a bridge for reading and writing development include; (a) when the writing structure is familiar to the students and is being used to explore new science content, (b) when the writing structure is open ended so the students are not confined to a spe-cific pattern, and (c) when reading for information is connected to students' own questions.

EFFECTIVE STRATEGIES FOR USING INTERDISCIPLINARY LANGUAGE ARTS AN SCIENCE INSTRUCTION IN ELEMENTARY CLASSROOMS

From the sample studies shared in this chapter, it is apparent that ele-mentary teachers can use action research to explore the kinds of interdis-ciplinary language arts and science instruction that are most effective to use in elementary classrooms. Through training in action research strate-gies and support in implementing these designs, the teachers are able to discern for themselves which instructional approaches actually make the best impact on student learning of language arts and science objectives. I draw some case-to-case generalizations to identify promising and robust patterns for language arts and science instruction in the previous action research studies.

All teachers used strategies that encouraged their students to think about the relationships between language arts and science. Stine and Akerson (2001) tested a variety of graphic organizers to discern the kinds of metacognitive strategies that would be most effective. Nixon and Akerson (2004), Liu and Akerson (2002), and Akins and Akerson (2003) gave students specific prompts so students would consider and then record their views in writing. However, Nixon found that certain writing styles prohibited expression of science learning and constrained students to certain formats. She found that if the writing structures were either open ended, if the structures were already known by the students, or if they were in response to students' own questions, they would be better able to share their developing science conceptions. Liu also found that more capable students showed less growth in their use of writing for science learning simply because they already had developed a high level of writing skills. Thus, to best fit all students, interdisciplinary writing and science instruction should use writing in an open-ended fashion, not constrained by particular writing structures, and if the goal is to use writing to explore developing science concepts, assessment should allow for creative spellings and developing grammar.

One method Akins, Nixon, and Liu found helpful for the use of writing to support science was science journals. Akins used two kinds of journals—journals specific to science content, and journals that she called "connection journals" through which she required students to note any connections they saw between the disciplines. Akins' open-ended content journals encouraged students to share their developing ideas using writing structures that were best for each student, particularly given the wide range of student ability in her class. Her "connection journals" served as a metacognitive strategy that explicitly required students to recognize and describe relationships between language arts, science, and social studies. Liu used a structured writing form, and found that it was more effective in helping lower ability students improve their writing to learn science. Nixon found that open-ended structures in science journals encouraged all students to better record their science ideas, and that to force a specific writing structure on students' science recording inhibited their description of their science ideas.

Akins and Nixon both recommend from their findings that in order for effective interdisciplinary instruction to take place, there should also be specific disciplinary instruction. For example, Akins found that the fourth graders initially could not distinguish between social studies and science. She needed to do some explicit instruction to help them understand what social studies and science were before they were able to discern connections between the disciplines. Nixon also found that students needed to know the writing structure before they could use it to explore new science understandings. Therefore, she also recommends that time be spent in specific disciplinary instruction on the writing structure so students can learn the structure before using it to explore new science content. Stine's findings also support the idea that time must be given to teach students to use specific metacognitive organizers before they can use them effectively to explore developing ideas about science content. From these studies falls the recommendation that it is necessary to have time for explicit disciplinary instruction, as well as for interdisciplinary instruction during which connections between disciplines are emphasized.

In Nixon's study in which she explored the relationship of interdisciplinary reading and science, she found that students could be taught to use reading to support acquisition of science content. Students in her study initially did not read resources to answer their science questions, but after being directed by her to do so, they began to use their textbook as a resource to answer their own questions. However, using the text and nonfiction books as a resource for science content did not encourage students to select more science trade books to read on their own. It cannot be assumed that because students use texts as resources that they will necessarily begin to read more science books. Stine found that students could be taught to glean more from the science textbook if they used graphic organizers to structure their learning.

It is apparent that there are many effective ways of using interdisciplinary science and language arts instruction to enhance elementary students' learning. However, without research on the effectiveness of different approaches, it cannot be presumed that all strategies are equal at helping students meet objectives for both language arts and science. More research on interdisciplinary language arts and science instruction is necessary at different grade levels to explore these ideas. From these studies, it is apparent that students need to be made explicitly aware of the natures of the disciplines, connections between the disciplines, and use appropriate strategies that encourage development of both disciplines' objectives. Some would question whether action research can provide robust enough designs to be able to draw reasonable conclusions. However, I would argue that these rigorously designed and conducted teacher research studies can provide information regarding interdisciplinary language arts and science instruction that we may not have just by researching others' classrooms. These studies provide insight into issues that are important to teachers, conducted by teachers in their own classrooms, which then helps the teachers know which strategies are particularly effective at helping their students.

APPLICATIONS TO CLASSROOM PRACTICE

If you are an elementary methods instructor, you can use action research strategies to help your preservice teachers explore science teaching strategies, including interdisciplinary language arts and science instruction. They will require explicit instruction and support in designing and carrying out the research study (Akerson & Roth McDuffie, 2006), but the advantages of such instruction can help them become more familiar with appropriate methods for teaching science and language arts in an interdisciplinary fashion.

If you are an elementary teacher, you can take a local class in action research methods, or find a group of like-minded teachers with whom to collaborate, and explore your own evidence-based teaching strategies. The Hubbard and Power (1993) book provides a very good start for designing your own research.

FOR FURTHER THOUGHT

1. What are some questions you might raise if you were conducting an action research study exploring effective interdisciplinary language arts and science instruction?
2. What are some constraints to carrying out such a study? How might you overcome those constraints?
3. What are some ways to become familiar with action research methods?
4. Choose one of the questions you raised for question 1—design a brief plan for how you might carry out that study.

REFERENCES

Akerson, V. L., & Roth McDuffie, A. (2006). The elementary teacher as researcher. In K. Appleton (Ed.), *Elementary science teacher education: International perspectives on contemporary issues and practice* (pp. 259–274). Mahwah, NJ: Lawrence Erlbaum Associates.

Akins, A., & Akerson, V. L. (2003). Connecting science, social studies, and language arts: An interdisciplinary approach. *Educational Action Research, 10,* 479–497.

Casteel, C. P., & Isom, B. A. (1994). Reciprocal processes in science and literacy. *Reading Teacher, 47,* 538–545.

Cox, C. A., & Carpenter, J. R. (1989). Improving attitudes toward teaching science and reducing science anxiety through increasing confidence in science ability in inservice elementary school teachers. *Journal of Elementary Science Education, 1*(2), 14–34.

Feldman, A., & Minstrell, J. (2000). Action research as a research methodology for the study of teaching and learning of science. In A. E. Kelly & R. A. Lesh (Eds.), *Handbook of research design in mathematics and science education* (pp. 429–456). Mahwah, NJ: Lawrence Erlbaum Associates.

Flick, L. B. (1995). Navigating a sea of ideas: Teacher and students negotiate a course toward mutual relevance. *Journal of Research in Science Teaching, 32,* 1065–1082.

Hopkins, D. (1993). *A teacher's guide to classroom research.* Philadelphia: Open University Press.

Hubbard, R., & Power, B. (1993). *The art of classroom inquiry: A handbook for teacher researchers.* Portsmouth, NH: Heinemann.

Lederman, N. G., & Niess, M. L. (1997). Integrated, interdisciplinary, or thematic instruction? Is this a question, or is it questionable semantics? *School Science and Mathematics, 97,* 57–58.

Liu, Z., & Akerson, V. L. (2002, May). Science and language links: A fourth grade intern's attempt to increase language skills through science. *Electronic Journal of Literacy Through Science, 1,* Article 4. Retrieved May 31, 2002 from http: //sweeneyhall.sjsu.edu/ejlts/vol1–2.htm

Nixon, D. T., & Akerson, V. L. (2004). Building bridges: Using science as a tool to teach reading and writing. *Educational Action Research, 12,* 197–217.

Perkes, V. A. (1975). Relationships between a teacher's background and sensed adequacy to teach elementary science. *Journal of Research in Science Teaching, 12,* 85–88.

Reutzel, R. D., & Cooter, R. B. (1999). *Teaching children to read* (3rd ed). New Jersey: Merrill.

Stine, E. O., & Akerson, V. L. (2001, January). *Determining how to use graphic organizers in a sixth grade science classroom.* Paper presented at the annual meeting of the Association for the Education of Teachers in Science, Costa Mesa, CA.

Tilgner, P. J. (1990). Avoiding science in the elementary school. *Science Education, 74,* 421–431.

Van Zee, E. (1998). Preparing teachers as researchers in courses on methods of teaching science. *Journal of Research in Science Teaching, 35,* 791–809.

Part IV

CONCLUSIONS AND RECOMMENDATIONS

In Chapter 16, we draw together common themes regarding research on what children can gain from interdisciplinary instruction, as well as how to appropriately prepare teachers to effectively use such instruction. Additionally, we make recommendations for future research.

16

What Do We Know From Our Research? What Do We Still Need to Know? Conclusions and Recommendations

Valarie L. Akerson
Indiana University

Terrell A. Young
Washington State University

The reader can see from the chapters in this book that there has been much work exploring interdisciplinary science and language arts instruction at the elementary level. It is clear from Akerson and Young's as well as Richards' chapter that there are many different definitions of interdisciplinary instruction. Indeed, the authors of these two chapters hold different viewpoints of the definitions themselves, with Akerson and Young ascribing to the view that interdisciplinary instruction leaves the subjects themselves intact while making clear connections between the disciplines, and Richards viewing the idea through the lens that combining two or more subjects is considered interdisciplinary, through the use of multiple terms like multidisciplinary teaching, transdisciplinary teaching, themed units, nested integration, webbed curricula, cross-curricular or integrated curricula teaching approaches. Despite the disagreement on an exact definition or terminology for interdisciplinary instruction, all authors in this book agree that interdisciplinary instruction includes instruction in some combination of two or more subjects simultaneously.

Richards also provides a thorough historical perspective that shows that interdisciplinary instruction is not new, but can be based on cognitive theory, and justified through learning styles and a pedagogy that is a synthesis of two or more disciplines. It is an idea and approach for teaching that has been advocated for many years. In addition to the cognitive and learning styles theoretical framework for interdisciplinary instruction, Sadler and Akerson and Young note that literacy is part of science literacy, which also justifies the use of interdisciplinary science and language arts instruction. In order to be scientifically literate, the public needs to possess language literacy, enabling them to communicate scientific understandings. Sadler also adds the sociocultural perspective on science literacy as further justification for such instruction, noting that science can provide a purposeful use of communication for learning and conceptualizing ideas, supported by a situated way of knowing (e.g., Brown, Collins, & Duguid, 1989). This situated perspective allows for written, verbal, and mathematical communication to take place surrounding the cognitive processes of learning the science content.

Regarding research on what children can gain from interdisciplinary language arts and science instruction, many of our authors have been working with science notebooking (Crowther & Cannon; Morrison; Powell & Aram). Morrison has found science notebooking effective as an assessment tool for both the teachers and the students to track development of content knowledge. She found that it requires much support of teachers, as well as of the students, and much practice by the students to be able to record their ideas rather than believe they are required to write particular answers. It was very difficult for the students to use the notebooks at first, but they became better accustomed to the writing after some experience. Morrison also found that teachers were better able to track the development of their students' science understandings when the notebooks were left more open ended without using a required format in which the students were required to respond.

Crowther and Cannon developed a method called THC that enabled them to help teachers help their students to organize their thoughts and investigations through writing in ways that mimic what scientists might do. This structure allows students to activate their primary knowledge (what do I think about the subject), plan a way to find out (how might I find out), and then draw conclusions (what do I conclude from my investigation). While providing some organization for recording in science notebooks, this method is still open ended enough to allow the kind of structure that encourages rather than discourages student writing, and would readily follow the recommendations from the Morrison study.

Building on using science notebooks to help elementary students learn science, Powell and Aram explored having students publish their science writings in a variety of formats as evidence of their ways of knowing science. They found that these published works of science writings mimic the publishing of scientific work done by scientists. They note that the scientific inquiry motivates students to write, and that publishing their results and work in a variety of formats gives students real reasons to write about their study, providing the context required for authentic writing, as would be advocated by Sadler in Chapter 3.

Crowther and his colleagues Michael Robinson, Amy Edmundson, and Alan Colburn also explored the use of writing strategies to support ELL learners' development of science content knowledge. Their recommendations include modifying lessons to include writing and oral language communications using an inquiry format with the 5E model. Gile also found that using writing within an inquiry format "worked" for primary students' science understandings. She found that the writing helped the students "think like scientists." She also found that science motivated the students to read and to write, to better conceptualize ideas for themselves, and to communicate their understandings to others.

Regarding preparing teachers to effectively use interdisciplinary science and language arts instruction, once again, science notebooking and the use of science journals was a theme in the research, but this time as a way to help teachers use their own writing to explore their understandings (Morrison) and to help teachers interpret students' writing (Britsch & Shepardson). Morrison found that preservice elementary teachers were able to use science notebooking as formative assessments of student science content knowledge. She also found that preservice teachers became more adept at using their own science notebooks over the course of the semester, becoming more dependent on their notebooks to explore their own thinking. The preservice teachers created individual formats in their notebooks that enabled them to record their ideas and thoughts regarding their learning. Britsch and Shepardson used an approach to develop inservice teachers' abilities to interpret children's science journals. Teachers analyzed vignettes; their analysis of journals depended on their own science conceptions. They used journals to identify children's prior conceptions, spent time discussing what to look for in journal entries. The teachers designed and conducted case studies as teacher researchers, which helped their understandings and interpretations of entries. Teachers viewed scientific literacy as including verbal (oral and written) and visual modes to represent meaning. Britsch and

Shepardson found that journaling is multimodal—it is more than a paper and pencil task.

Bintz and Moore and Graves and Phillipson explored science through argumentation as well as by using literature and critical literacy with preservice teachers. Bintz and Moore have developed methods for using children's literature to address themes of science instruction in science courses. Graves and Phillipson explored how critical literacy can be used in science methods courses to help preservice teachers develop argumentation skills, and to develop more appropriate understanding of the very nature of science. They did this by leading science methods and language arts methods students through debates regarding whether intelligent design is a science, for instance.

There are difficulties and successes in using interdisciplinary instruction with preservice teachers, particularly when preparing them to use the same kinds of instruction with their own elementary students (Richards & Shea; Akerson). Richards and Shea found that preservice teachers were stressed and experienced self-doubt in using interdisciplinary instruction (time management, group supervision). They also found that by the end of the semester, the preservice teachers had gained more positive viewpoints about their teaching experiences, and recognized the power of integrating science and language arts instruction for their own students. Thus, the difficulty became a success. Similarly, another difficulty became a success with preparing preservice teachers to conduct action research (Akerson). The preservice teachers described in this chapter experienced difficulties in learning how to conduct action research, and in the kinds of instruction that enabled them to use interdisciplinary language arts with science. However, these teachers also found a positive light as they recognized they could explore interdisciplinary instructional strategies in their own teaching settings. They became more confident in their own abilities to conduct classroom-focused research that explored questions they wanted answered. Looking at these kinds of studies as a whole enabled conclusions to be drawn regarding effective instructional practice. The preservice teachers could discover for themselves when interdisciplinary approaches were appropriate and when they were not.

Two chapters also emphasized the use of literacy and interdisciplinary instruction to teach science content to preservice teachers (Lu; Bintz & Moore). Lu used semiotics to integrated geosciences into literacy with her preservice teachers. She found that science motivated her students to read and write. Bintz and Moore developed a structure for teaching science to preservice teachers using children's literature as a centerpiece. The children's literature provided a framework for the preservice teachers to use in their field experiences and future teaching settings.

We can make some recommendations for interdisciplinary instruction with elementary students, and for teacher preparation based on the work of the authors in this book. First, there is obviously no "one size fits all" approach to interdisciplinary instruction with children. It seems that more open-ended strategies that provide some guidance for organizing thoughts, but that do not impose particular formats are important for children to be able to write about their developing ideas about science content (Crowther & Cannon; Morrison), but then later, the children can be asked to use particular writing formats as they formally publish their science writings (Powell & Aram). Adaptation of lessons, and inclusion of writing and reading in inquiry lessons, can be helpful for both ELL and primary students as they learn science content and develop in their reading and writing literacy (Crowther, Robinson, Edmundson, & Colburn; Gile).

Regarding preparing elementary teachers (preservice and inservice) to effectively use interdisciplinary language arts and science instruction, it is again the case that "one size does not fit all." Rather, it seems a combination of strategies can be effective in both methods courses as well as science courses for elementary teachers. It seems that elementary teachers can be trained to use interdisciplinary science and language arts instruction through science notebooking (Morrison) and through learning to interpret elementary students' journal writings (Britsch & Shepardson). Both Britsch and Shepardson, and Akerson also used action research to help inservice (Britsch & Shepardson) and preservice (Akerson) teachers. The action research approach may hold promise in both helping teachers develop strategies for interdisciplinary instruction, and for tracking the influence of that instruction on elementary student knowledge. Also, it seems important to adjust strategies to the particular students involved. Morrison found that for using science notebooking, the preservice teachers individualized their notebooks to what was most useful for them while meeting the course objectives, rather than using one single teacher imposed format.

While we have emphasized interdisciplinary language arts and science instruction in this volume, the work done by Richards and Shea and by Britsch and Shepardson indicate that the disciplines emphasized can be expanded. Richards and Shea were successful at including the arts with their preservice teachers, and Britsch and Shepardson found that interdisciplinary language arts and science instruction was multimodal including thought processes beyond a simple focus on reading and writing within science. Thus, approaches to develop teachers' instructional strategies should go beyond simply reading and writing, and also be multimodal.

Interdisciplinary approaches can be used to teach science content as well as in methods courses. Lu used geosciences as the content, and Bintz and Moore used children's literature to teach science content, as well as science processes. Graves and Phillipson focused on using critical literacy within a language arts methods course, using science content as the impetus for argumentation and debate that was the trigger for critical thinking, writing, and discussion.

Obviously there is room for much more research in interdisciplinary science and language arts instruction. A particularly fruitful arena for such research would be on children's learning of content, both language arts and science content. There is room for much more knowledge of children's content knowledge of science and language arts as a result of interdisciplinary instruction. We need to know the influence of such instruction on students of different grade levels—does engagement in scientific inquiry actually motivate students to read and write more about their ideas? At what grade levels are they capable of using different writing strategies in science? One difficulty here may be for researchers to get into classrooms to find elementary students as a research pool. Perhaps continued work with action research studies can hold a key in the research on elementary students' learning. As teachers learn to conduct action research on their interdisciplinary instruction, we can find out the influence of their instruction on elementary students' content knowledge in science and language arts.

Research needs to be conducted on particular approaches to be used when using writing with science. For instance, in both children and teachers, Morrison found that learners using science notebooks wrote more about their ideas and conceptions when the notebooks were less structured and they were allowed to individualize their notebooks. Crowther and Cannon found that the THC model provided enough structure for science notebooking for students to organize their thoughts, but not so much that it stifled expression of their ideas. Research needs to be conducted on the kinds of structures that should be in place for the best learning of science and language arts content using scientific notebooking, and with what kinds of students. Research also needs to be conducted to find out when it is appropriate to then take students to the next level and have them publish their science writings as a way of knowing (Powell & Aram). When is it appropriate to have students write in notebooks and then move their writing to a publishable form? What are appropriate teaching strategies for enabling elementary students of different grade levels to be able to publish their science writings? Crowther, Riboinson, Edmundson, and Colburn also found that giving ELL students more specific prompts was helpful in their learning of content through scientific inquiry—what is most appropriate for these students?

Given Sadler's introductory Chapter 3, one of our goals as elementary teachers is to help students become communities of learners, and enculturated into the worlds of science—for example, to be able to see how their work as students in school science is similar to, or different from, the work of scientists, and to be able to explore ideas through communication. One other research question could then be how can we use such interdisciplinary science and language arts instruction to help students become "communities of learners" and enculturated into the worlds of science? Would the context of inquiry science provide the kind of context required to develop appropriate writing, reading, and communications skills? Would the use of these skills to communicate ideas help students become part of a classroom scientific "community?" Do these communities develop differently depending on grade level of the students? Are they different for ELL students?

We conclude with the same questions with which we began "What strategies can we use to develop the best communities of learners in elementary science classrooms?" and "How can we best prepare elementary teachers to use such instruction?" The chapters within this volume have shed some light on these questions, but we still have further to go in exploring the best approaches.

REFERENCE

Brown, J. S., Collins, A., & Duguid, P. (1989). Situated learning and the culture of learning. *Educational Researcher, 18*, 32–42.

Author Index

A

Abell, J., 20, 21
Abell, S. K., 49, 200
Aguirre, M., 111
Aikenhead, G. S., 70
Akerson, V. L., 3, 65, 174, 175, 177, 283, 285, 286, 287, 289, 291
Akins, A., 174, 286, 289, 290
Allen, P., 163, 164
Alvermann, D. E., 69, 79, 181
Amaral, O., 106, 107
American Association for the Advancement of Science (AAAS), 6, 7, 70, 219, 226, 231
Anderson, N., 177
Anderson, T. H., 86
Anfara, V., 179
Applebee, A. N., 24, 50
Armbruster, B. B., 64, 86
Ashley, C., 173, 174, 179
Atkins, J. M., 116, 119
Atkinson, D., 69
Atwell, N., 96
Audet, R. H., 49, 198, 199
Au, K., 64
Ayala, C., 50, 199

B

Baker, F., 174
Baker, L., 4, 63
Barab, S. A., 42

Barber, J., 79, 85, 97
Barnard, B., 100
Bass, K. M., 51, 69, 199
Baxter, G. P., 51, 69, 199
Baylor, B., 18
Bazerman, C., 86
Beach, R., 266
Becijos, J., 112
Beers, S., 15, 17, 21, 22, 23
Bell, B., 50, 210
Beller, C., 113
Benke, G., 71
Bernard, H., 180
Berson, M., 223
Biklen, S., 203
Bintz, W. P., 157, 160, 161, 165
Biondo, S., 22, 173, 182, 191
Bisanz, G. L., 4
Black, P., 198, 199, 210
Bluth, G. J., 82
Bogdan, R., 203
Boix Mansilla, B. V., 17, 19, 20, 21, 22, 24, 174, 175
Bonds, C., 22, 23
Borko, H., 198
Boscolo, P., 71
Boyd, C., 147
Boyer Commission, The, 174
Brandt, D. M., 82, 220
Branley, F. M., 270
Bransford, J. D., 66, 67
Bravo, M., 110

Subject Index

Note: Page numbers in *italics* indicate figures and tables.